スター・ウォーズ

新たなる希望

"WHERE DO YOU THINK YOU'RE GOING?"

STAR WARS: A NEW HOPE — MANGA is a translation which was first published in Japan by Media Works. In Japan, manga is normally read from right-to-left. In order to conform to Western standards, the art in this book was copied in a mirror-image to facilitate left-to-right reading of the pages. This, of course, can cause some confusion in a story such as STAR WARS: A NEW HOPE — MANGA where readers are somewhat familiar with the material and so will notice characters both moving and appearing in an opposite fashion from that which they did in the film. We apologize for any confusion this may cause and hope that it will not detract from your enjoyment of this volume.

ピキュー
ピ
いいか もう私を当てにするなよ 絶対に助けてやらないからな
これ以上わけのわからないことに巻き込まれるのはもうごめんだよ！

WHAT MISSION? WHAT ARE YOU TALKING ABOUT?
I'VE JUST ABOUT HAD ENOUGH OF YOU! GO THAT WAY!
YOU'LL BE MAL-FUNCTIONING WITHIN A DAY, YOU NEARSIGHTED SCRAP PILE!
VEE-BEE! BOOP!

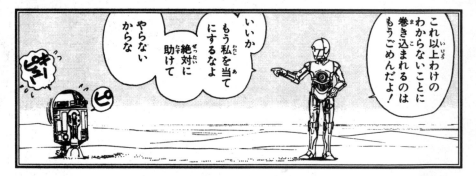

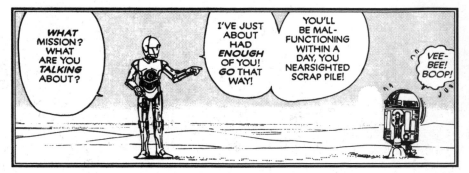

A long time ago in a galaxy far, far away....

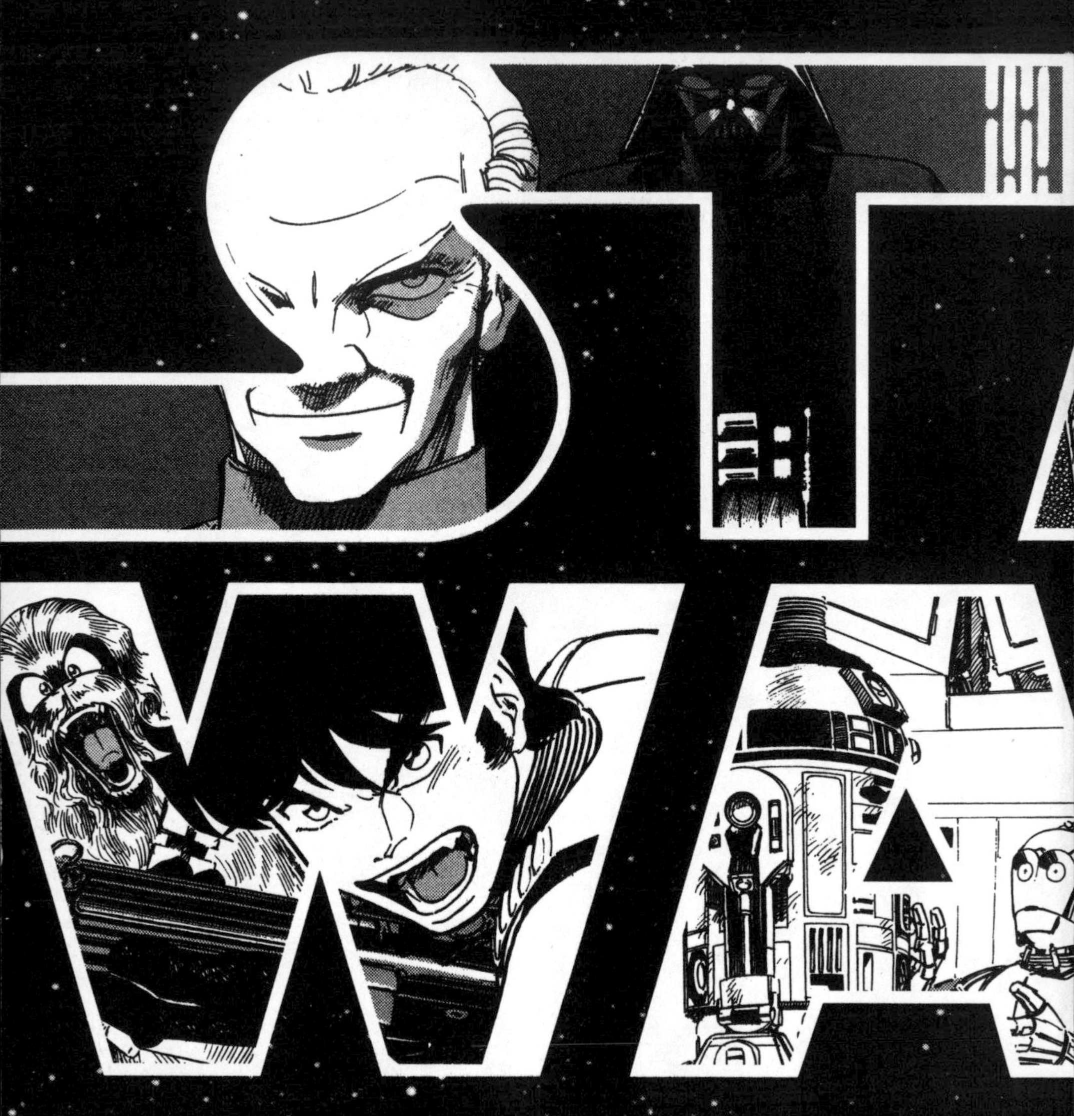

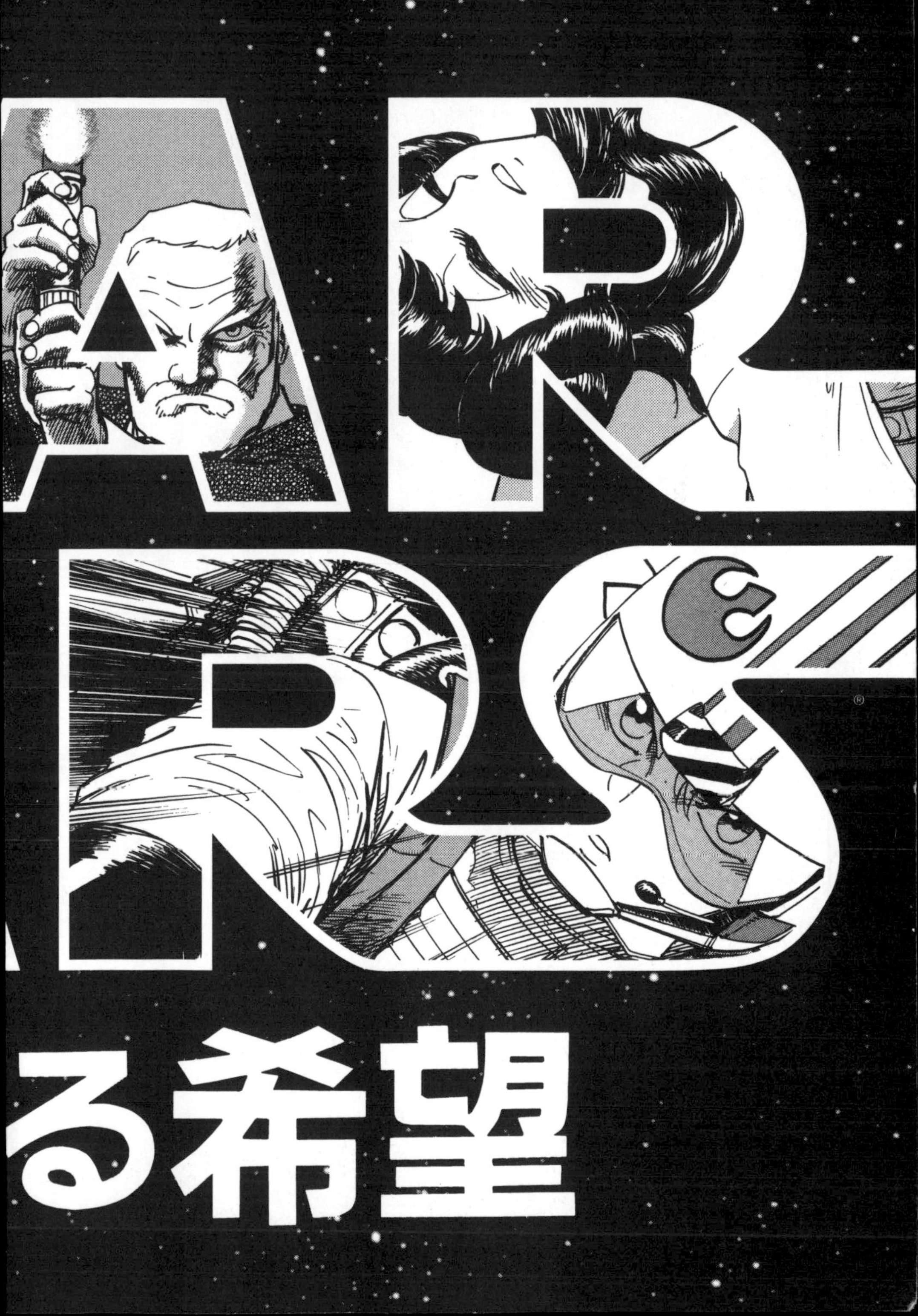

る希望

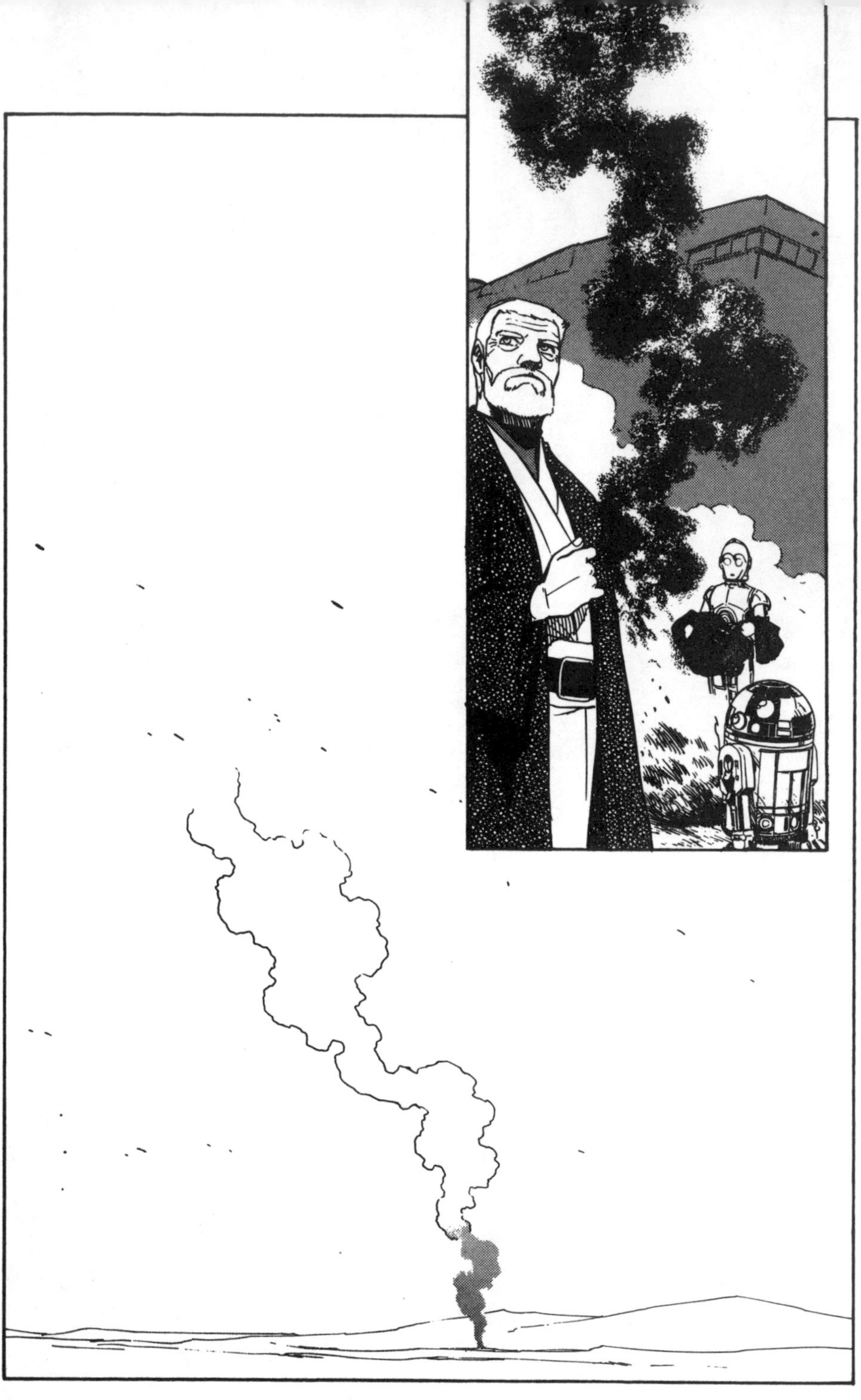

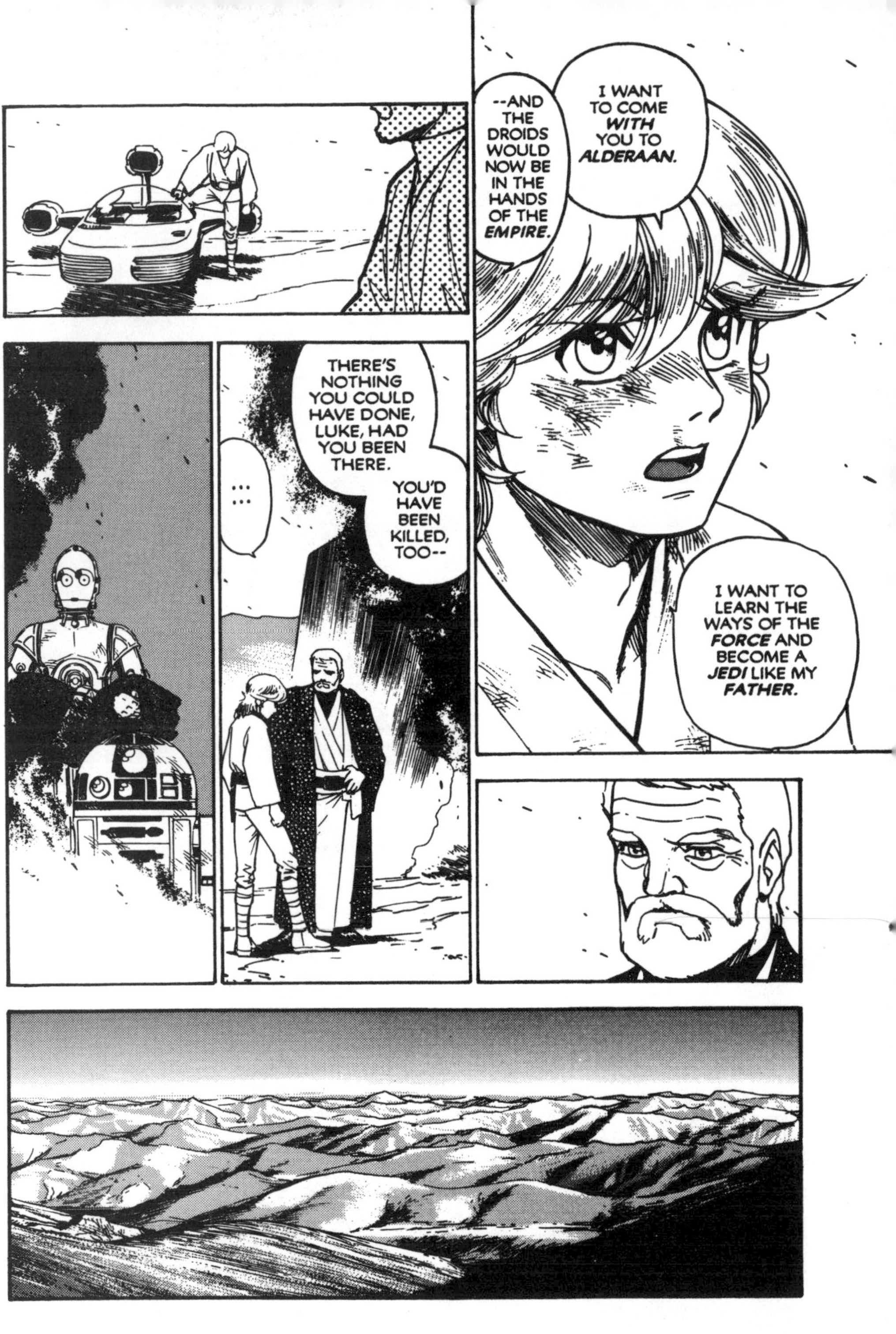
THERE'S NOTHING YOU COULD HAVE DONE, LUKE, HAD YOU BEEN THERE.
... ...
YOU'D HAVE BEEN KILLED, TOO--
--AND THE DROIDS WOULD NOW BE IN THE HANDS OF THE EMPIRE.
I WANT TO COME WITH YOU TO ALDERAAN.
I WANT TO LEARN THE WAYS OF THE FORCE AND BECOME A JEDI LIKE MY FATHER.

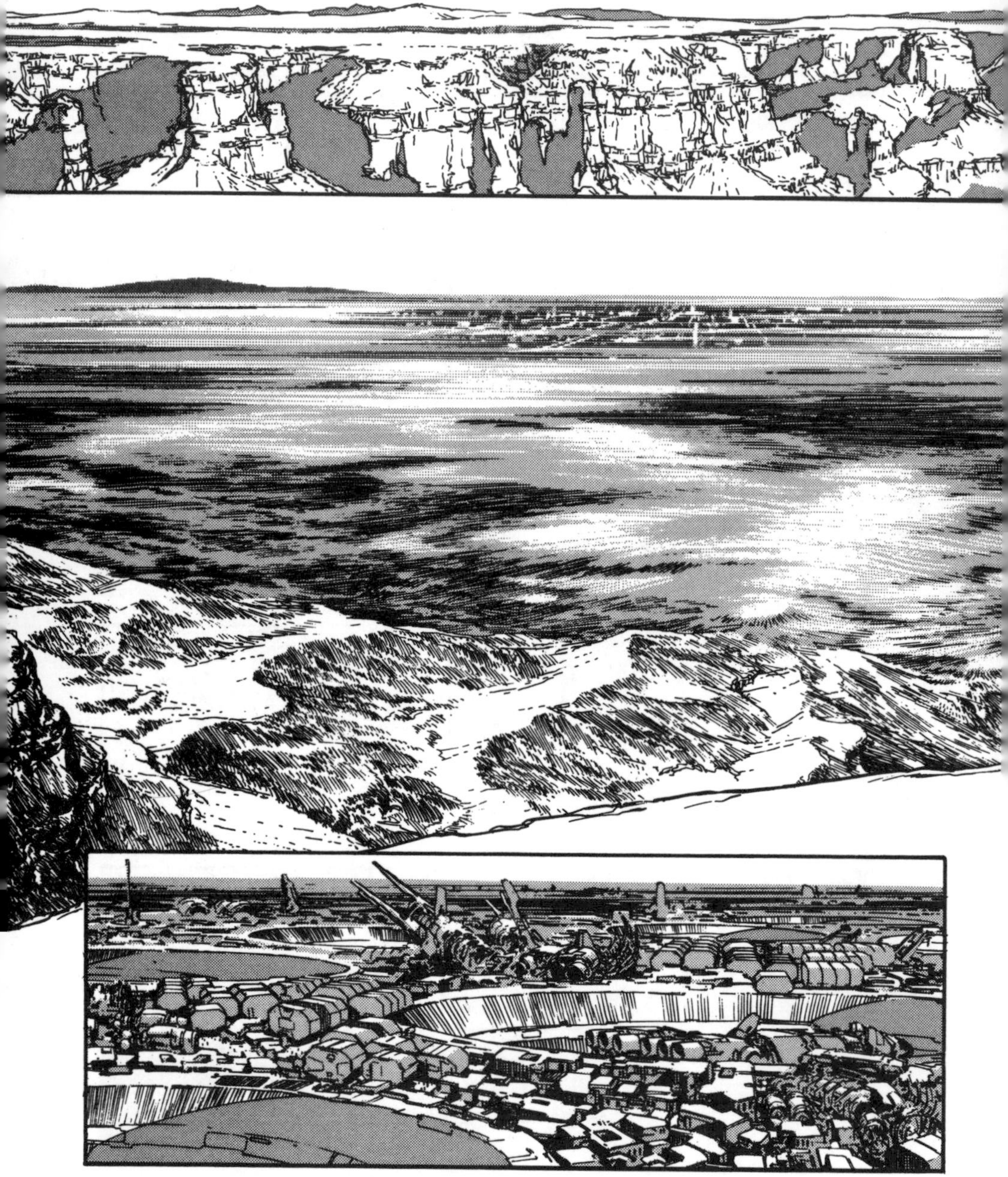

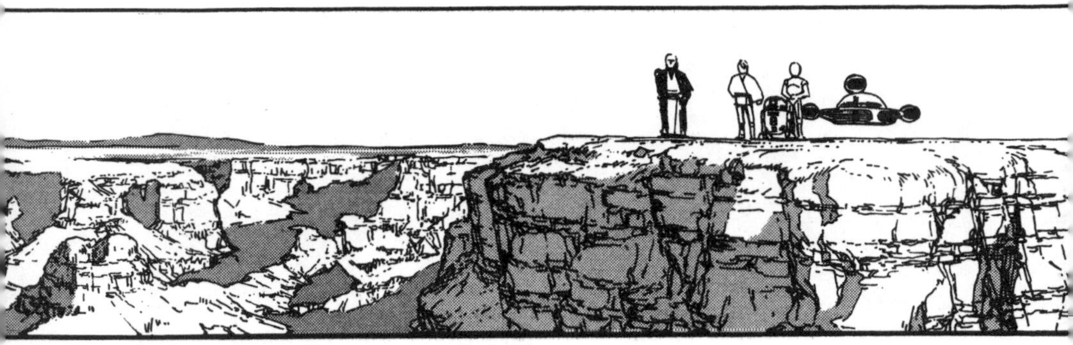

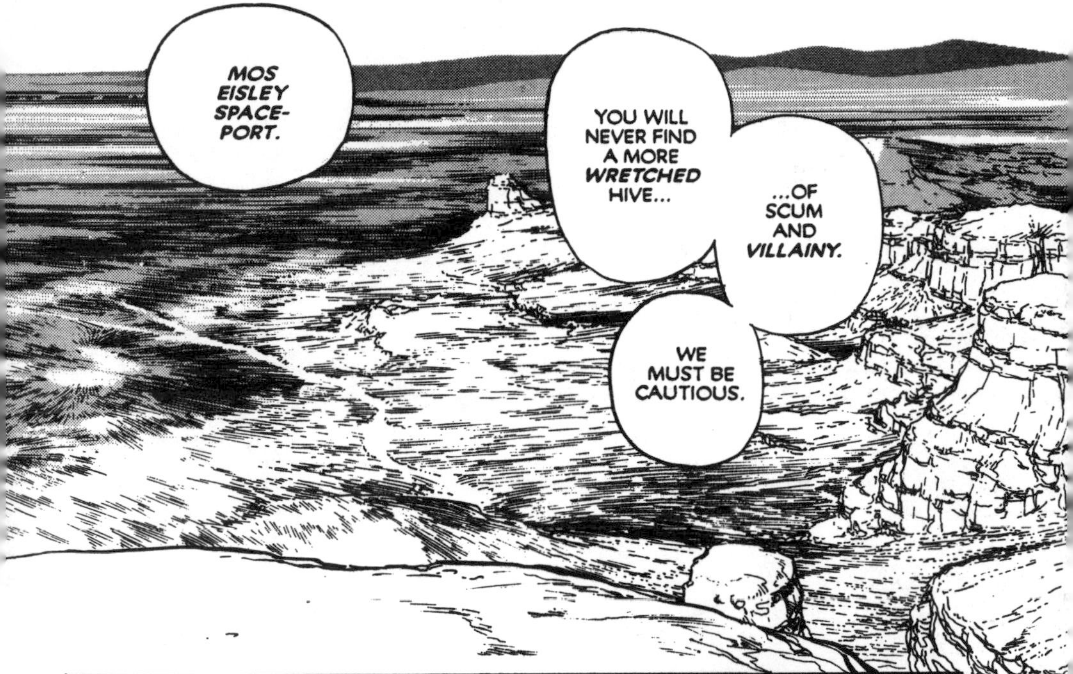
MOS EISLEY SPACE-PORT.
YOU WILL NEVER FIND A MORE *WRETCHED* HIVE...
...OF SCUM AND *VILLAINY.*
WE MUST BE CAUTIOUS.

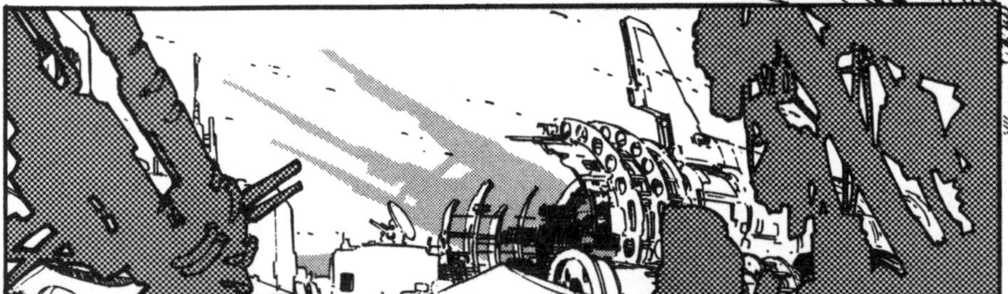

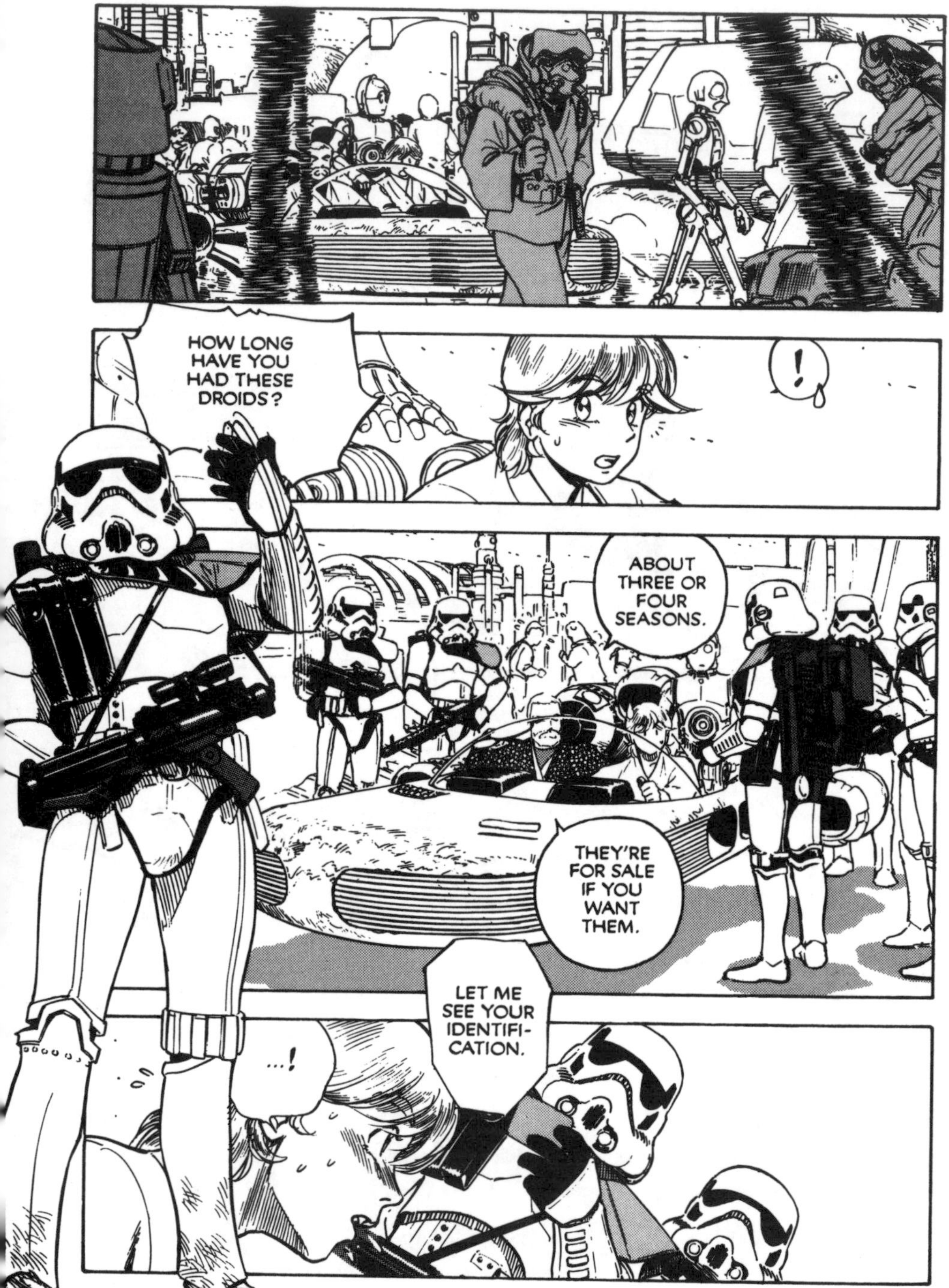
HOW LONG HAVE YOU HAD THESE DROIDS?
!
ABOUT THREE OR FOUR SEASONS.
THEY'RE FOR SALE IF YOU WANT THEM.
...!
LET ME SEE YOUR IDENTIFI-CATION.

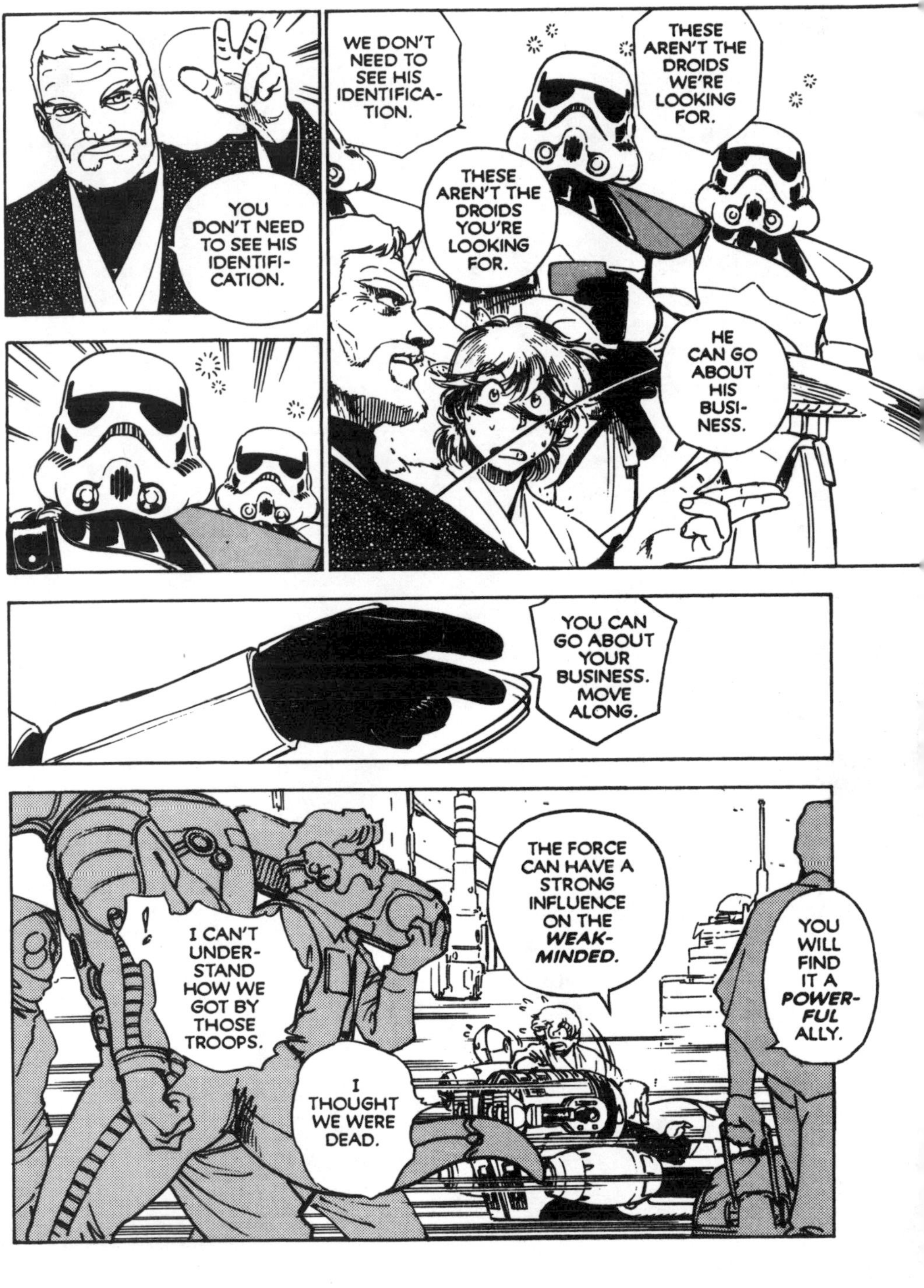
YOU DON'T NEED TO SEE HIS IDENTIFI-CATION.
WE DON'T NEED TO SEE HIS IDENTIFICA-TION.
THESE AREN'T THE DROIDS YOU'RE LOOKING FOR.
THESE AREN'T THE DROIDS WE'RE LOOKING FOR.
HE CAN GO ABOUT HIS BUSI-NESS.
YOU CAN GO ABOUT YOUR BUSINESS. MOVE ALONG.
!
I CAN'T UNDER-STAND HOW WE GOT BY THOSE TROOPS.
I THOUGHT WE WERE DEAD.
THE FORCE CAN HAVE A STRONG INFLUENCE ON THE ***WEAK-MINDED.***
YOU WILL FIND IT A ***POWER-FUL*** ALLY.

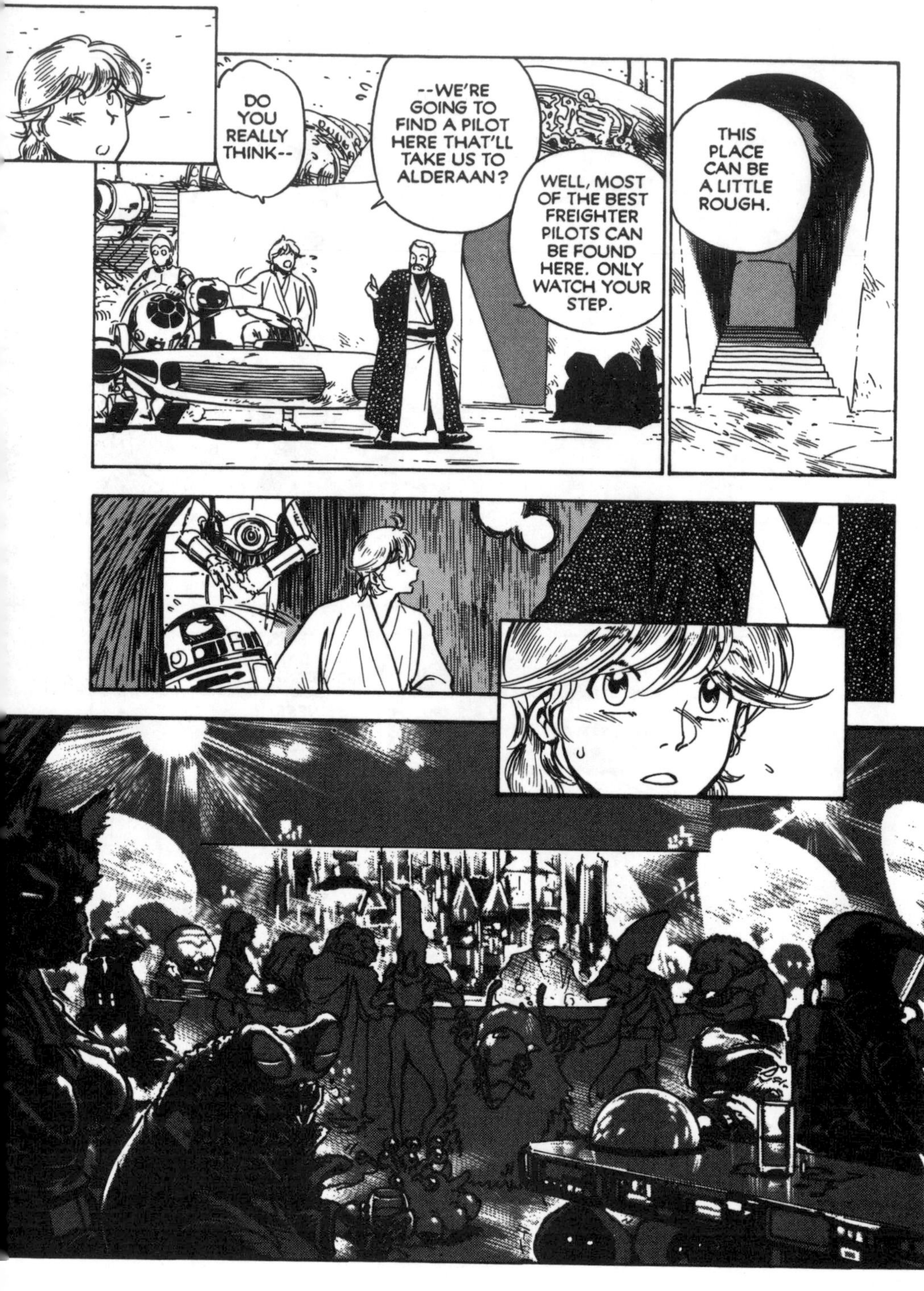
DO YOU REALLY THINK--
--WE'RE GOING TO FIND A PILOT HERE THAT'LL TAKE US TO ALDERAAN?
WELL, MOST OF THE BEST FREIGHTER PILOTS CAN BE FOUND HERE. ONLY WATCH YOUR STEP.
THIS PLACE CAN BE A LITTLE ROUGH.

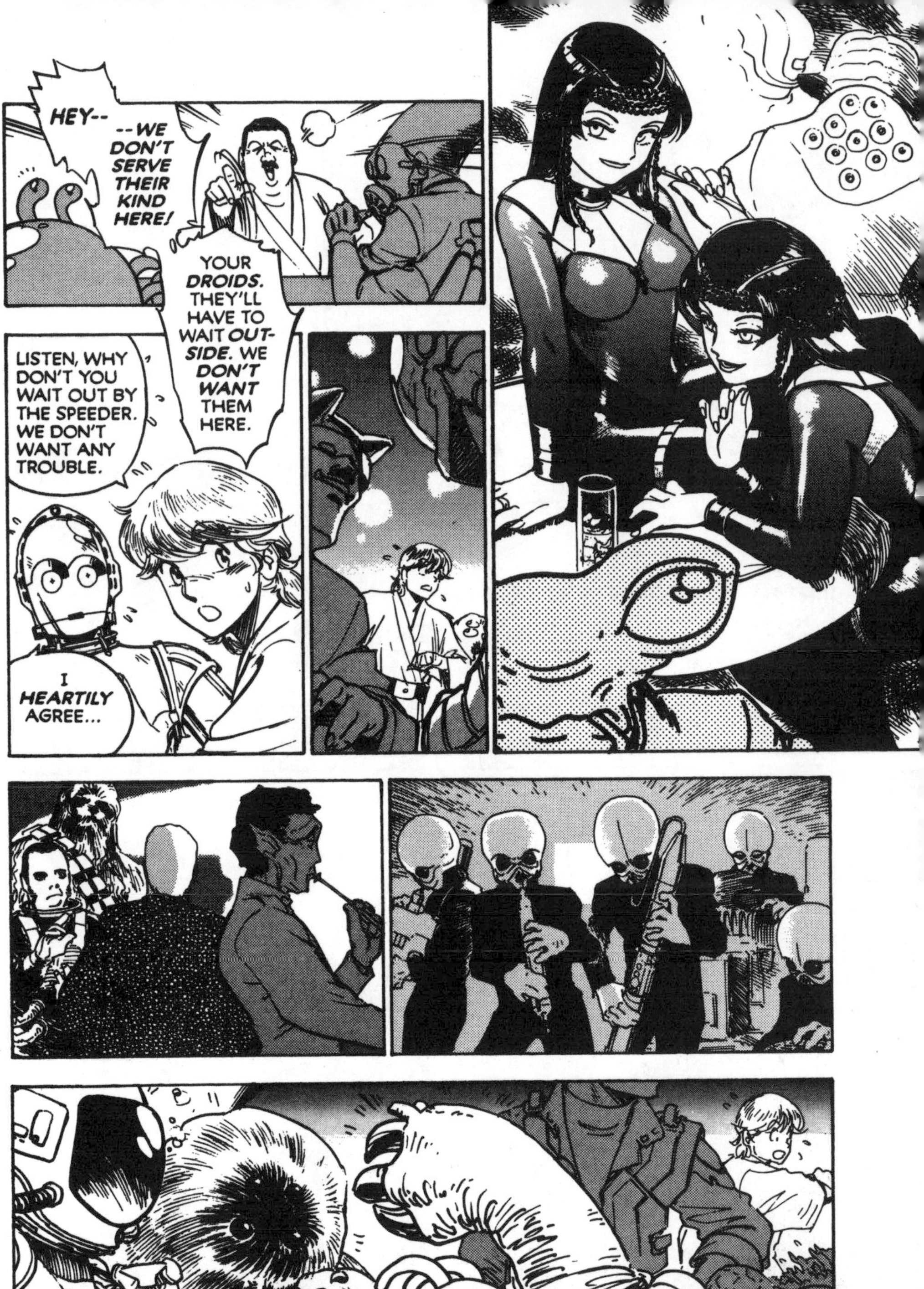
HEY--
--WE DON'T SERVE THEIR KIND HERE!
YOUR DROIDS. THEY'LL HAVE TO WAIT OUTSIDE. WE DON'T WANT THEM HERE.
LISTEN, WHY DON'T YOU WAIT OUT BY THE SPEEDER. WE DON'T WANT ANY TROUBLE.
I HEARTILY AGREE...

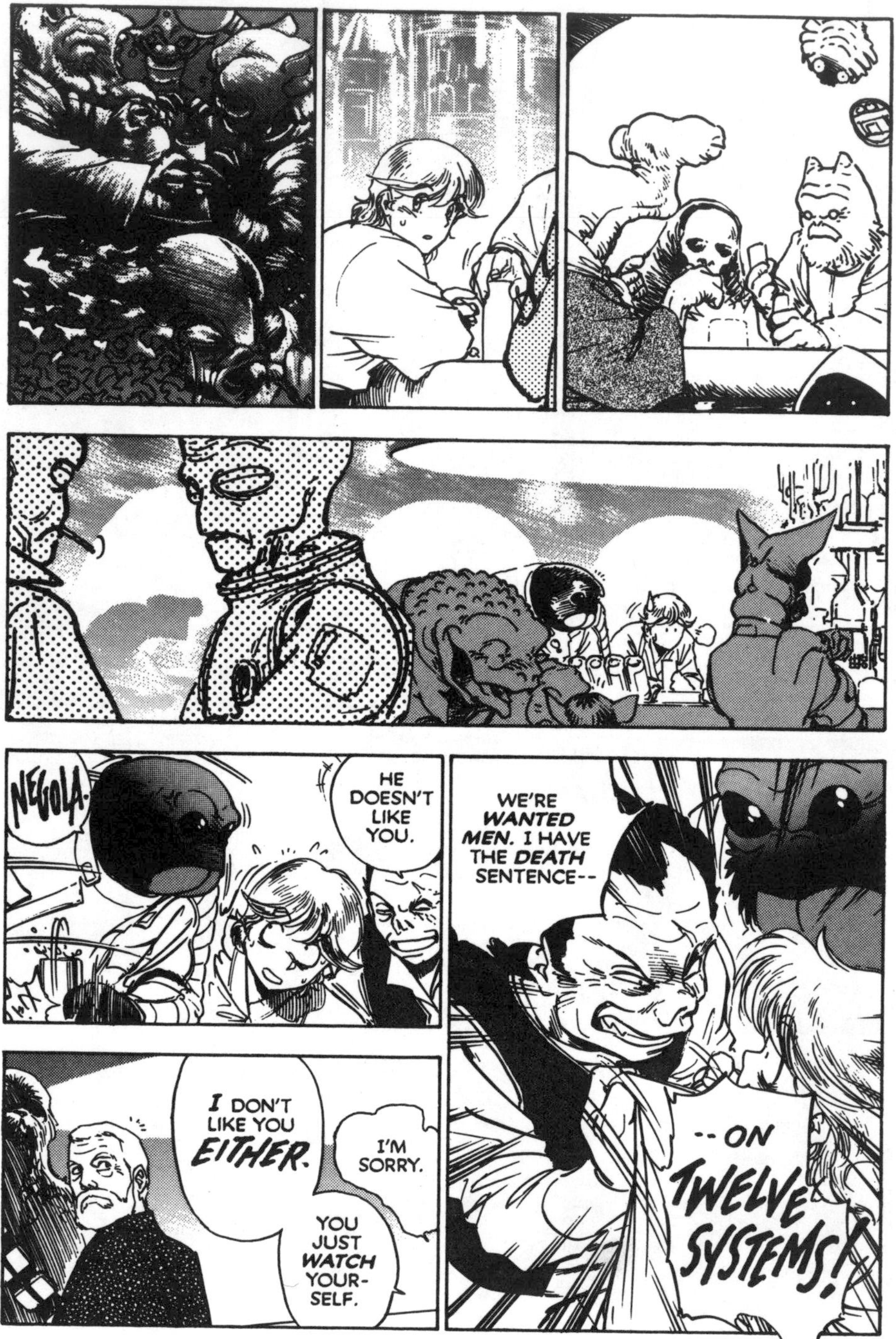
NEGOLA-
HE DOESN'T LIKE YOU.
I DON'T LIKE YOU EITHER.
I'M SORRY.
YOU JUST WATCH YOURSELF.
WE'RE WANTED MEN. I HAVE THE DEATH SENTENCE--
--ON TWELVE SYSTEMS!

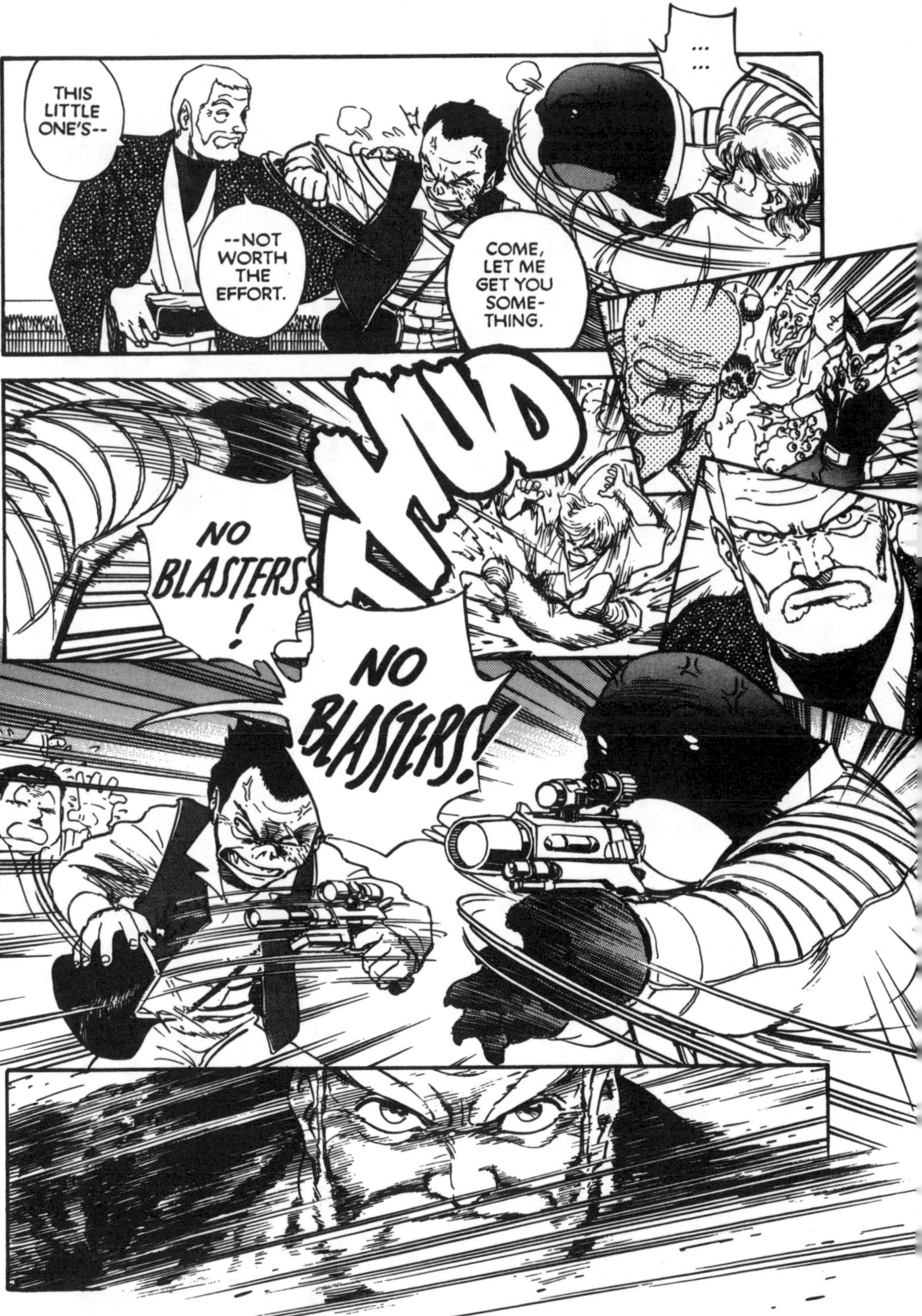
THIS LITTLE ONE'S--
--NOT WORTH THE EFFORT.
COME, LET ME GET YOU SOMETHING.
...
...
THUD
NO BLASTERS!
NO BLASTERS!

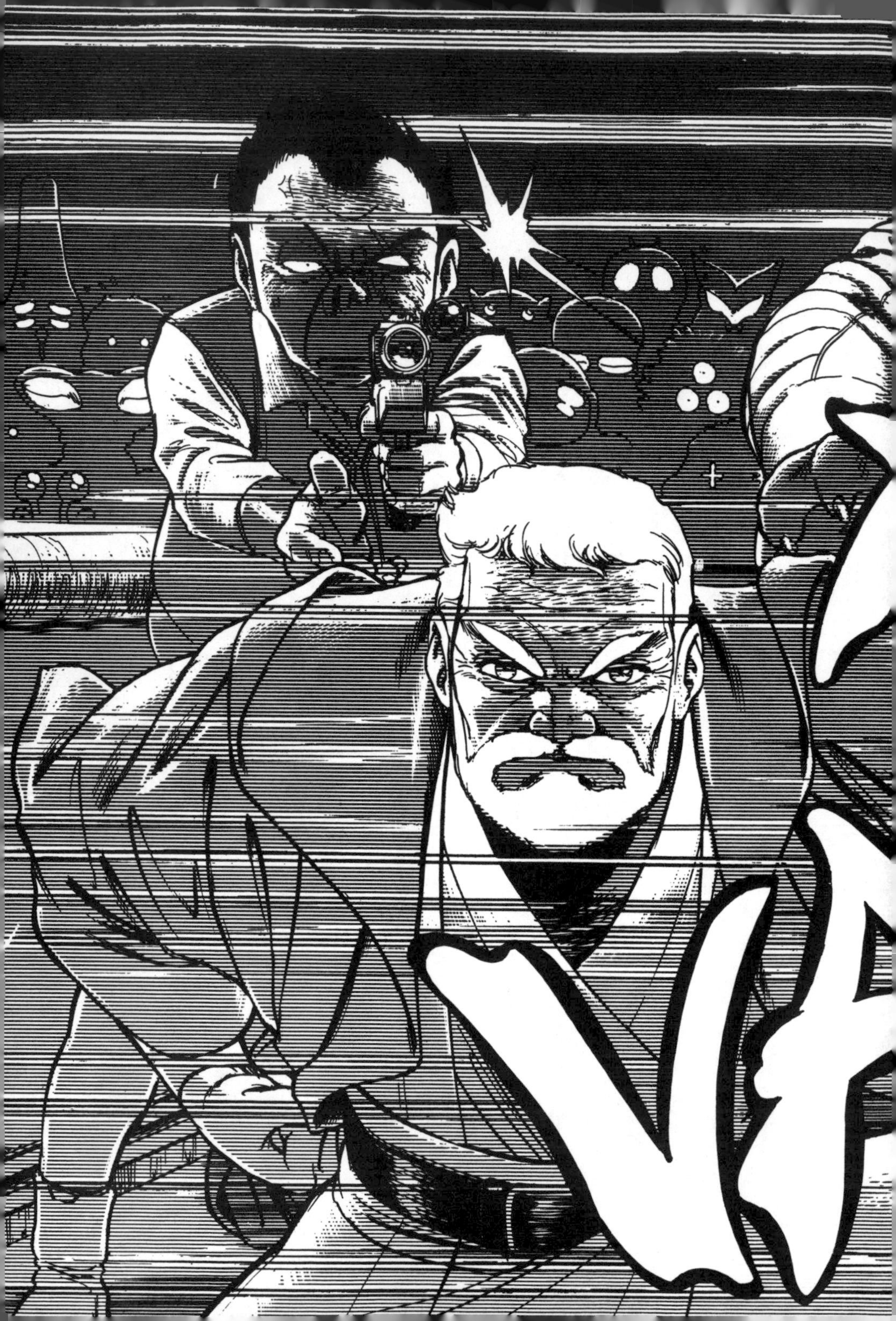

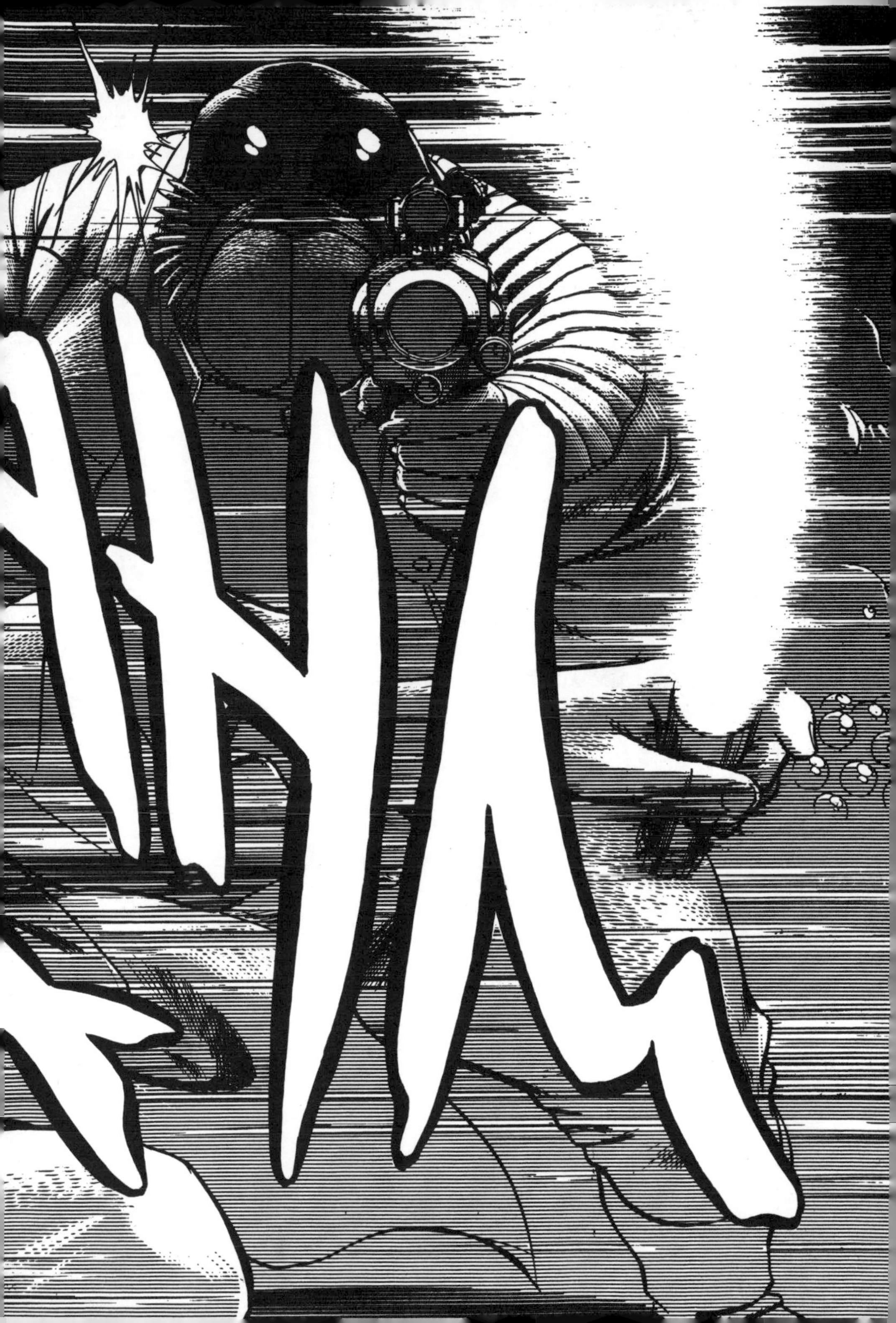

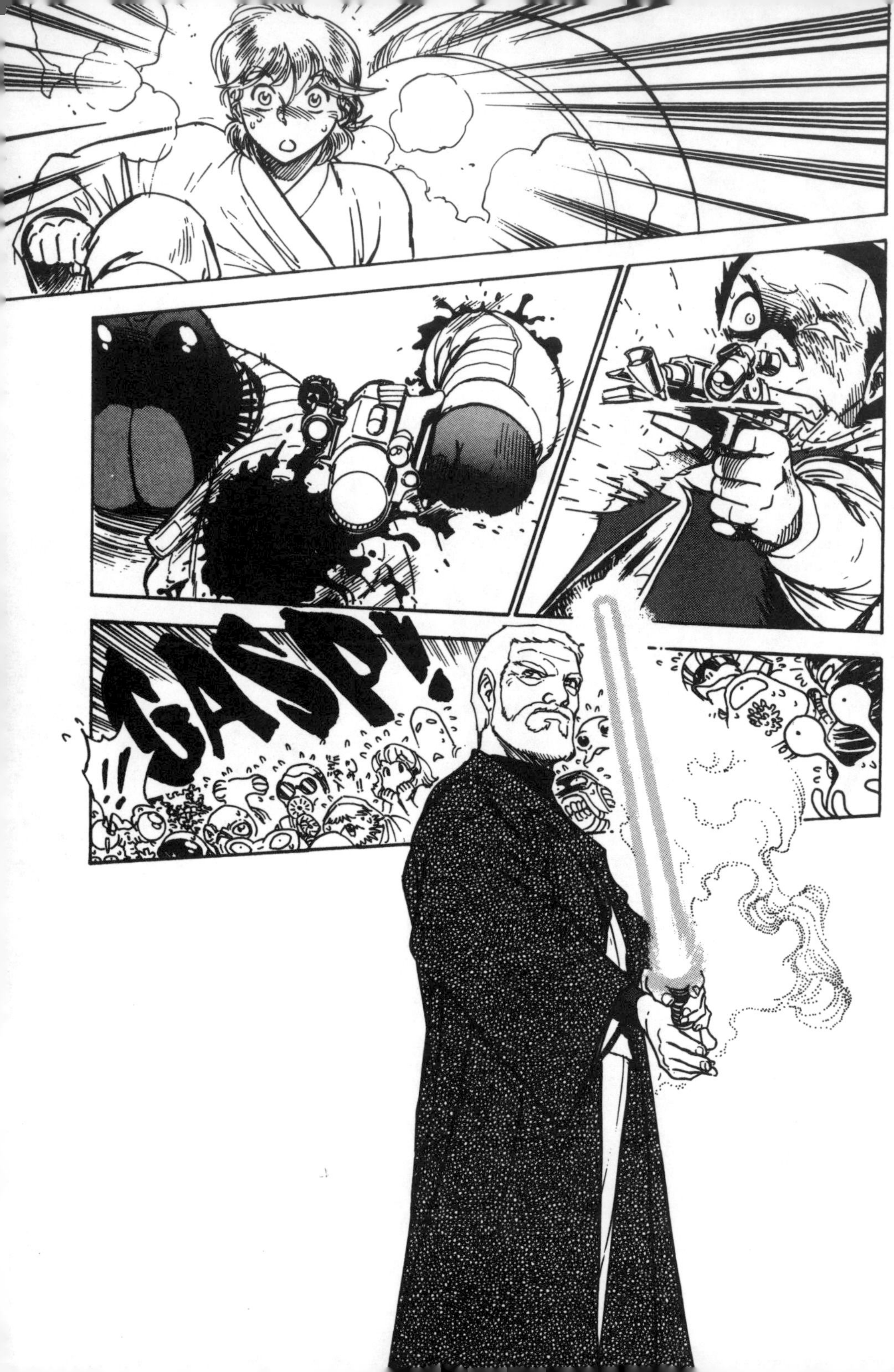
GASP!
!!

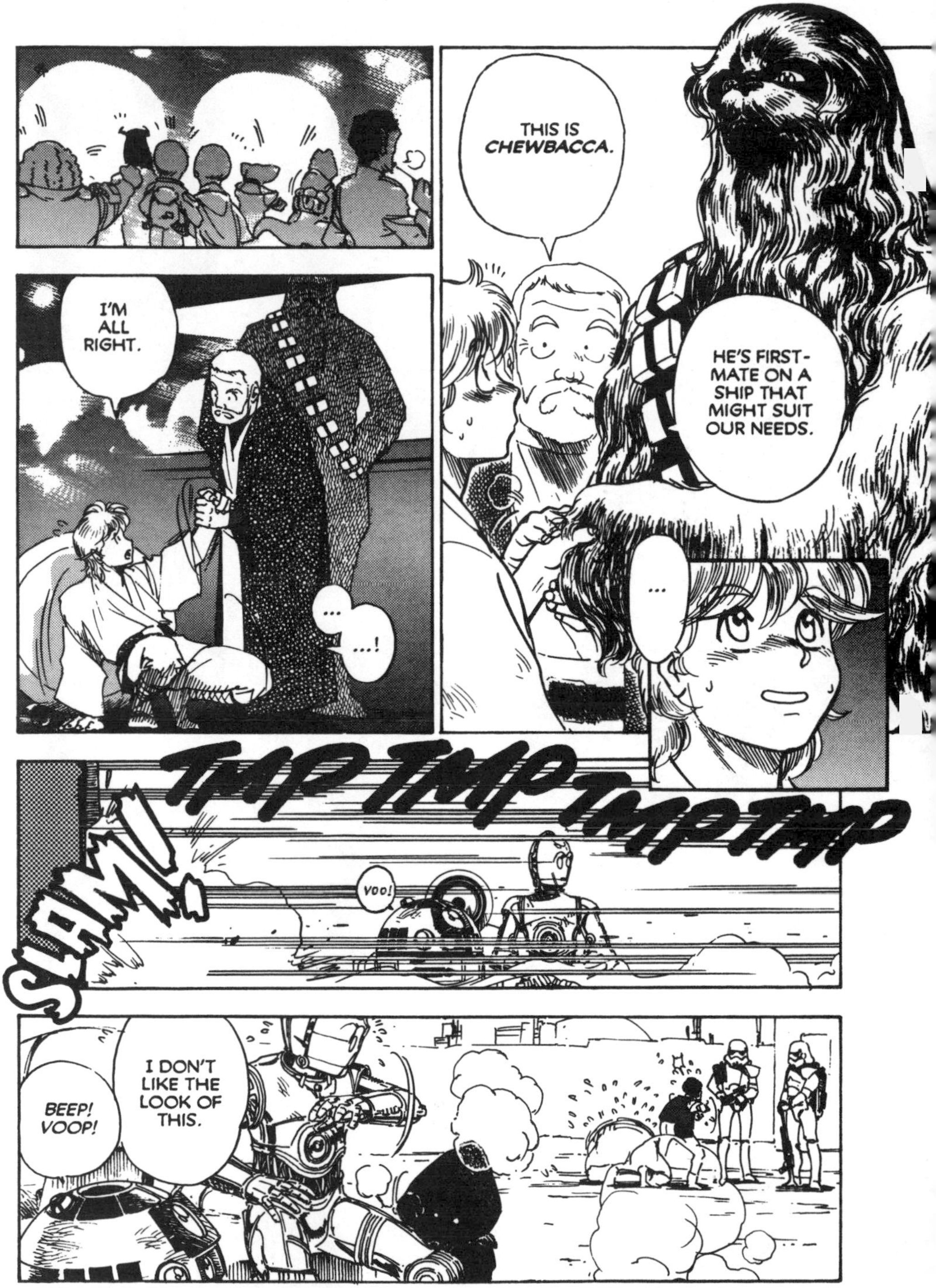
I'M ALL RIGHT.
...
...!
THIS IS *CHEWBACCA.*
HE'S FIRST-MATE ON A SHIP THAT MIGHT SUIT OUR NEEDS.
...
SLAM!
TMP TMP TMP TMP
VOO!
BEEP! VOOP!
I DON'T LIKE THE LOOK OF THIS.

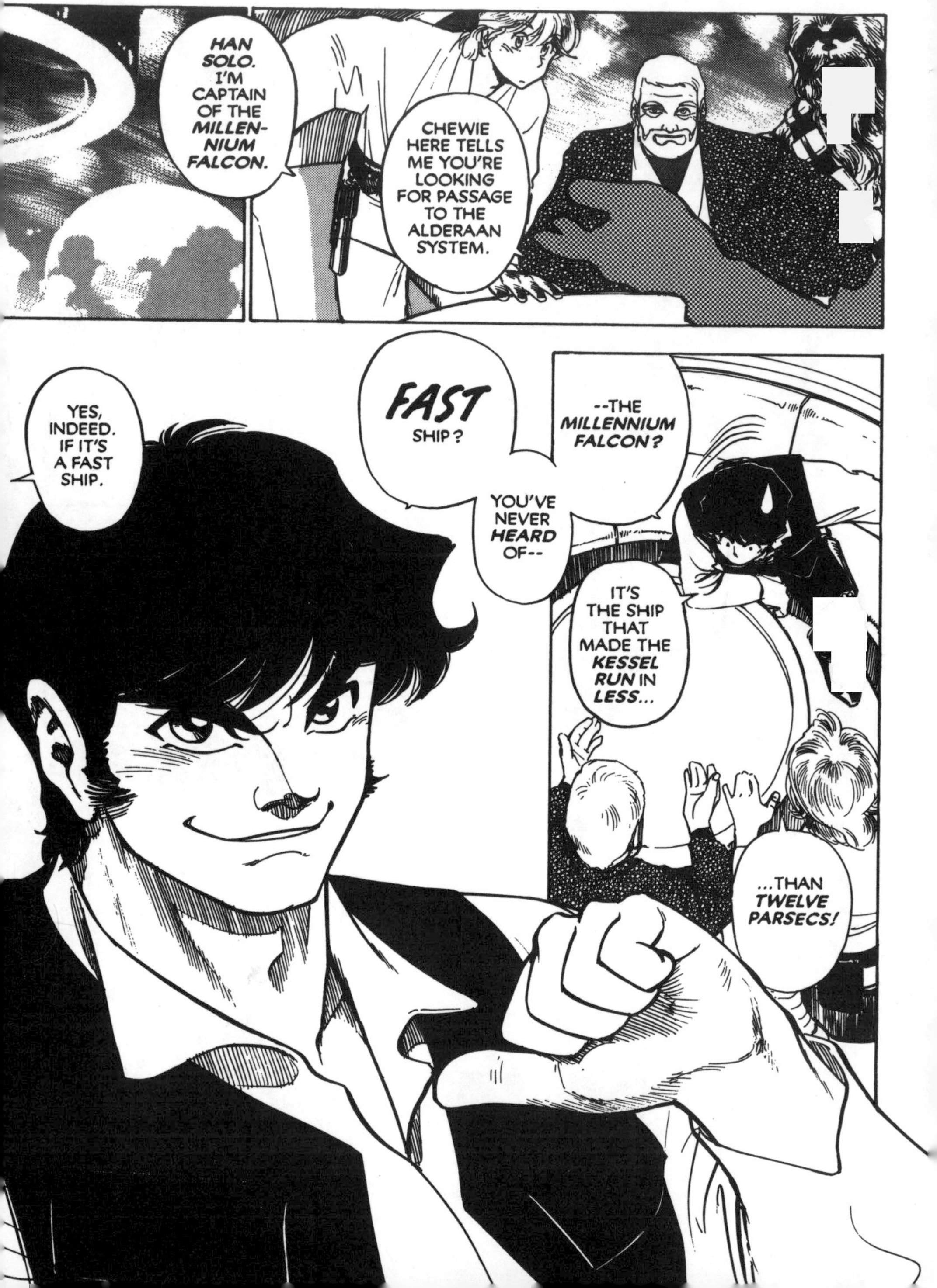
HAN SOLO. I'M CAPTAIN OF THE MILLENNIUM FALCON.
CHEWIE HERE TELLS ME YOU'RE LOOKING FOR PASSAGE TO THE ALDERAAN SYSTEM.
YES, INDEED. IF IT'S A FAST SHIP.
FAST SHIP?
YOU'VE NEVER HEARD OF--
--THE MILLENNIUM FALCON?
IT'S THE SHIP THAT MADE THE KESSEL RUN IN LESS...
...THAN TWELVE PARSECS!

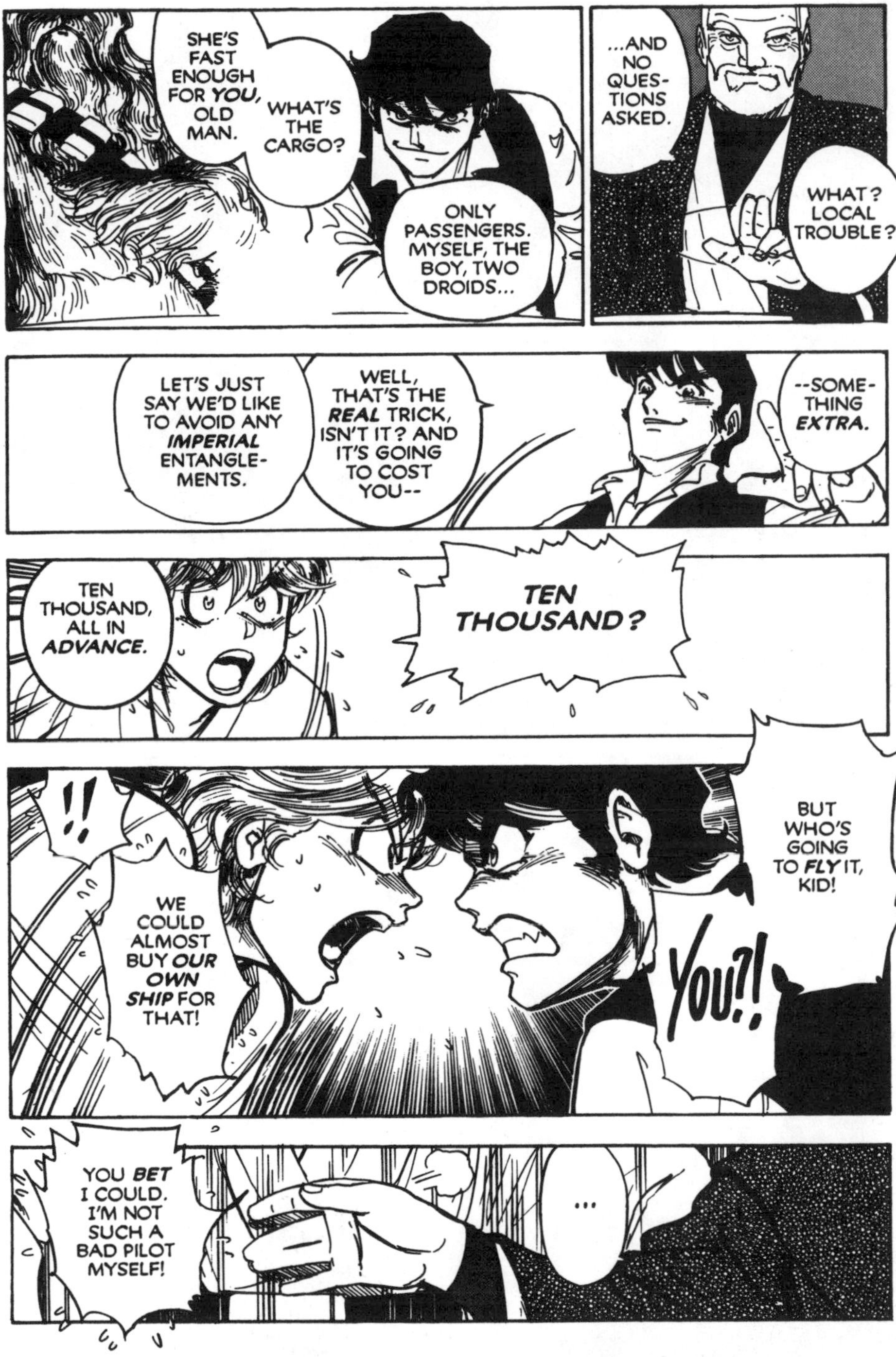
SHE'S FAST ENOUGH FOR YOU, OLD MAN.
WHAT'S THE CARGO?
ONLY PASSENGERS. MYSELF, THE BOY, TWO DROIDS...
...AND NO QUES-TIONS ASKED.
WHAT? LOCAL TROUBLE?
LET'S JUST SAY WE'D LIKE TO AVOID ANY IMPERIAL ENTANGLE-MENTS.
WELL, THAT'S THE REAL TRICK, ISN'T IT? AND IT'S GOING TO COST YOU--
--SOME-THING EXTRA.
TEN THOUSAND, ALL IN ADVANCE.
TEN THOUSAND?
!!
WE COULD ALMOST BUY OUR OWN SHIP FOR THAT!
BUT WHO'S GOING TO FLY IT, KID!
YOU?!
YOU BET I COULD. I'M NOT SUCH A BAD PILOT MYSELF!
...

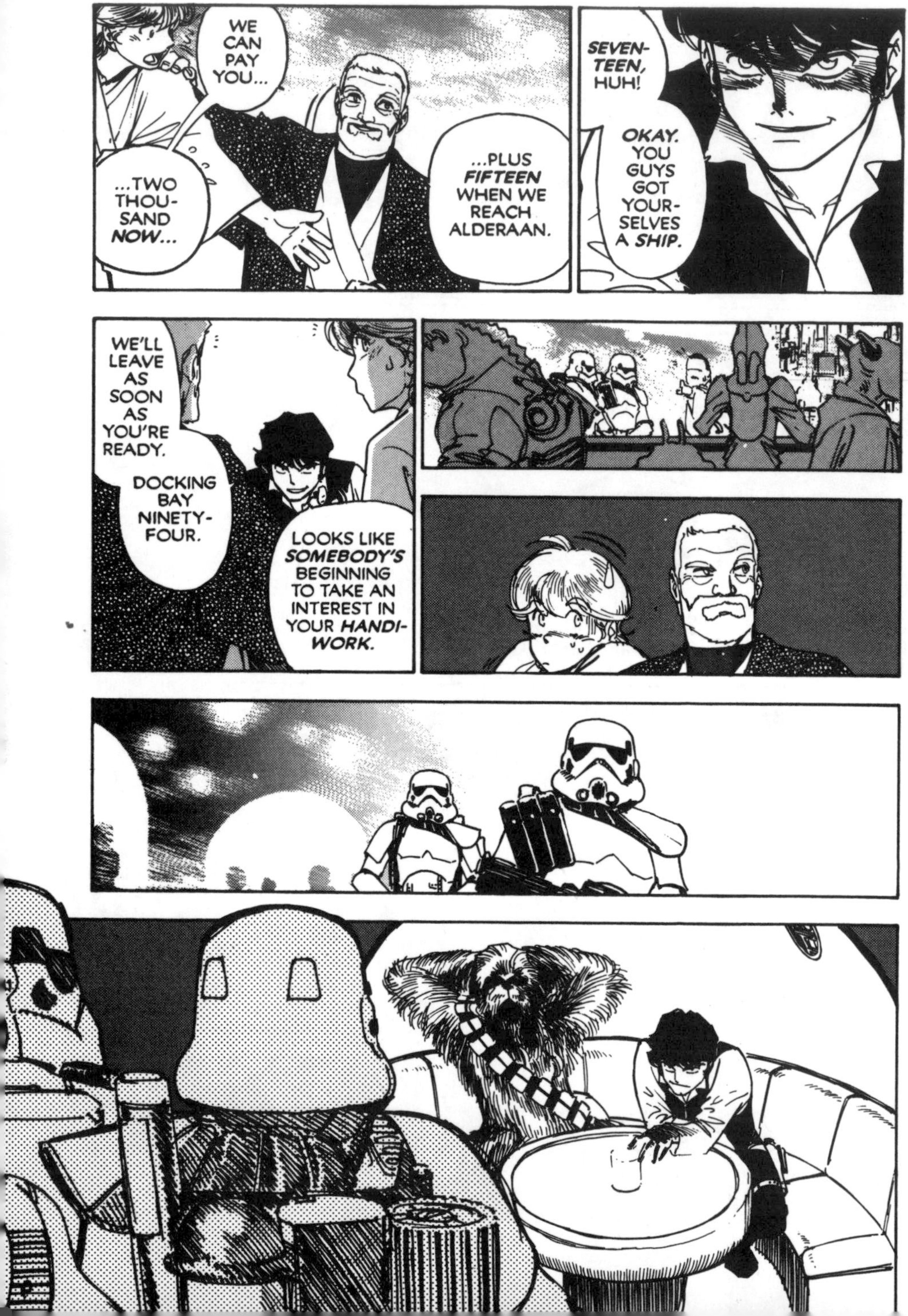
WE CAN PAY YOU...
...TWO THOU-SAND NOW...
...PLUS FIFTEEN WHEN WE REACH ALDERAAN.
SEVEN-TEEN, HUH!
OKAY. YOU GUYS GOT YOUR-SELVES A SHIP.
WE'LL LEAVE AS SOON AS YOU'RE READY.
DOCKING BAY NINETY-FOUR.
LOOKS LIKE SOMEBODY'S BEGINNING TO TAKE AN INTEREST IN YOUR HANDI-WORK.

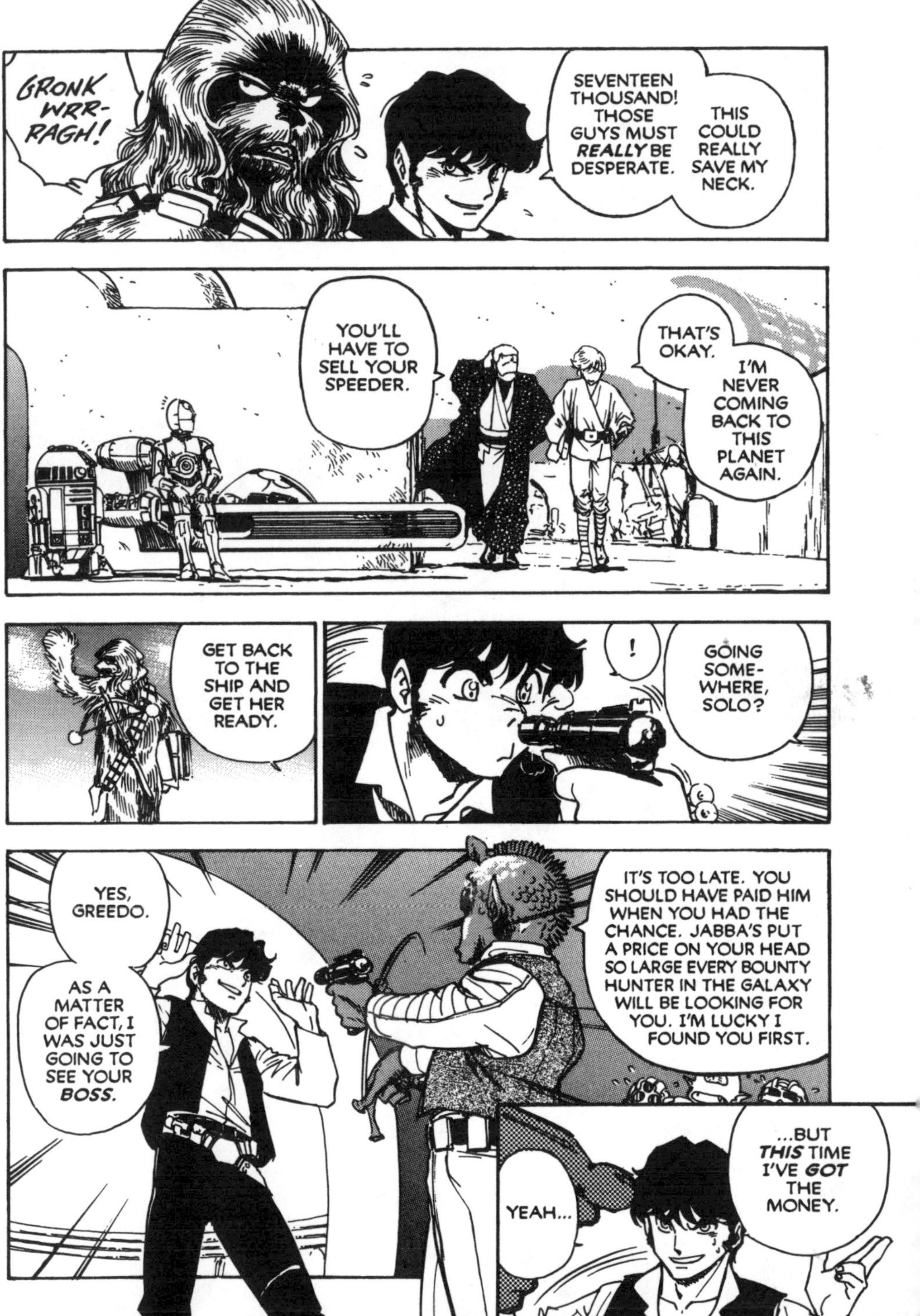
GRONK WRR-RAGH!
SEVENTEEN THOUSAND! THOSE GUYS MUST *REALLY* BE DESPERATE.
THIS COULD REALLY SAVE MY NECK.
YOU'LL HAVE TO SELL YOUR SPEEDER.
THAT'S OKAY.
I'M NEVER COMING BACK TO THIS PLANET AGAIN.
GET BACK TO THE SHIP AND GET HER READY.
!
GOING SOME-WHERE, SOLO?
YES, GREEDO.
AS A MATTER OF FACT, I WAS JUST GOING TO SEE YOUR *BOSS*.
IT'S TOO LATE. YOU SHOULD HAVE PAID HIM WHEN YOU HAD THE CHANCE. JABBA'S PUT A PRICE ON YOUR HEAD SO LARGE EVERY BOUNTY HUNTER IN THE GALAXY WILL BE LOOKING FOR YOU. I'M LUCKY I FOUND YOU FIRST.
YEAH...
...BUT *THIS* TIME I'VE *GOT* THE MONEY.

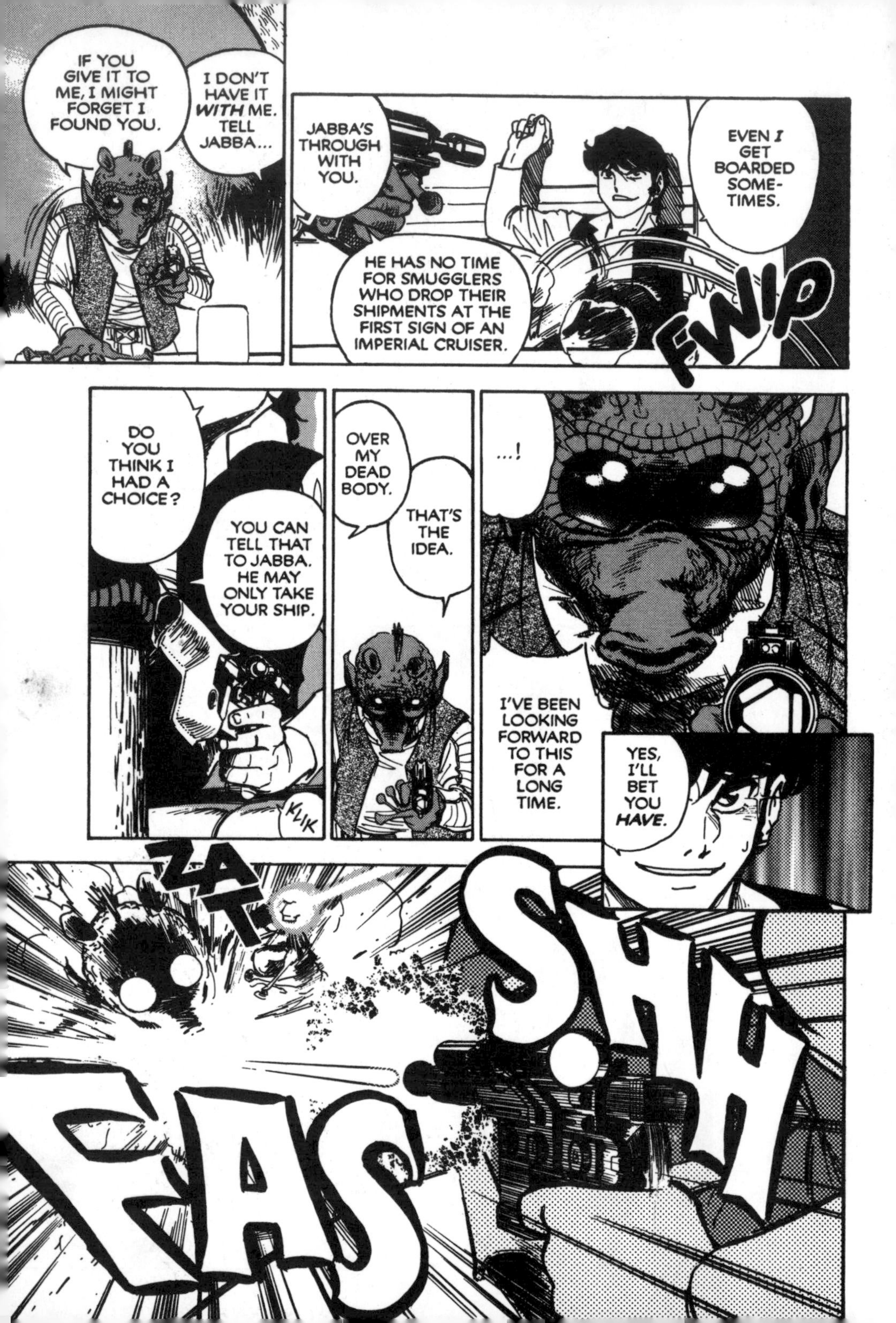
IF YOU GIVE IT TO ME, I MIGHT FORGET I FOUND YOU.
I DON'T HAVE IT *WITH* ME. TELL JABBA...
JABBA'S THROUGH WITH YOU.
HE HAS NO TIME FOR SMUGGLERS WHO DROP THEIR SHIPMENTS AT THE FIRST SIGN OF AN IMPERIAL CRUISER.
EVEN *I* GET BOARDED SOME-TIMES.
FWIP
DO YOU THINK I HAD A CHOICE?
YOU CAN TELL THAT TO JABBA. HE MAY ONLY TAKE YOUR SHIP.
KLIK
OVER MY DEAD BODY.
THAT'S THE IDEA.
...!
I'VE BEEN LOOKING FORWARD TO THIS FOR A LONG TIME.
YES, I'LL BET YOU *HAVE.*
ZAT

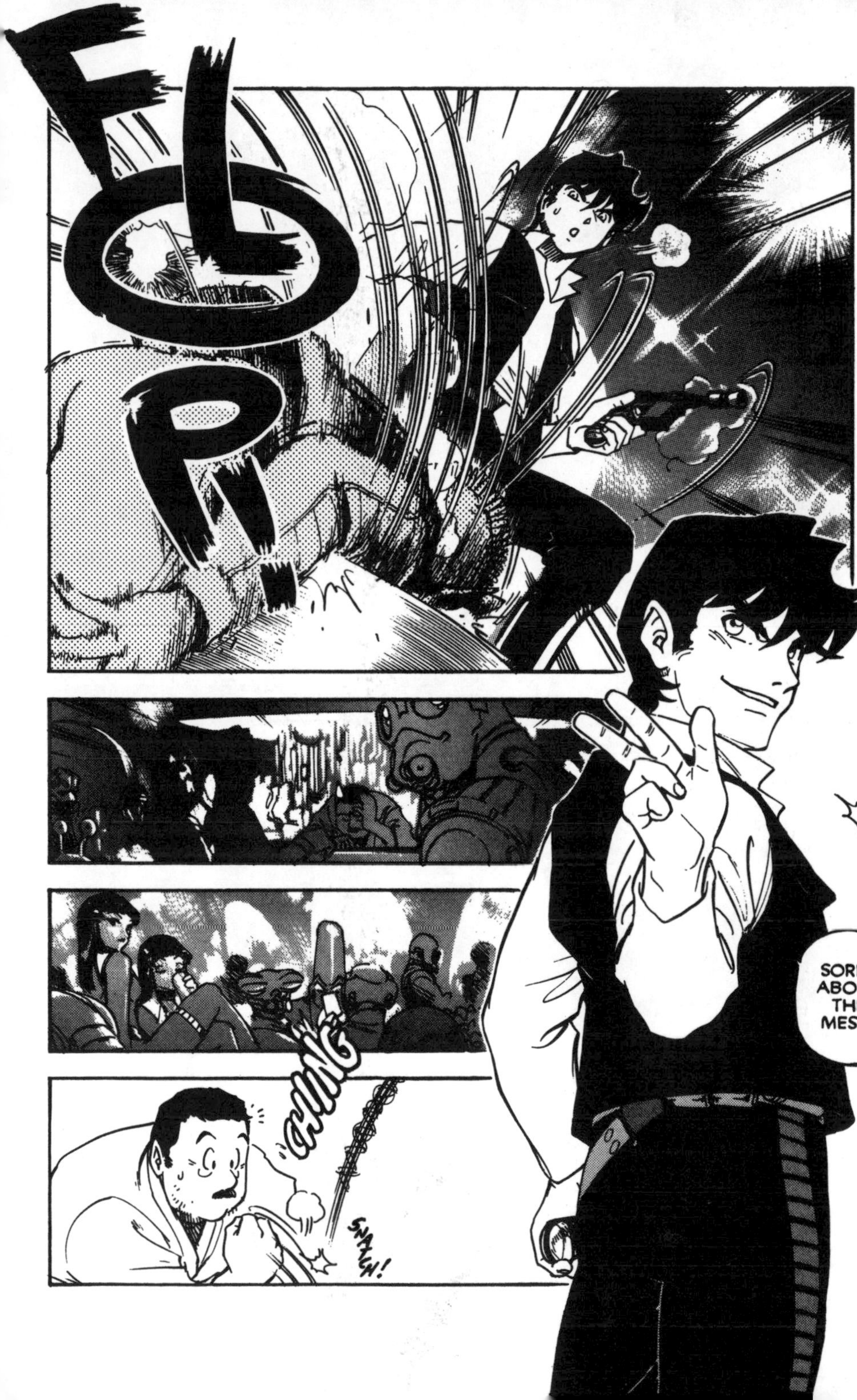
FLOP!
CHING
SNATCH!
SORRY ABOUT THE MESS.

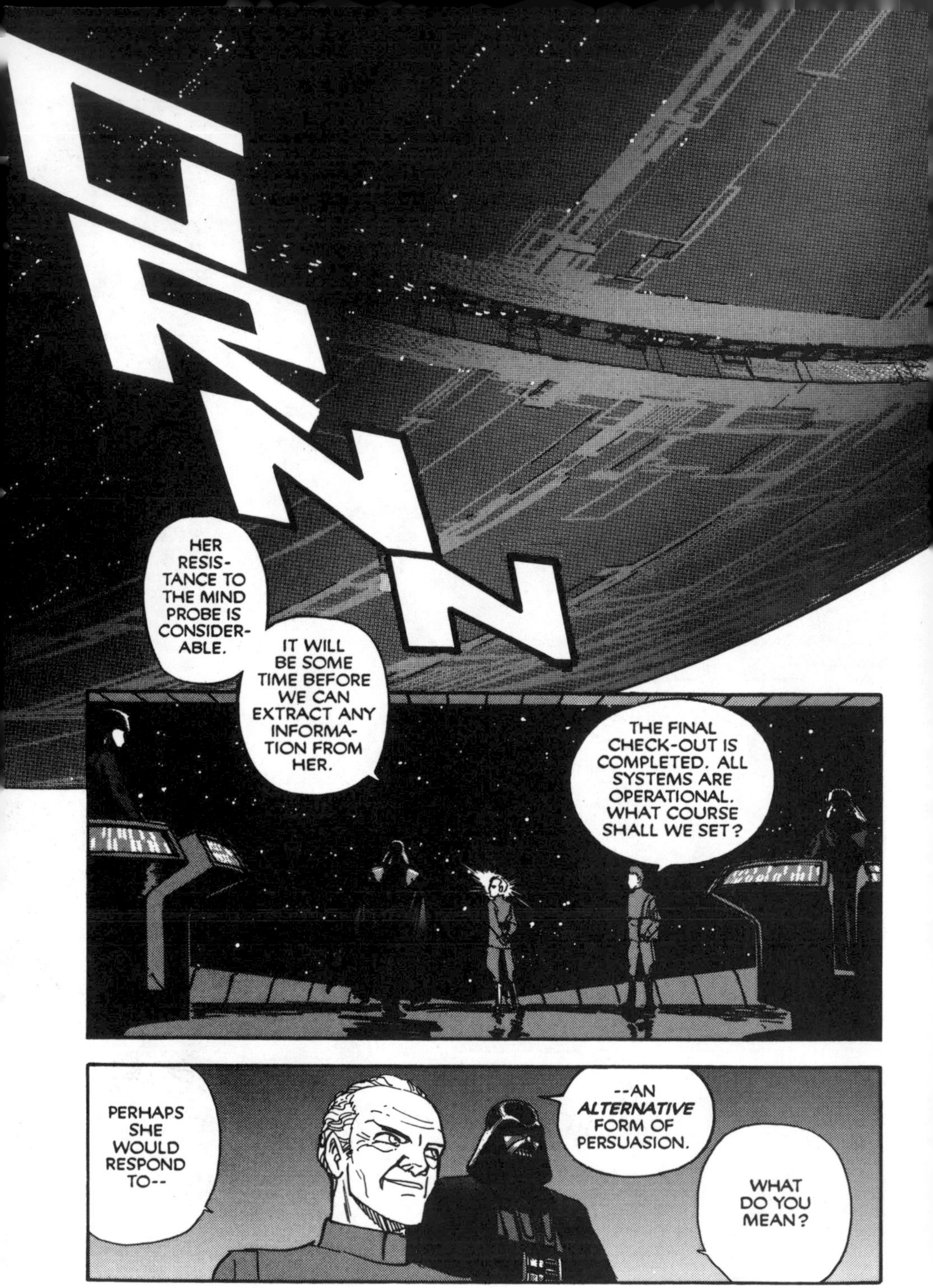
HER RESISTANCE TO THE MIND PROBE IS CONSIDERABLE.
IT WILL BE SOME TIME BEFORE WE CAN EXTRACT ANY INFORMATION FROM HER.
THE FINAL CHECK-OUT IS COMPLETED. ALL SYSTEMS ARE OPERATIONAL. WHAT COURSE SHALL WE SET?
PERHAPS SHE WOULD RESPOND TO--
--AN *ALTERNATIVE* FORM OF PERSUASION.
WHAT DO YOU MEAN?

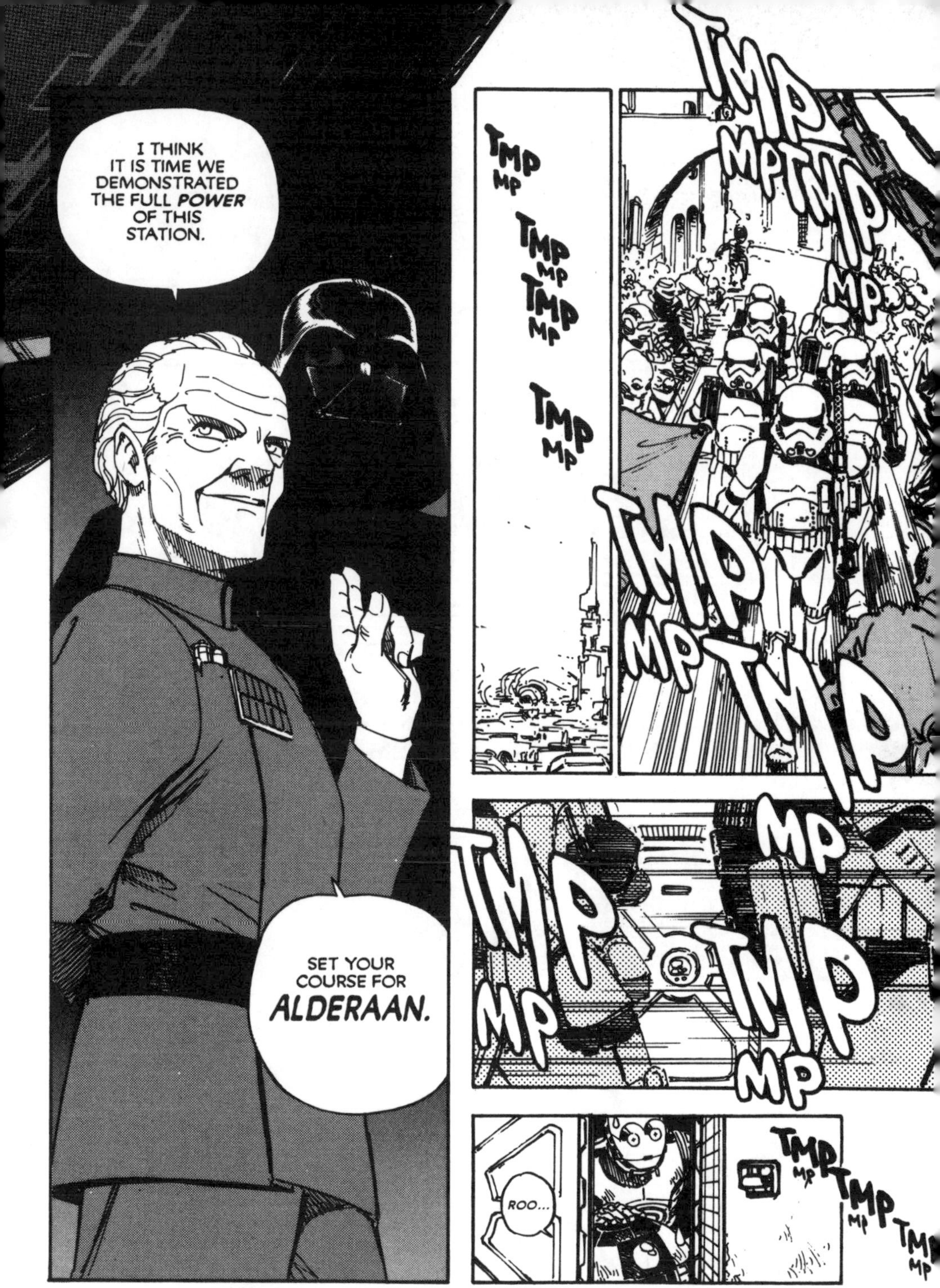
I THINK IT IS TIME WE DEMONSTRATED THE FULL *POWER* OF THIS STATION.
SET YOUR COURSE FOR **ALDERAAN.**
TMP MP TMP MP
TMP MP
TMP MP
TMP MP
TMP MP
TMP MP TMP MP
TMP MP TMP MP
TMP MP
ROO...
TMP MP TMP MP TMP MP

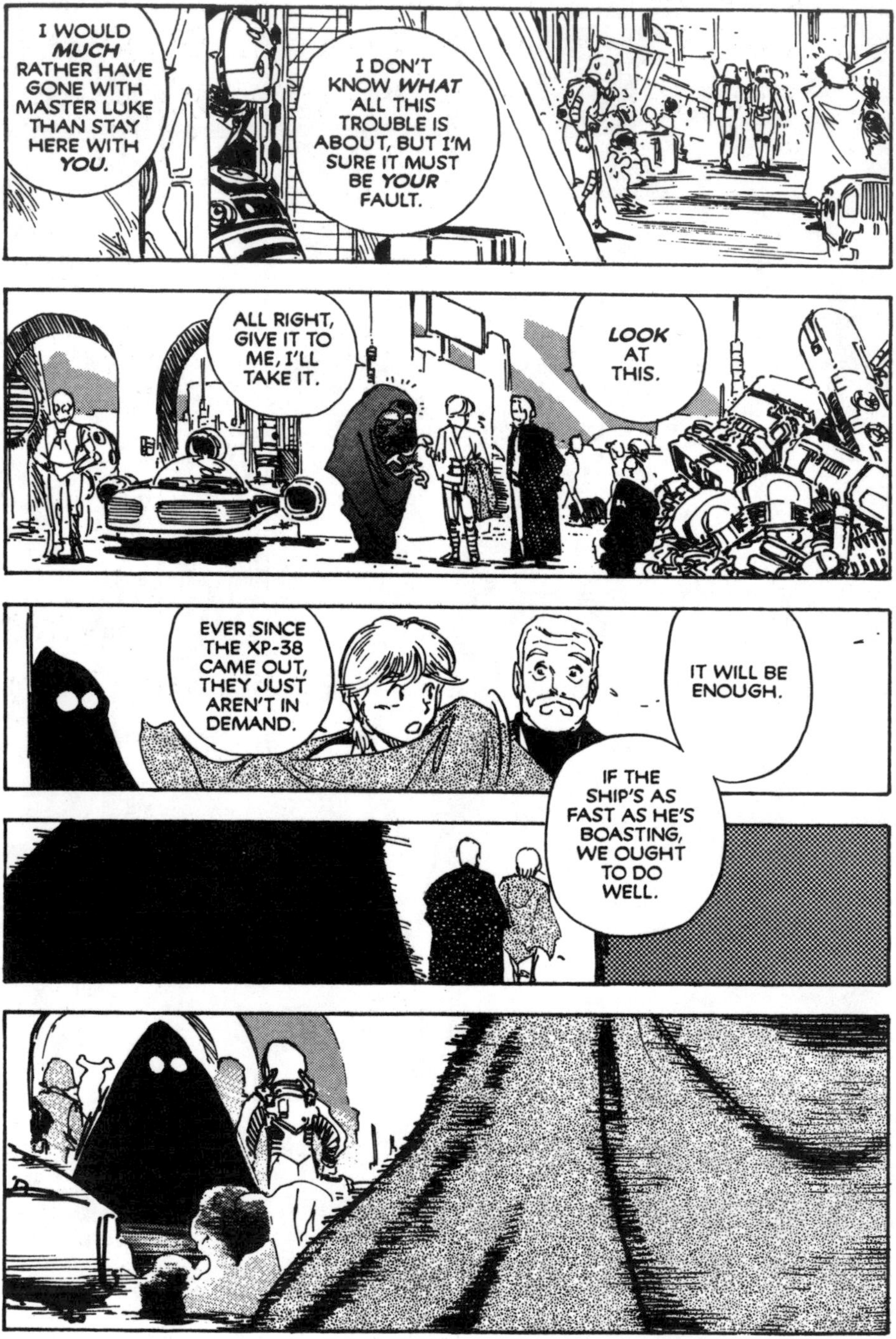
I WOULD *MUCH* RATHER HAVE GONE WITH MASTER LUKE THAN STAY HERE WITH *YOU.*
I DON'T KNOW *WHAT* ALL THIS TROUBLE IS ABOUT, BUT I'M SURE IT MUST BE *YOUR* FAULT.
ALL RIGHT, GIVE IT TO ME, I'LL TAKE IT.
LOOK AT THIS.
EVER SINCE THE XP-38 CAME OUT, THEY JUST AREN'T IN DEMAND.
IT WILL BE ENOUGH.
IF THE SHIP'S AS FAST AS HE'S BOASTING, WE OUGHT TO DO WELL.

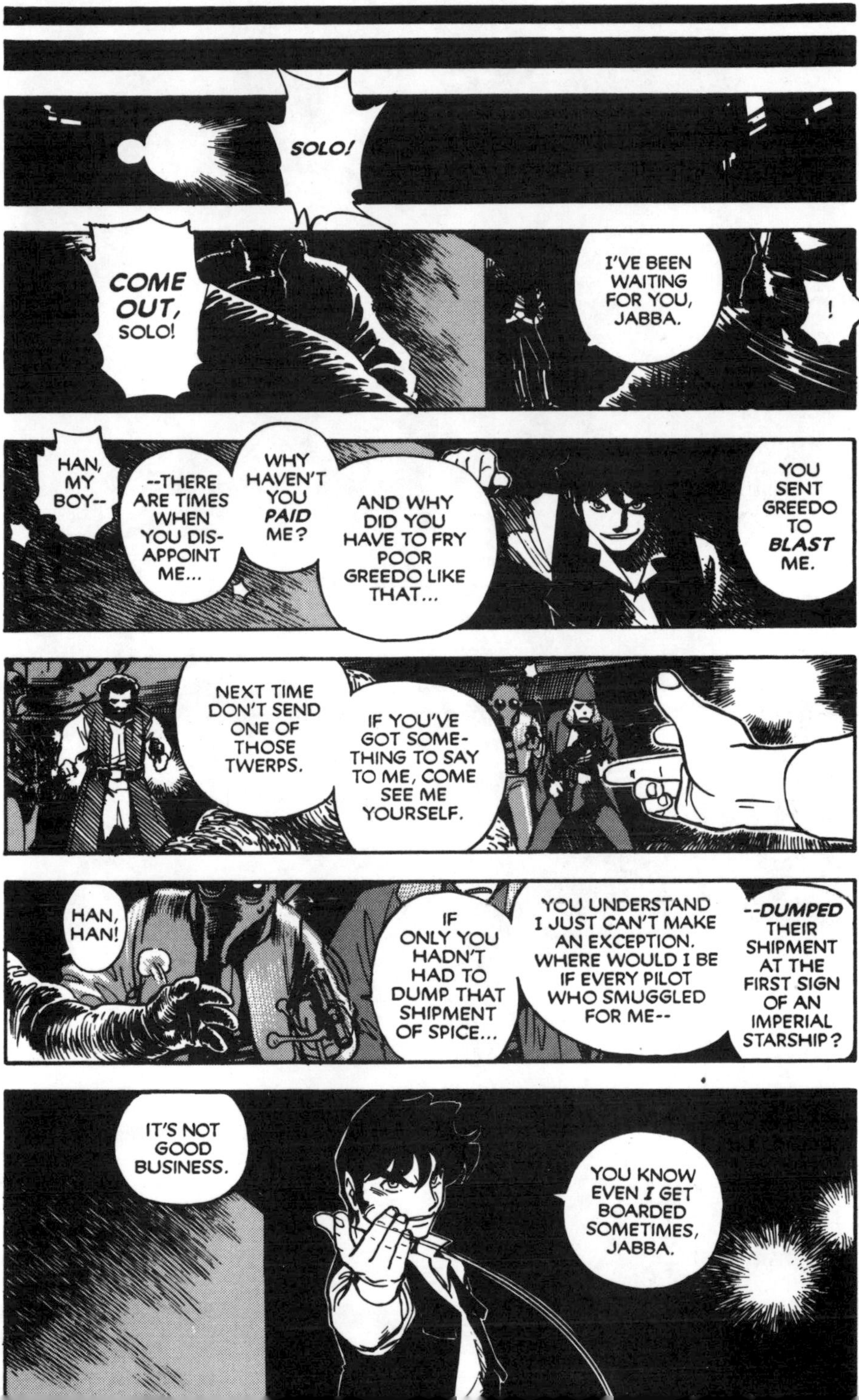
SOLO!
COME OUT, SOLO!
I'VE BEEN WAITING FOR YOU, JABBA.
!
HAN, MY BOY--
--THERE ARE TIMES WHEN YOU DIS-APPOINT ME...
WHY HAVEN'T YOU PAID ME?
AND WHY DID YOU HAVE TO FRY POOR GREEDO LIKE THAT...
YOU SENT GREEDO TO BLAST ME.
NEXT TIME DON'T SEND ONE OF THOSE TWERPS.
IF YOU'VE GOT SOME-THING TO SAY TO ME, COME SEE ME YOURSELF.
HAN, HAN!
IF ONLY YOU HADN'T HAD TO DUMP THAT SHIPMENT OF SPICE...
YOU UNDERSTAND I JUST CAN'T MAKE AN EXCEPTION. WHERE WOULD I BE IF EVERY PILOT WHO SMUGGLED FOR ME--
--DUMPED THEIR SHIPMENT AT THE FIRST SIGN OF AN IMPERIAL STARSHIP?
IT'S NOT GOOD BUSINESS.
YOU KNOW EVEN I GET BOARDED SOMETIMES, JABBA.

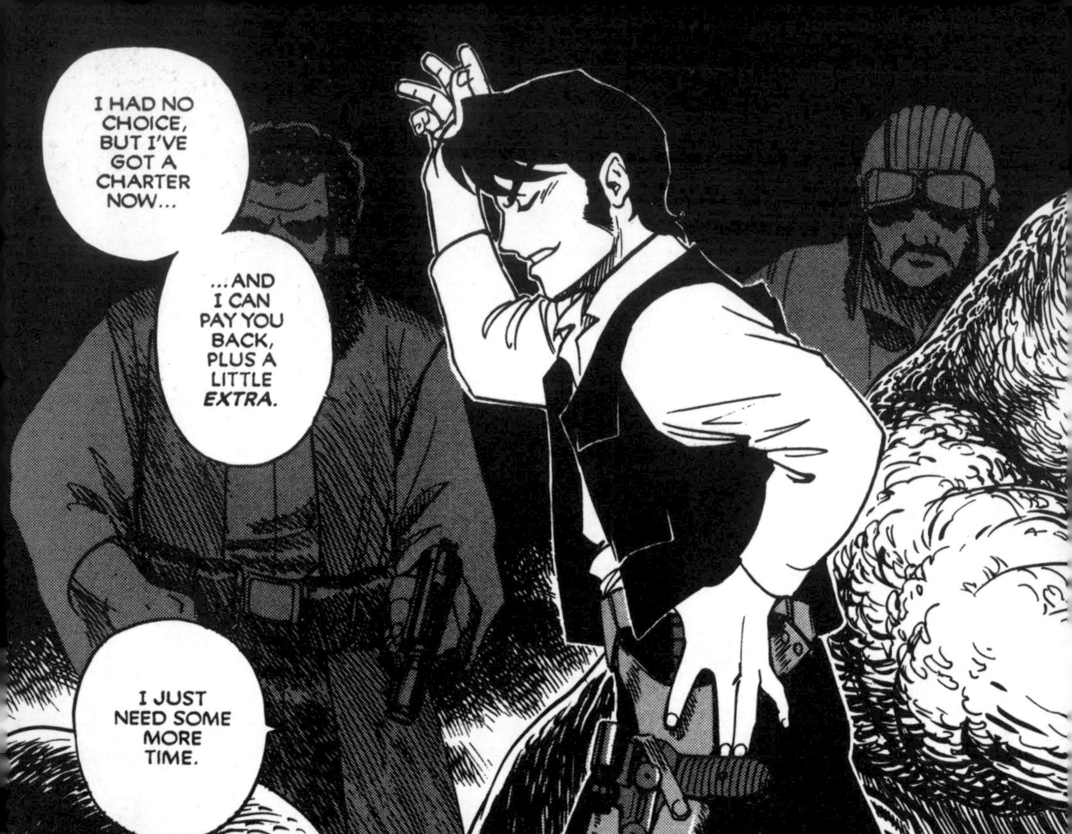
I HAD NO CHOICE, BUT I'VE GOT A CHARTER NOW...
...AND I CAN PAY YOU BACK, PLUS A LITTLE ***EXTRA***.
I JUST NEED SOME MORE TIME.

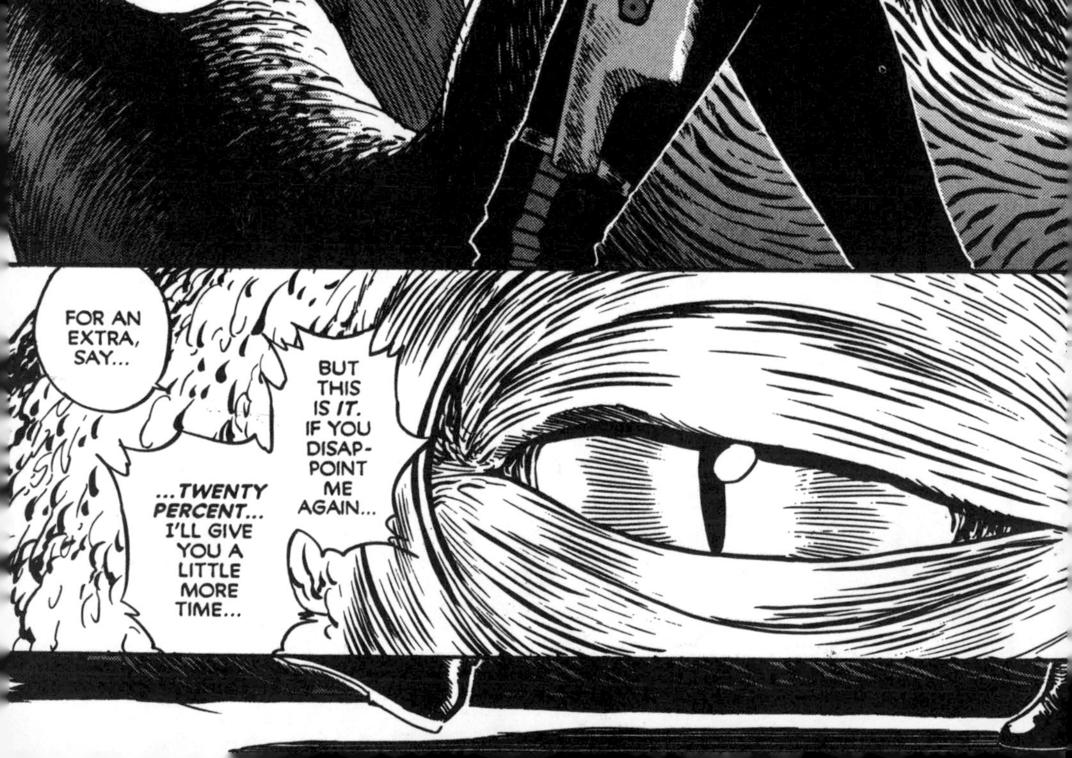
FOR AN EXTRA, SAY...
...TWENTY PERCENT... I'LL GIVE YOU A LITTLE MORE TIME...
BUT THIS IS ***IT***. IF YOU DISAPPOINT ME AGAIN...

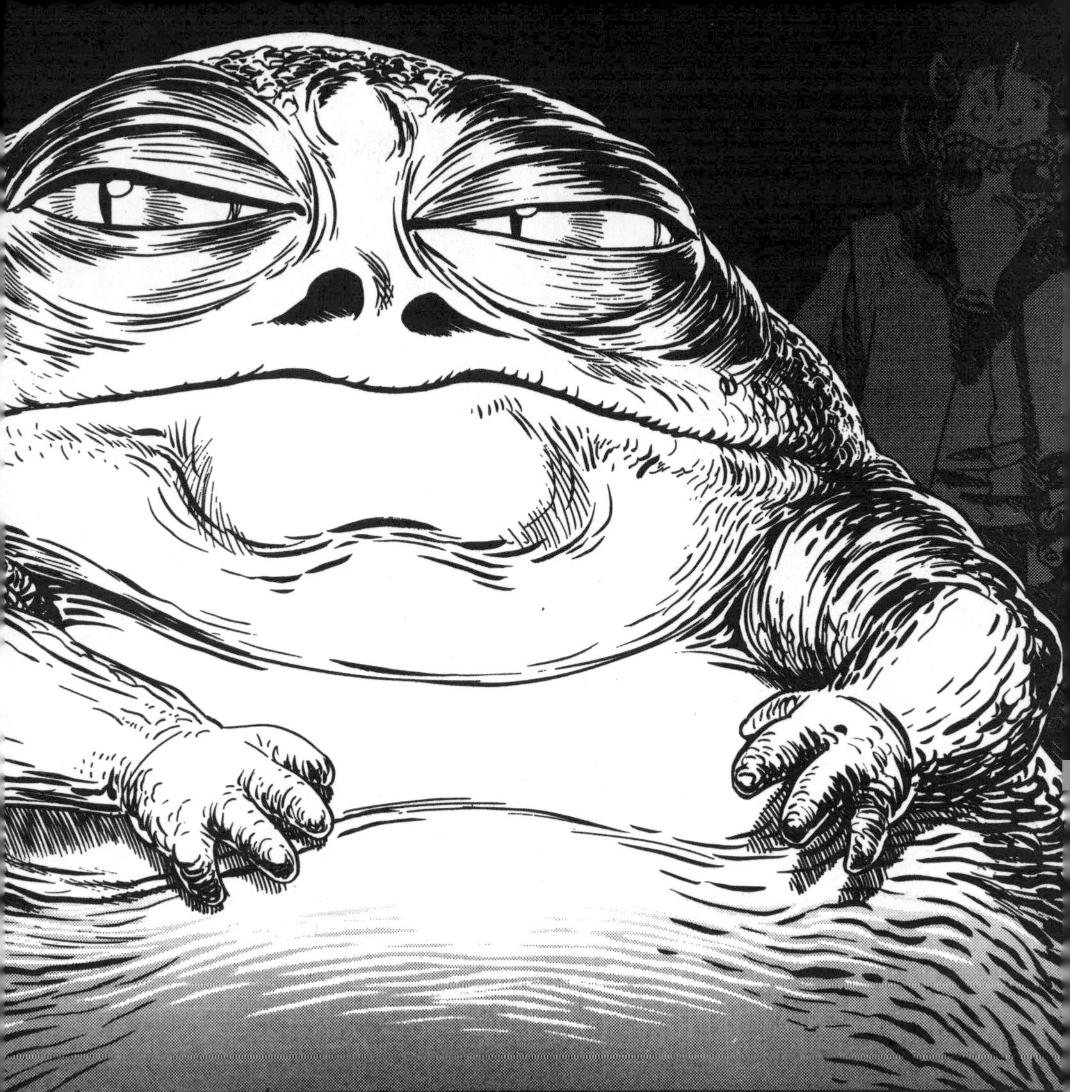

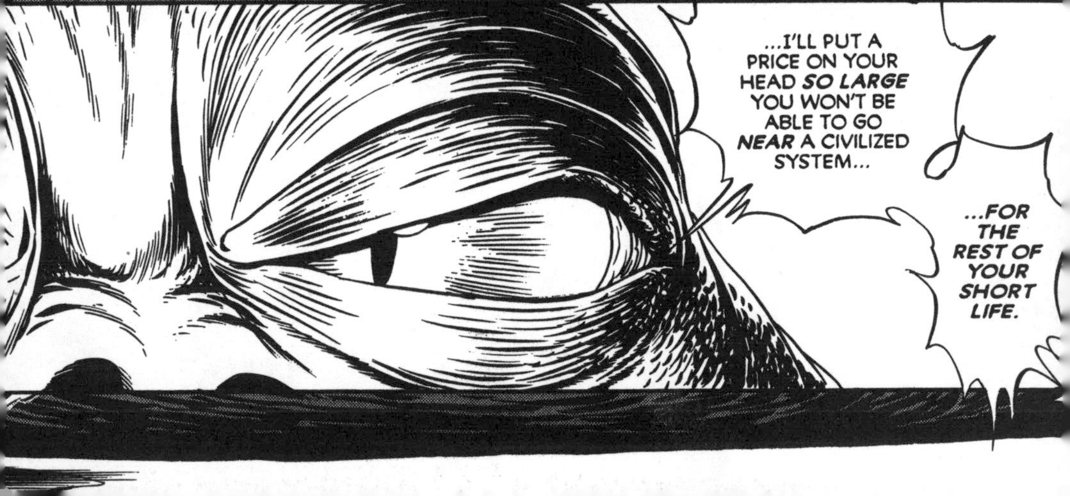
...I'LL PUT A PRICE ON YOUR HEAD SO LARGE YOU WON'T BE ABLE TO GO NEAR A CIVILIZED SYSTEM...
...FOR THE REST OF YOUR SHORT LIFE.

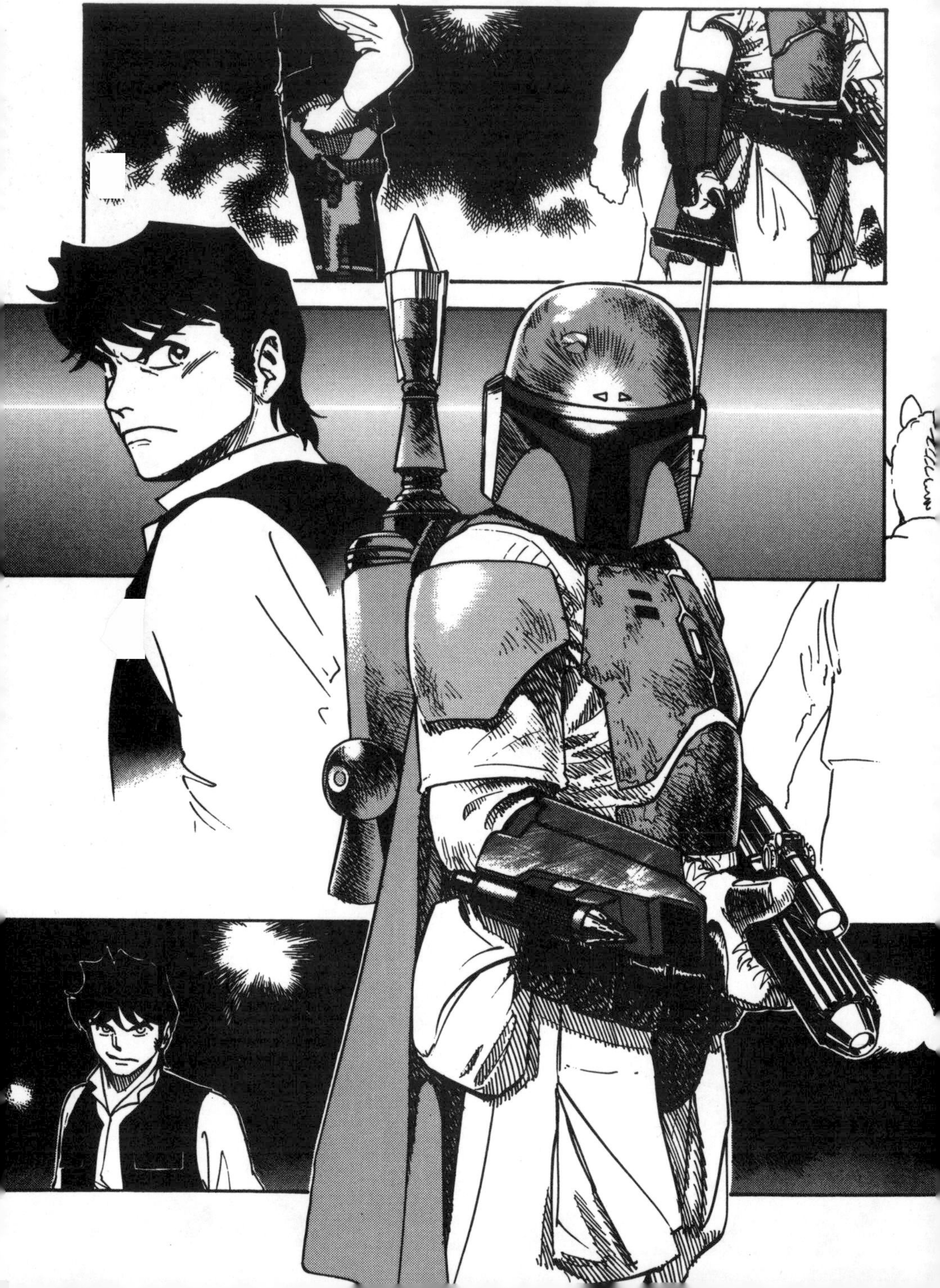

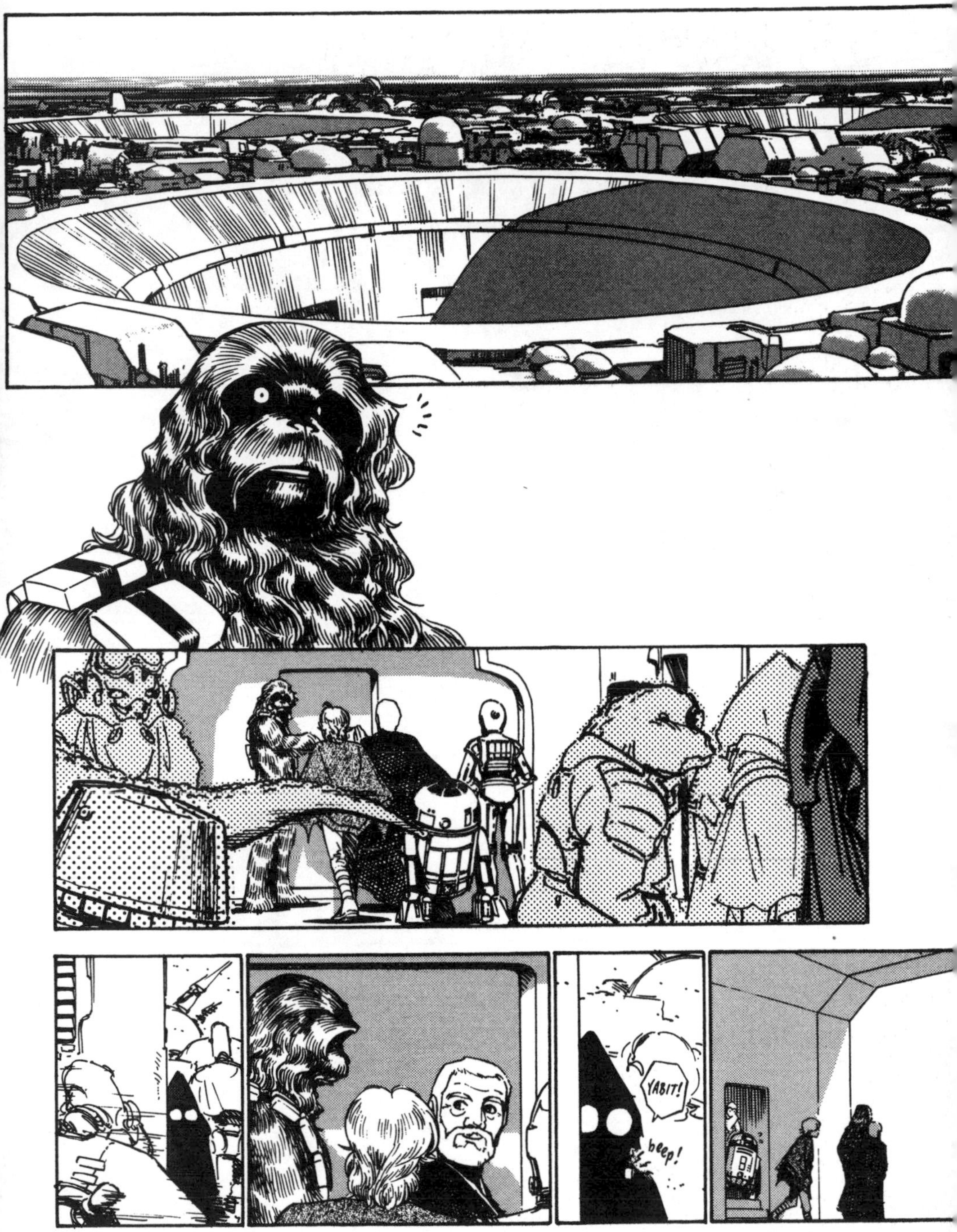
YABIT!
beep!

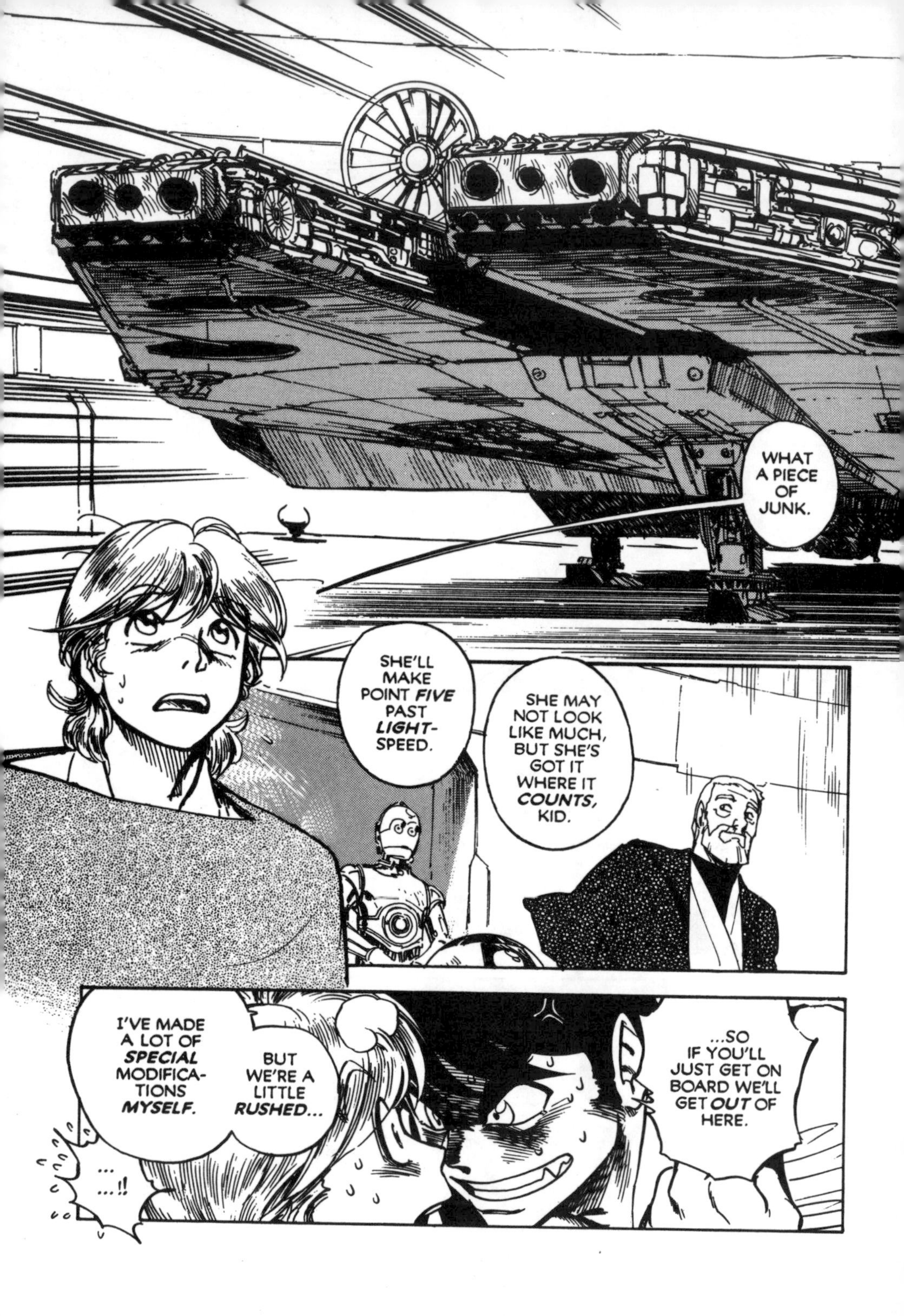
WHAT A PIECE OF JUNK.
SHE'LL MAKE POINT FIVE PAST LIGHT-SPEED.
SHE MAY NOT LOOK LIKE MUCH, BUT SHE'S GOT IT WHERE IT COUNTS, KID.
I'VE MADE A LOT OF SPECIAL MODIFICATIONS MYSELF.
BUT WE'RE A LITTLE RUSHED...
...SO IF YOU'LL JUST GET ON BOARD WE'LL GET OUT OF HERE.
... ...!!

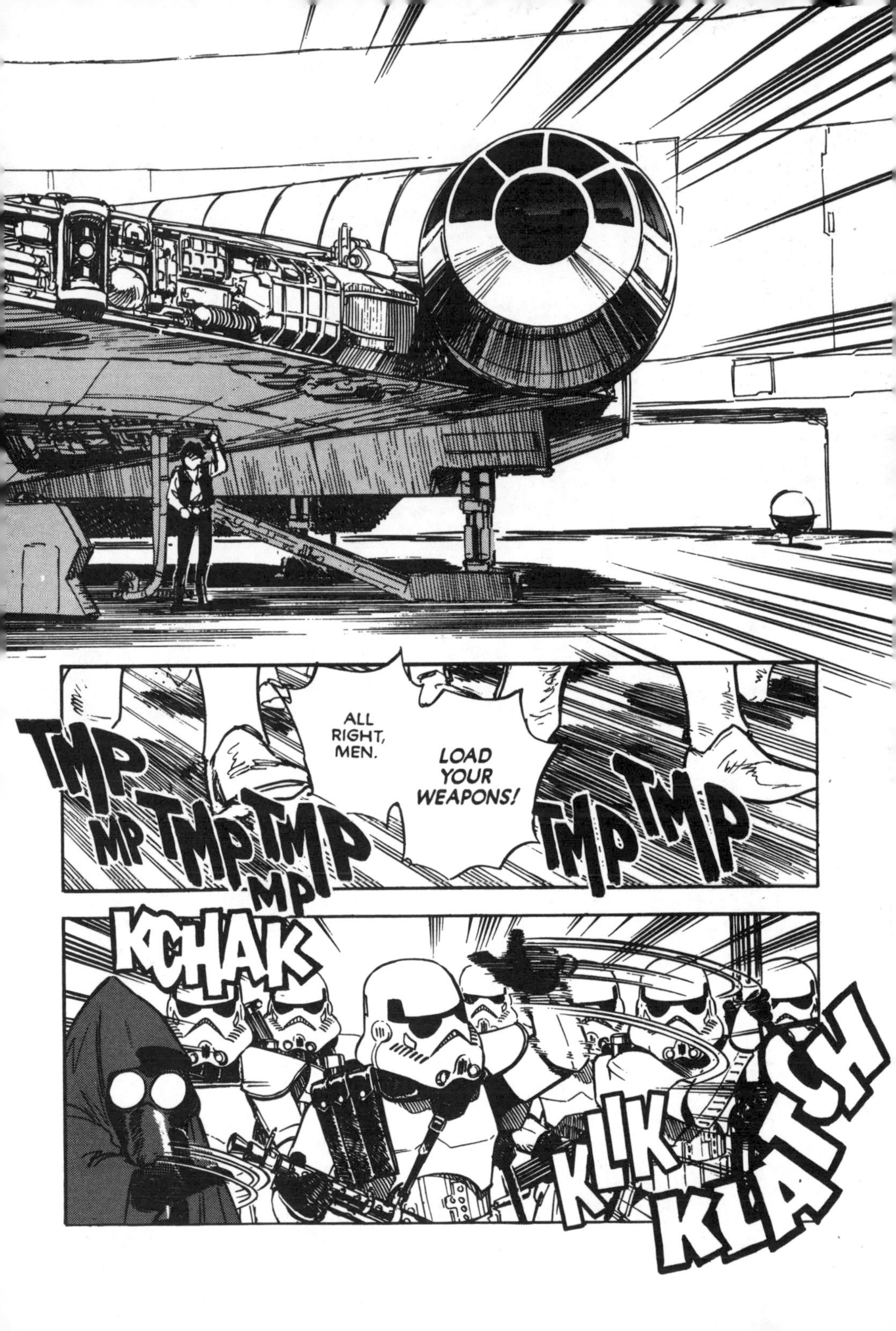
TMP MP TMP TMP MP
ALL RIGHT, MEN.
LOAD YOUR WEAPONS!
TMP TMP
KCHAK
KLIK KLATCH

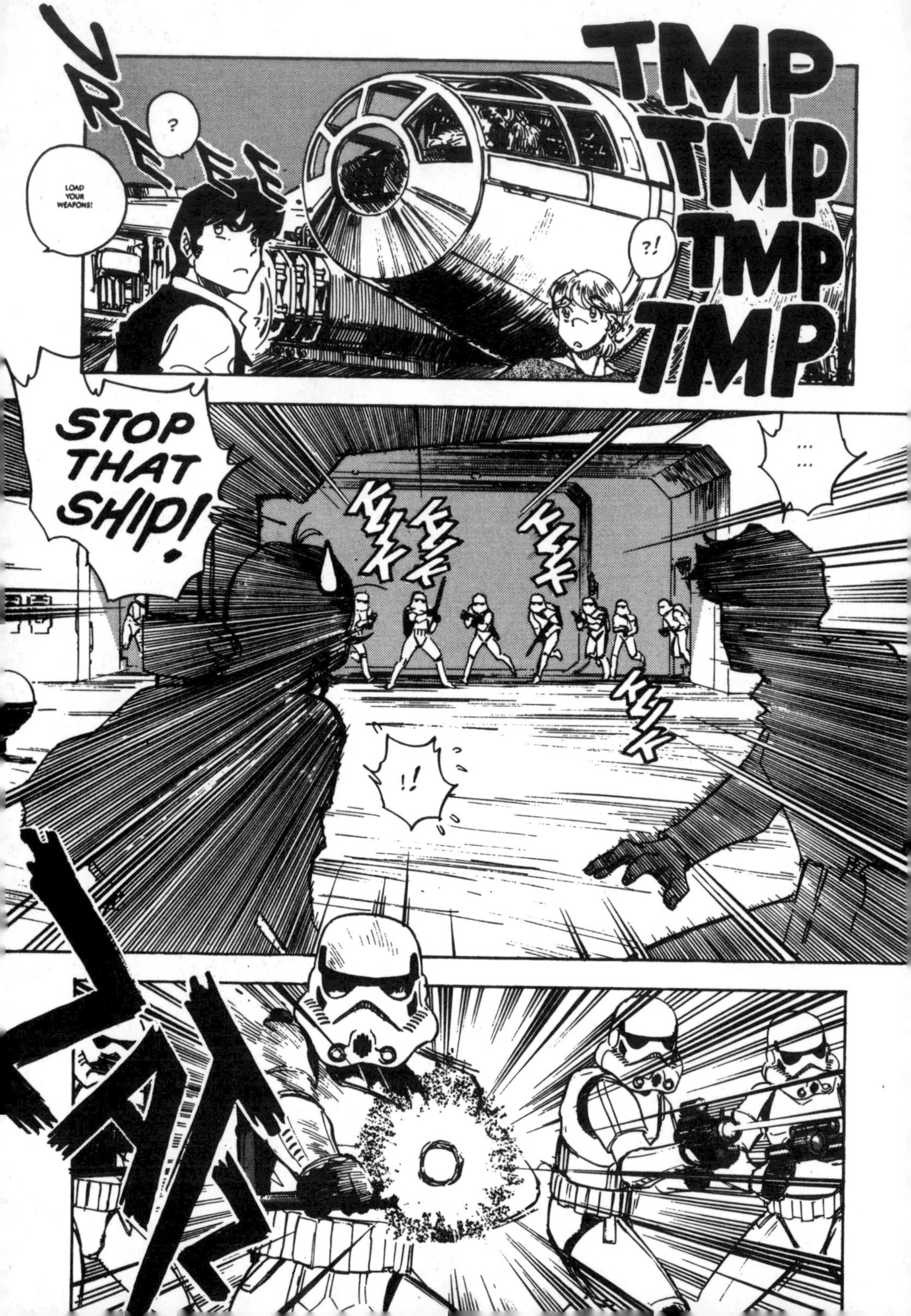
LOAD YOUR WEAPONS!
VREEEE
?
?!
TMP TMP TMP TMP
STOP THAT SHIP!
KLIK KLIK KLIK
... ...
!!
KLIK

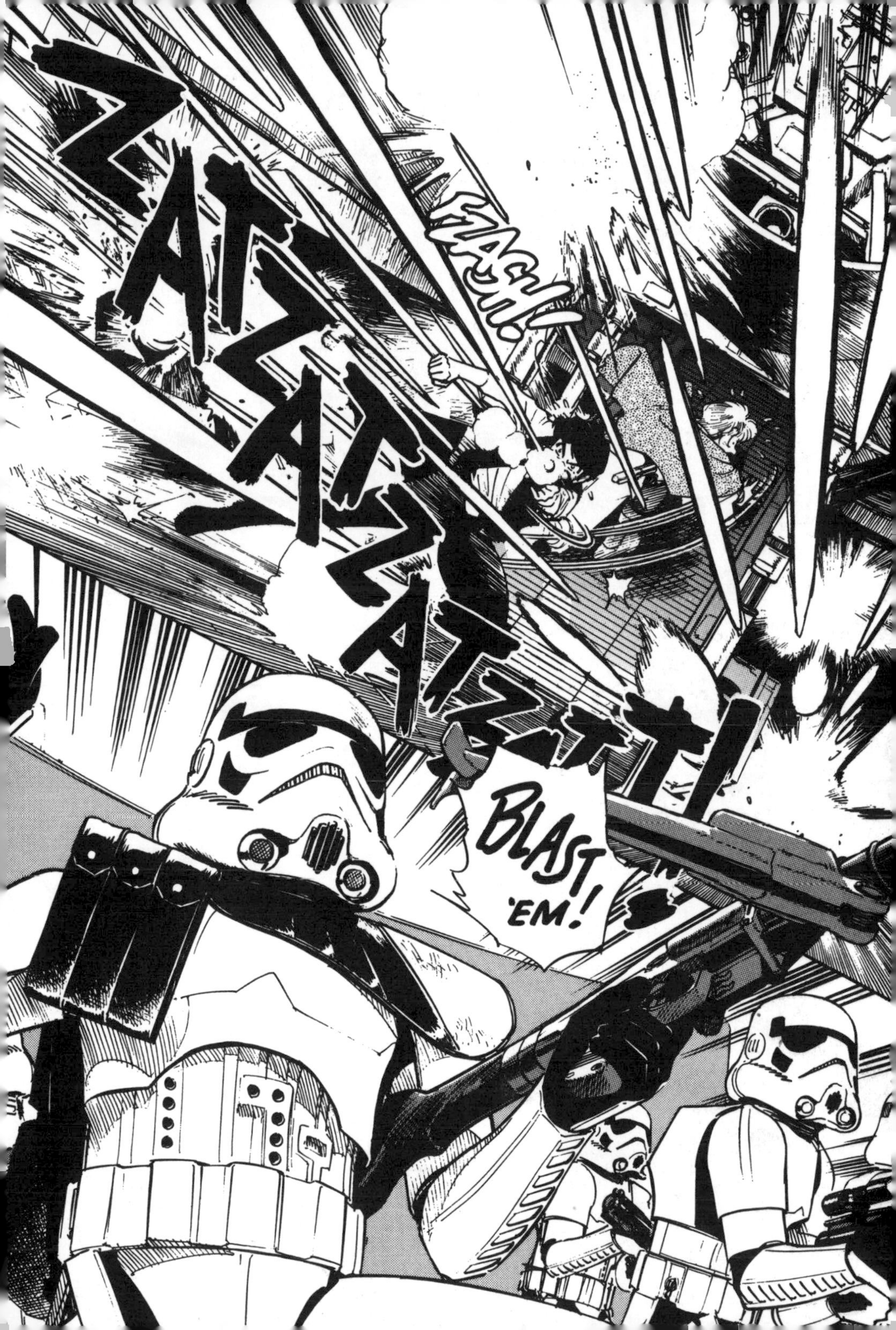
ZATZATZATZATTT!
ZZACH!!
BLAST 'EM!

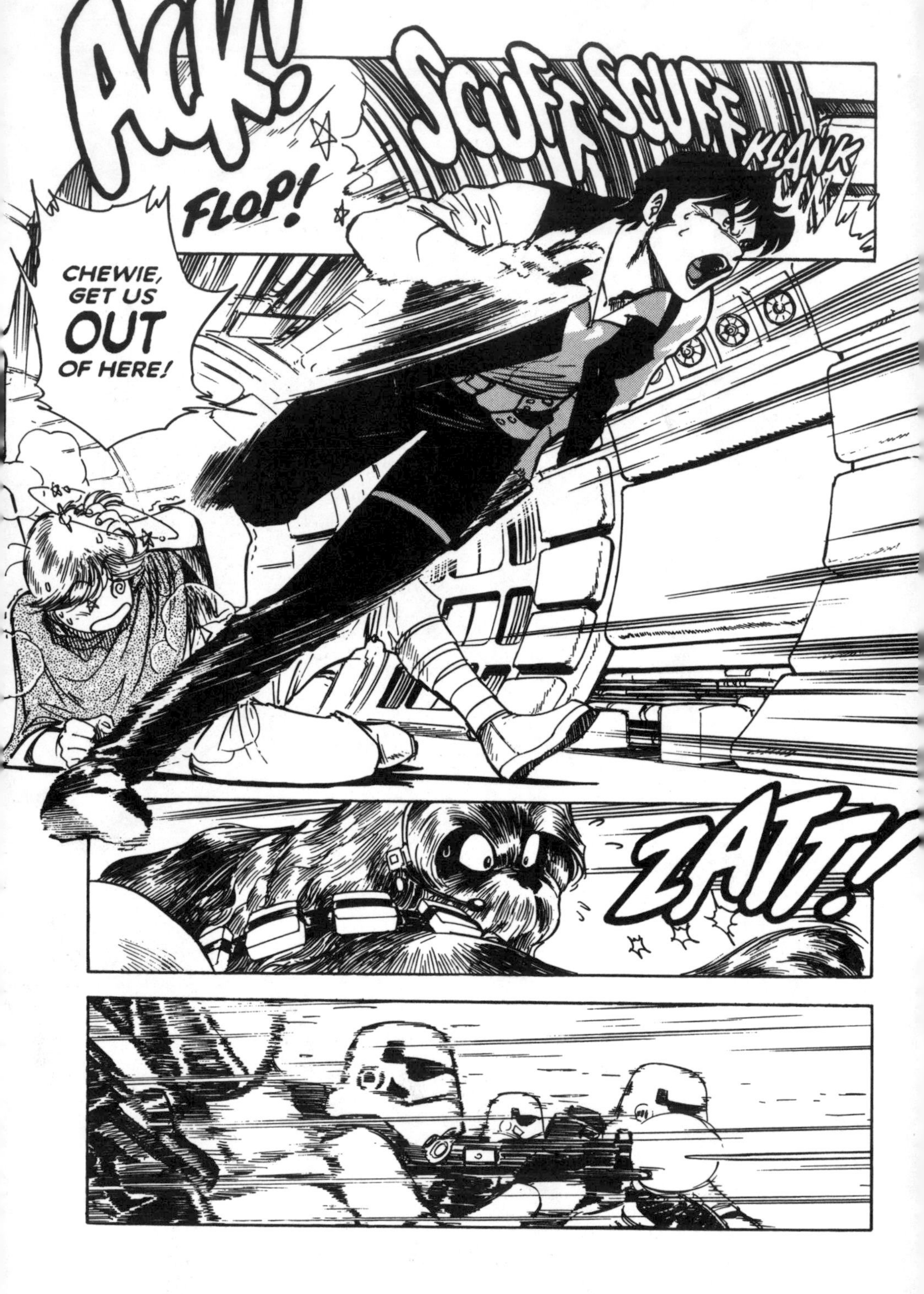
ACK!
SCUFF SCUFF
KLANK
FLOP!
CHEWIE, GET US OUT OF HERE!
ZAT!

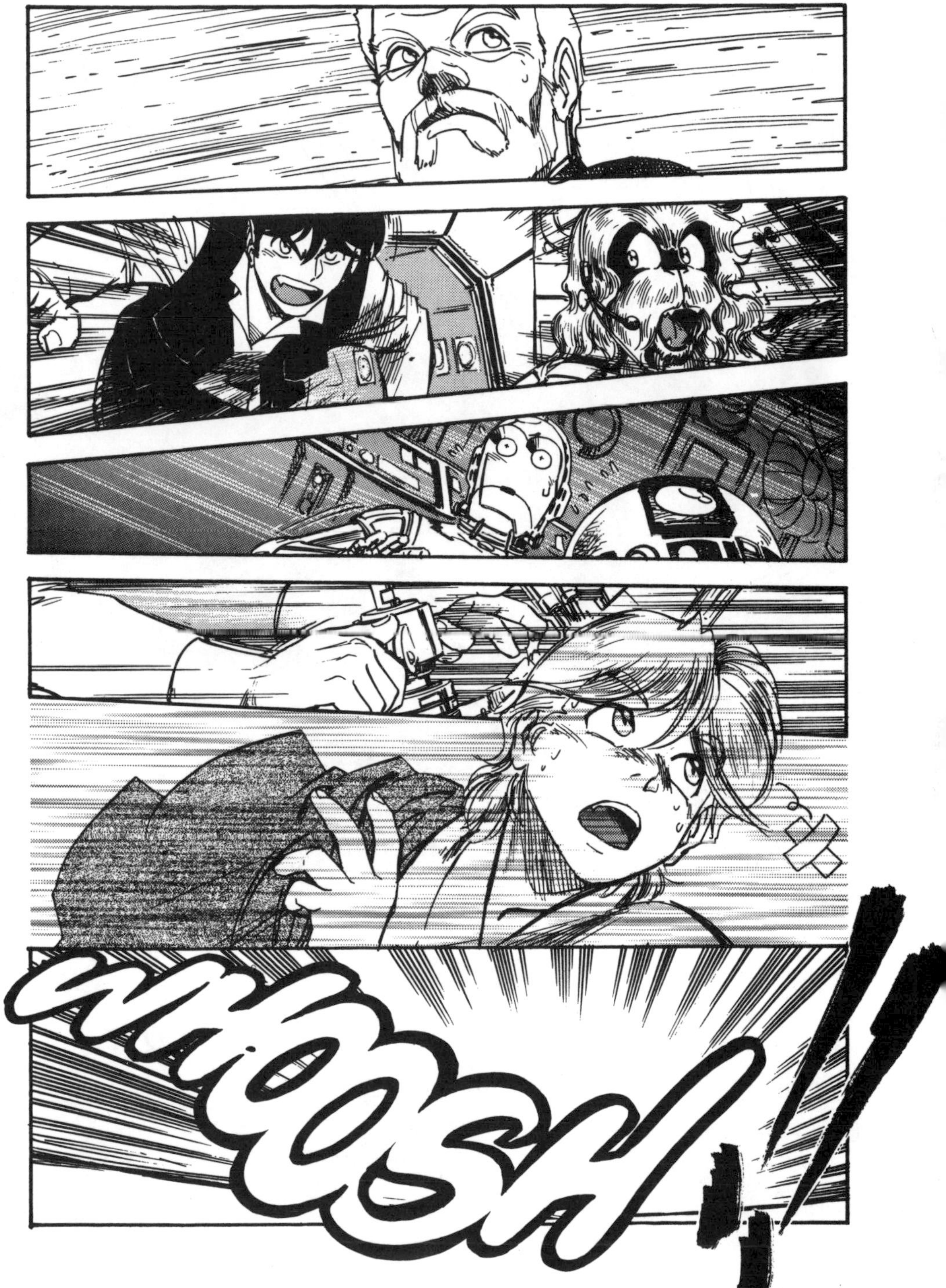
WHOOSH!!

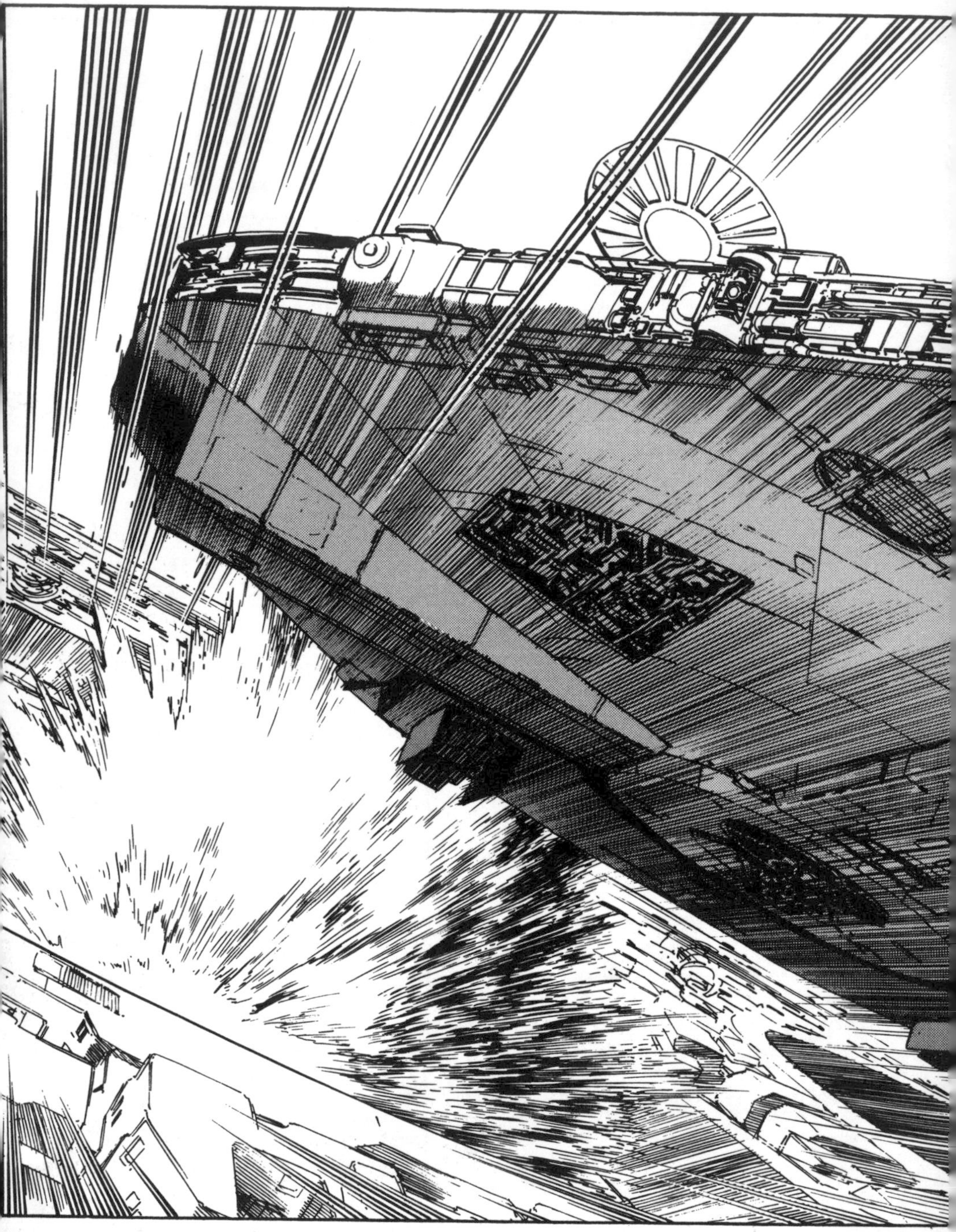

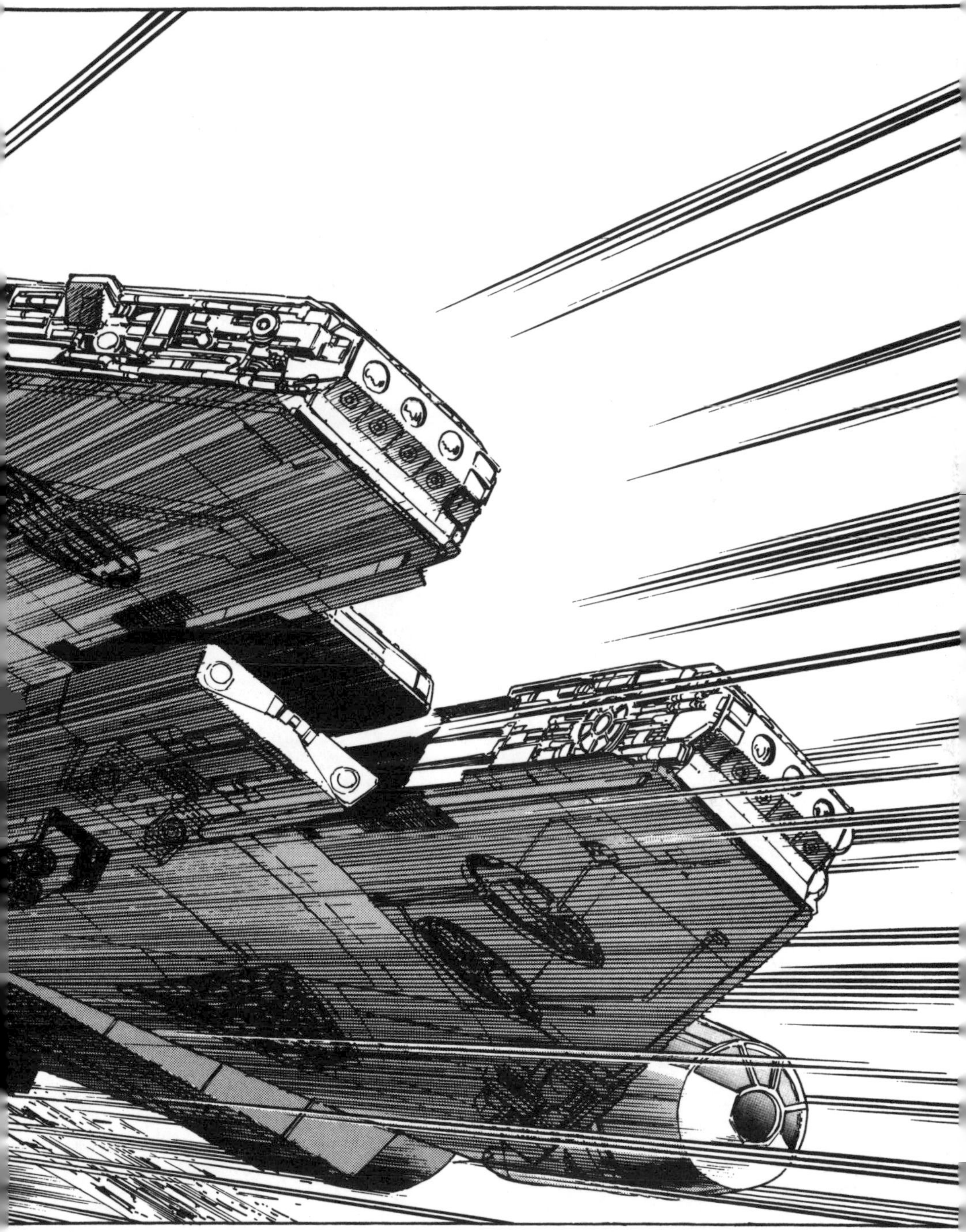

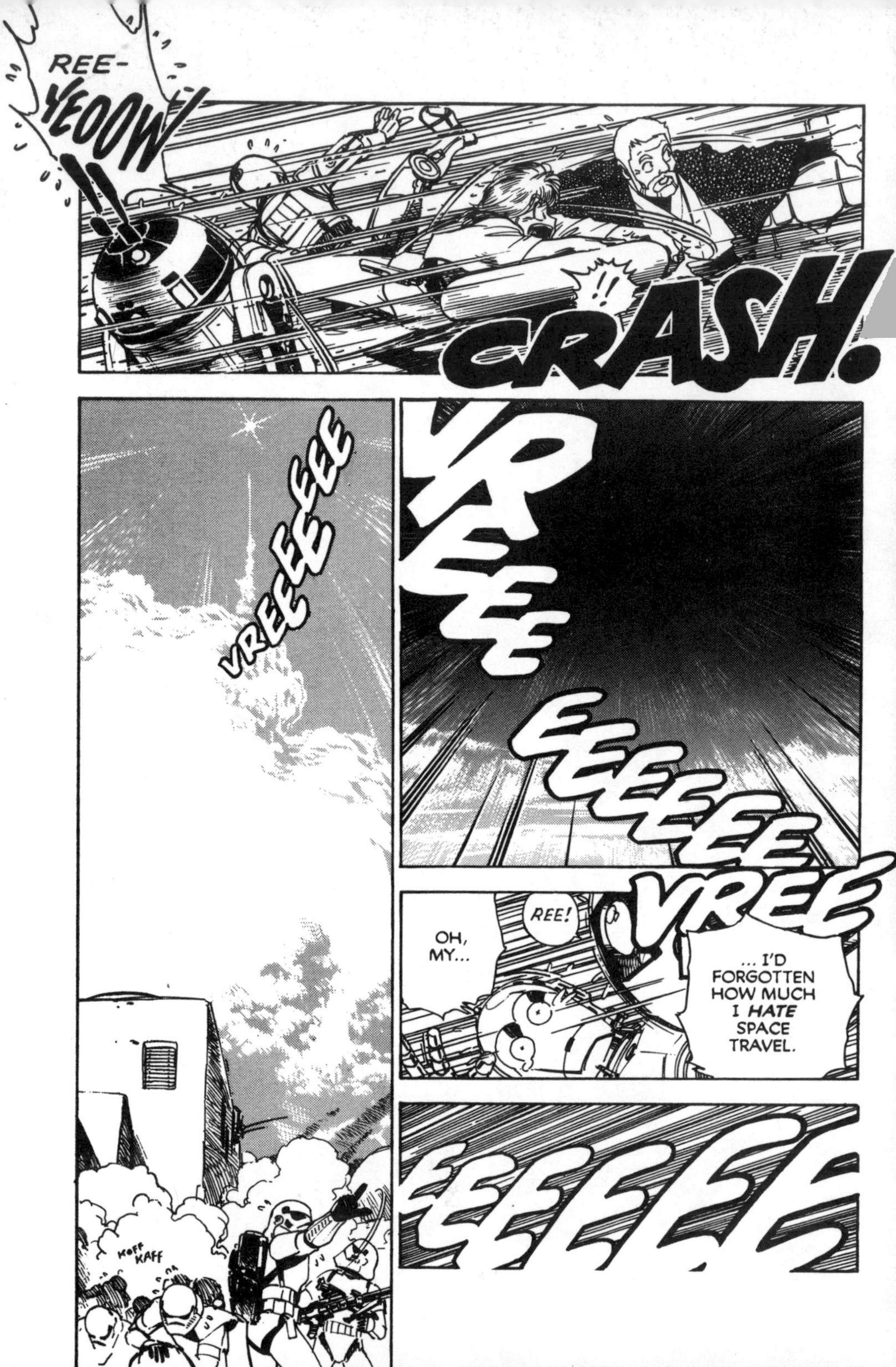
REE-
YEOOW!!
!!
CRASH.
VREEEEEEE
KOFF KAFF
VREEE
EEEEEEEE
VREE
REE!
OH, MY...
... I'D FORGOTTEN HOW MUCH I *HATE* SPACE TRAVEL.
EEEEEE

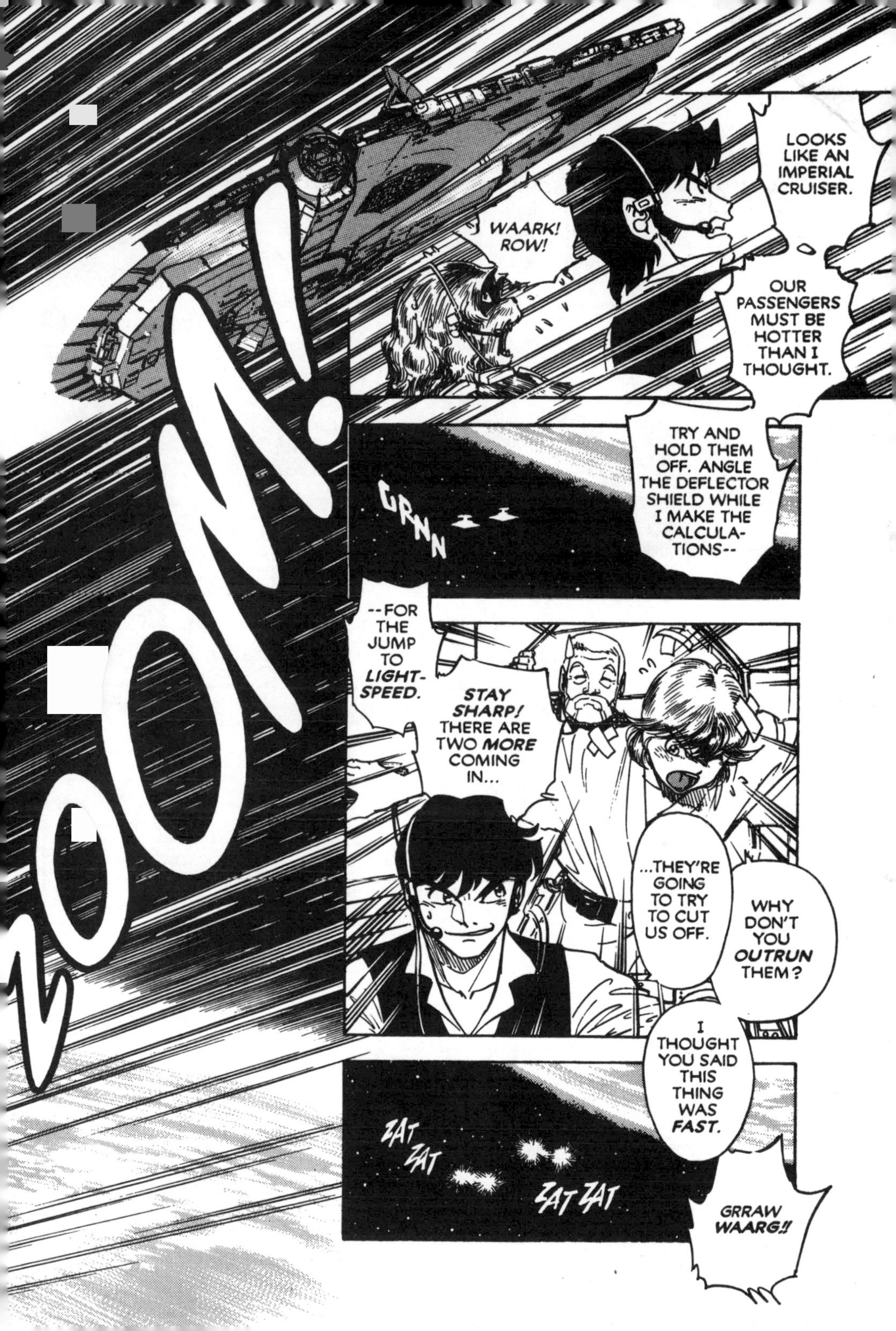
ZOOM!
LOOKS LIKE AN IMPERIAL CRUISER.
WAARK! ROW!
OUR PASSENGERS MUST BE HOTTER THAN I THOUGHT.
GRNN
TRY AND HOLD THEM OFF. ANGLE THE DEFLECTOR SHIELD WHILE I MAKE THE CALCULA-TIONS--
--FOR THE JUMP TO LIGHT-SPEED.
STAY SHARP! THERE ARE TWO MORE COMING IN...
...THEY'RE GOING TO TRY TO CUT US OFF.
WHY DON'T YOU OUTRUN THEM?
I THOUGHT YOU SAID THIS THING WAS FAST.
ZAT ZAT
ZAT ZAT
GRRAW WAARG!!

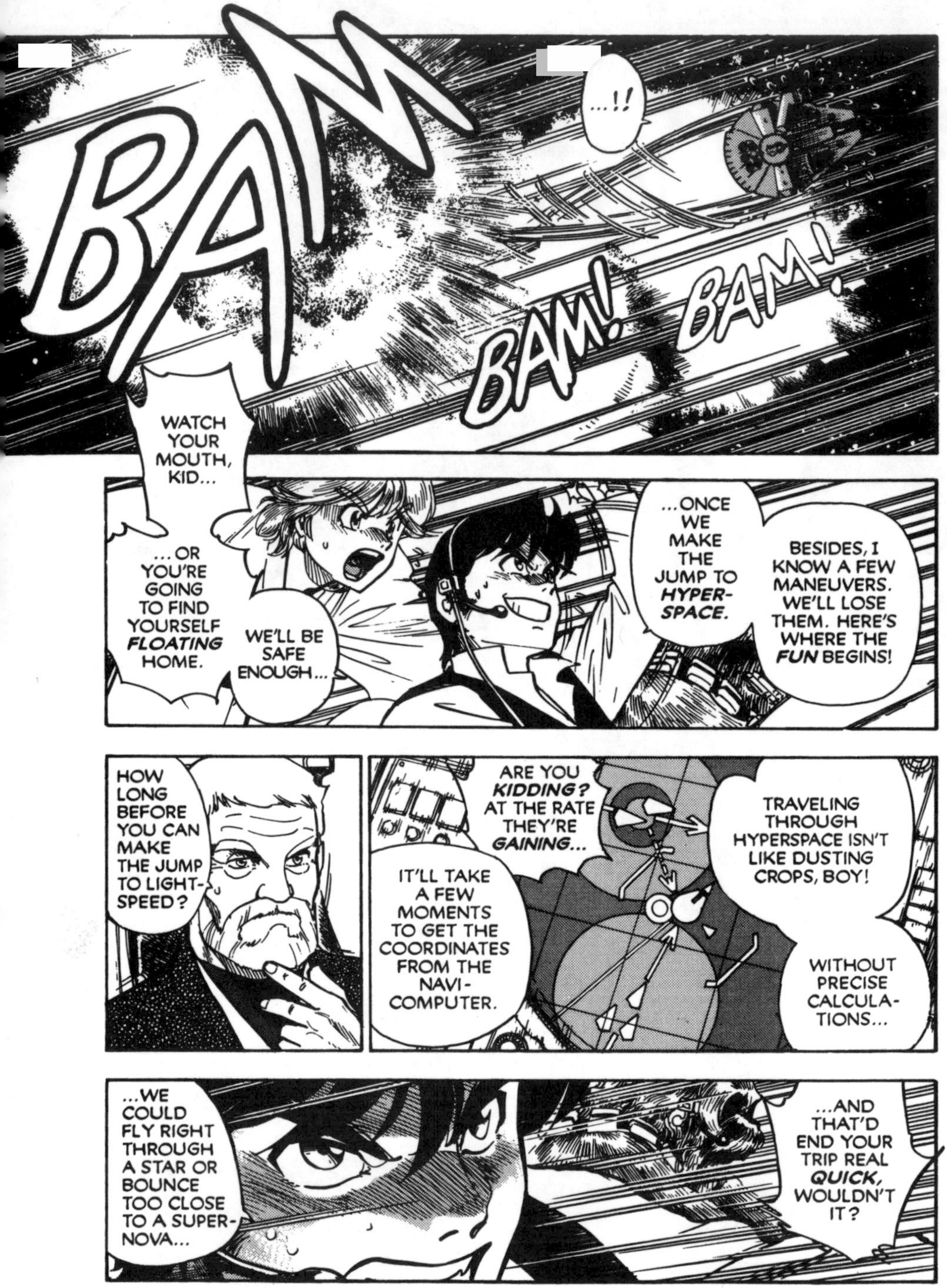
BAM
...!!
BAM! BAM!
WATCH YOUR MOUTH, KID...
...OR YOU'RE GOING TO FIND YOURSELF *FLOATING* HOME.
WE'LL BE SAFE ENOUGH...
...ONCE WE MAKE THE JUMP TO *HYPER-SPACE.*
BESIDES, I KNOW A FEW MANEUVERS. WE'LL LOSE THEM. HERE'S WHERE THE *FUN* BEGINS!
HOW LONG BEFORE YOU CAN MAKE THE JUMP TO LIGHT-SPEED?
ARE YOU *KIDDING?* AT THE RATE THEY'RE *GAINING...*
IT'LL TAKE A FEW MOMENTS TO GET THE COORDINATES FROM THE NAVI-COMPUTER.
TRAVELING THROUGH HYPERSPACE ISN'T LIKE DUSTING CROPS, BOY!
WITHOUT PRECISE CALCULA-TIONS...
...WE COULD FLY RIGHT THROUGH A STAR OR BOUNCE TOO CLOSE TO A SUPER-NOVA...
...AND THAT'D END YOUR TRIP REAL *QUICK,* WOULDN'T IT?

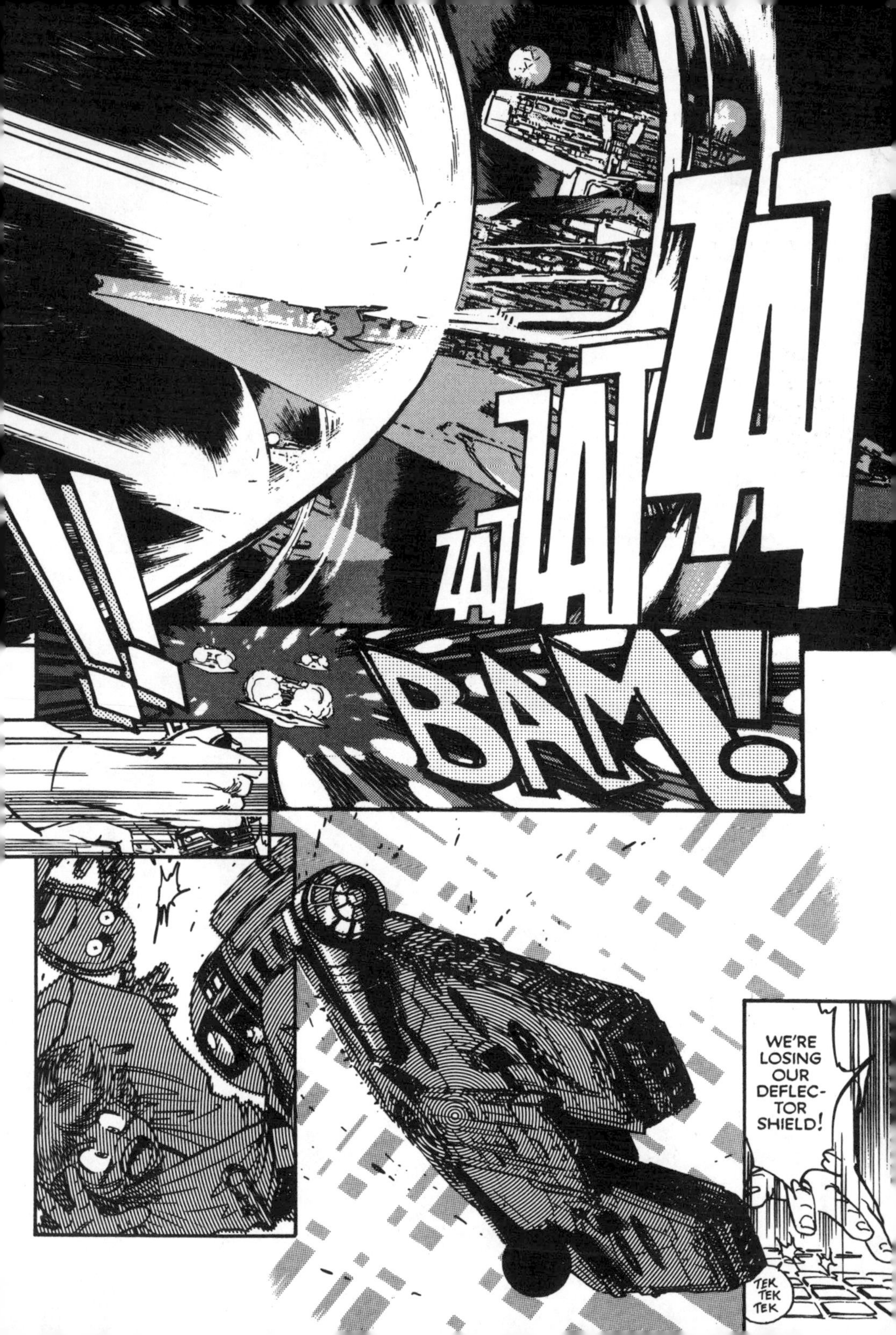
ZAT ZAT ZAT
BAM!
WE'RE LOSING OUR DEFLECTOR SHIELD!
TEK TEK TEK

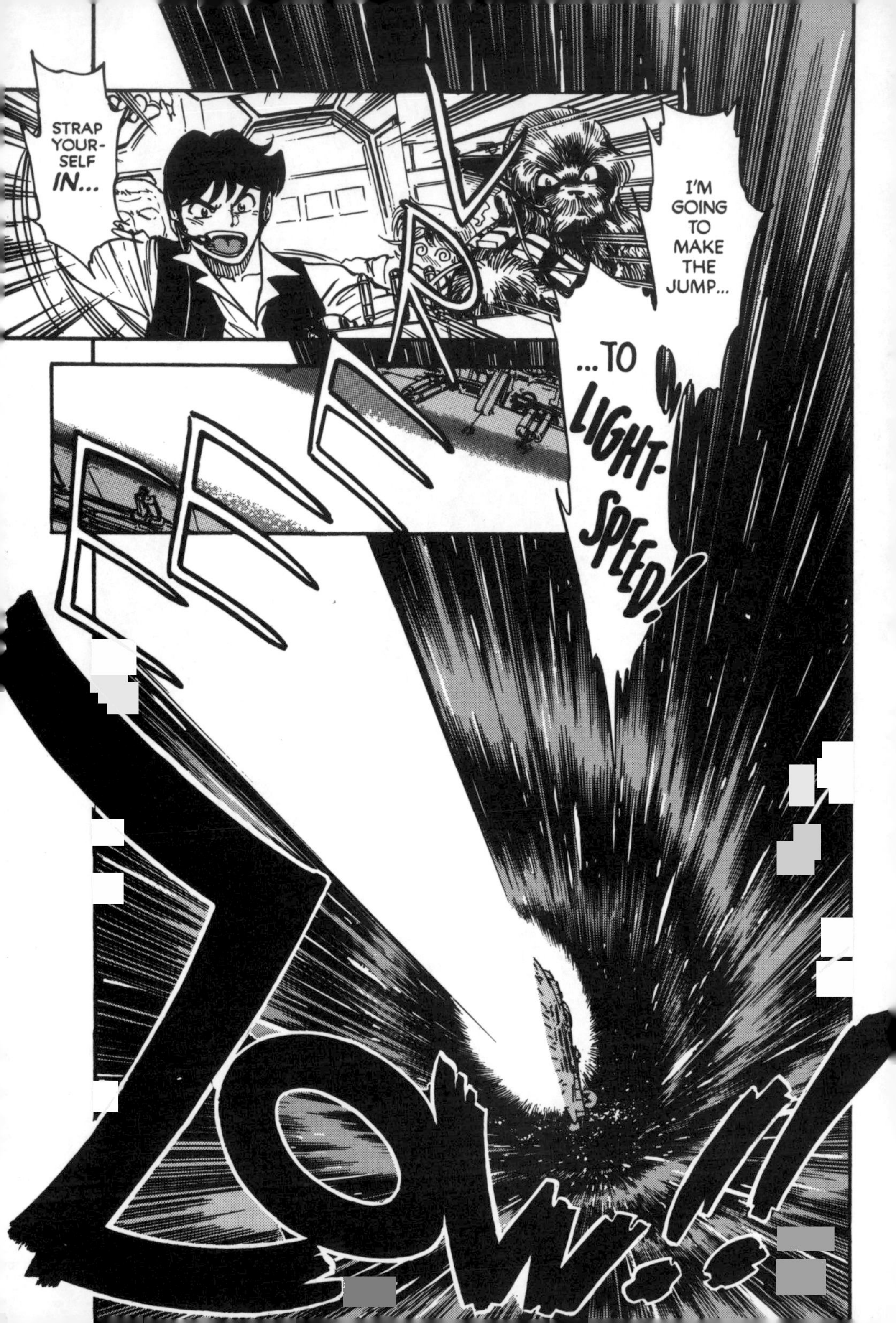
STRAP YOURSELF IN...
I'M GOING TO MAKE THE JUMP...
...TO LIGHT-SPEED!
ZOW!!

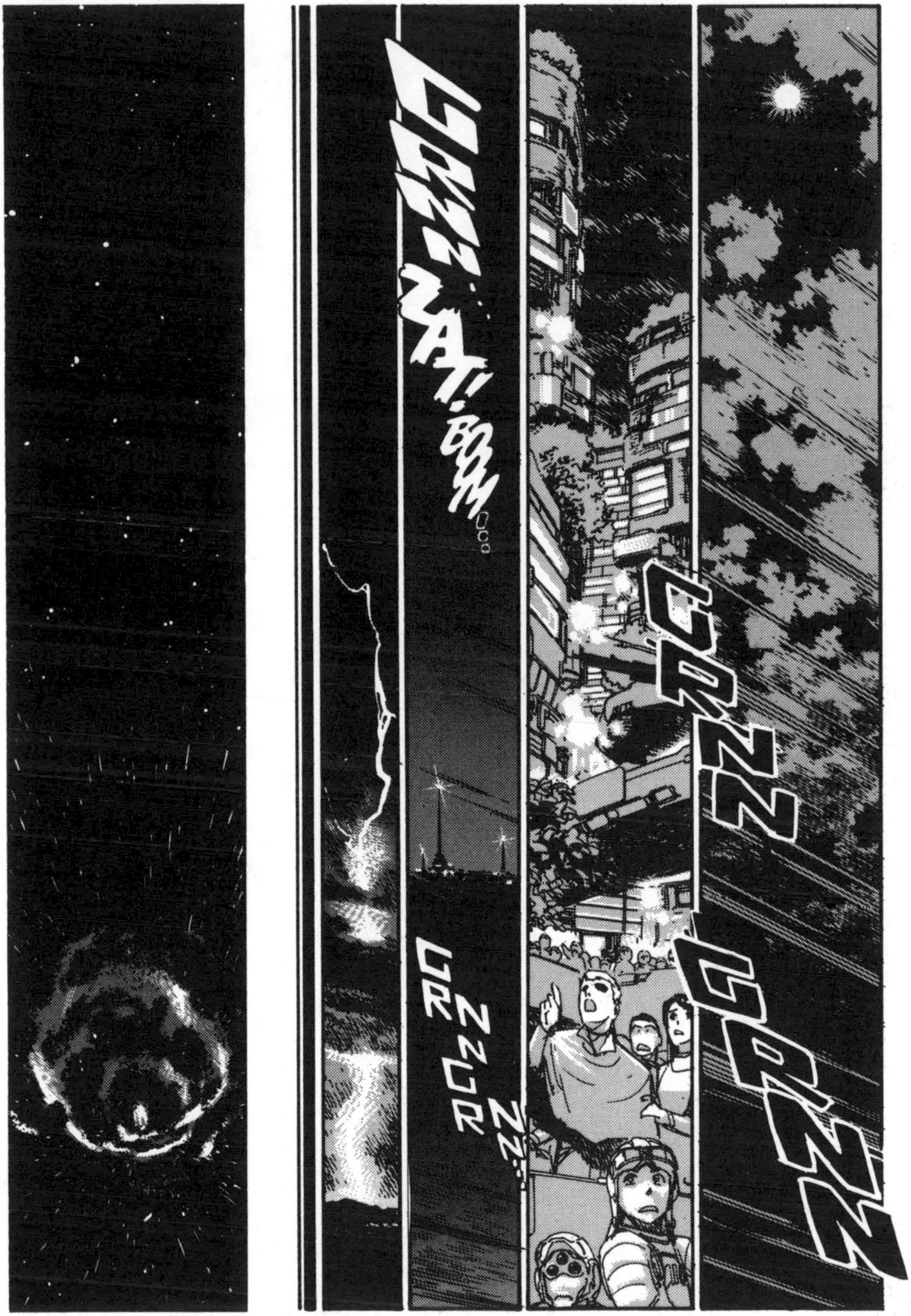
GRNN ZAT! BOOM...
GRNN GRNN...
GRNN
GRNN

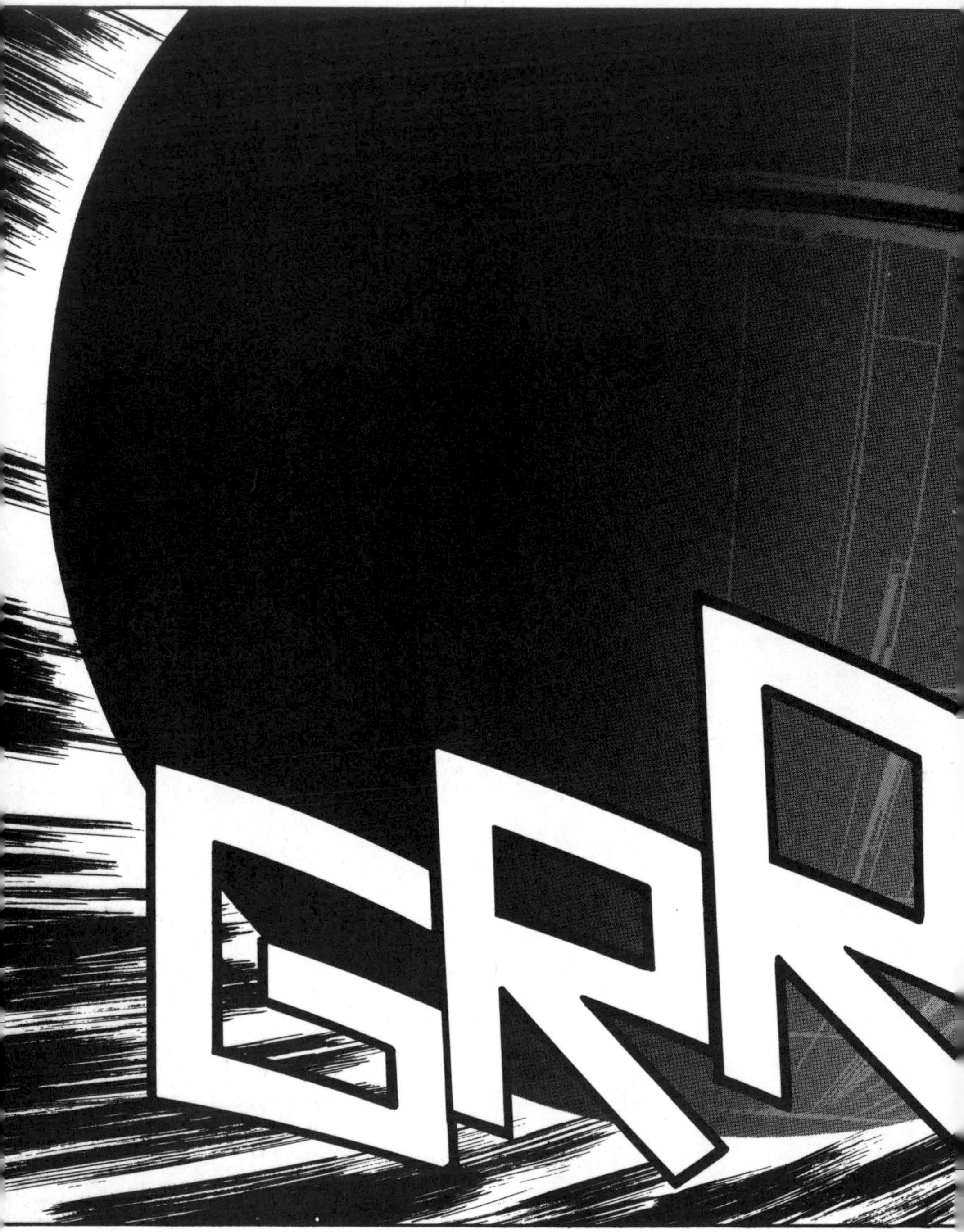
GRRR

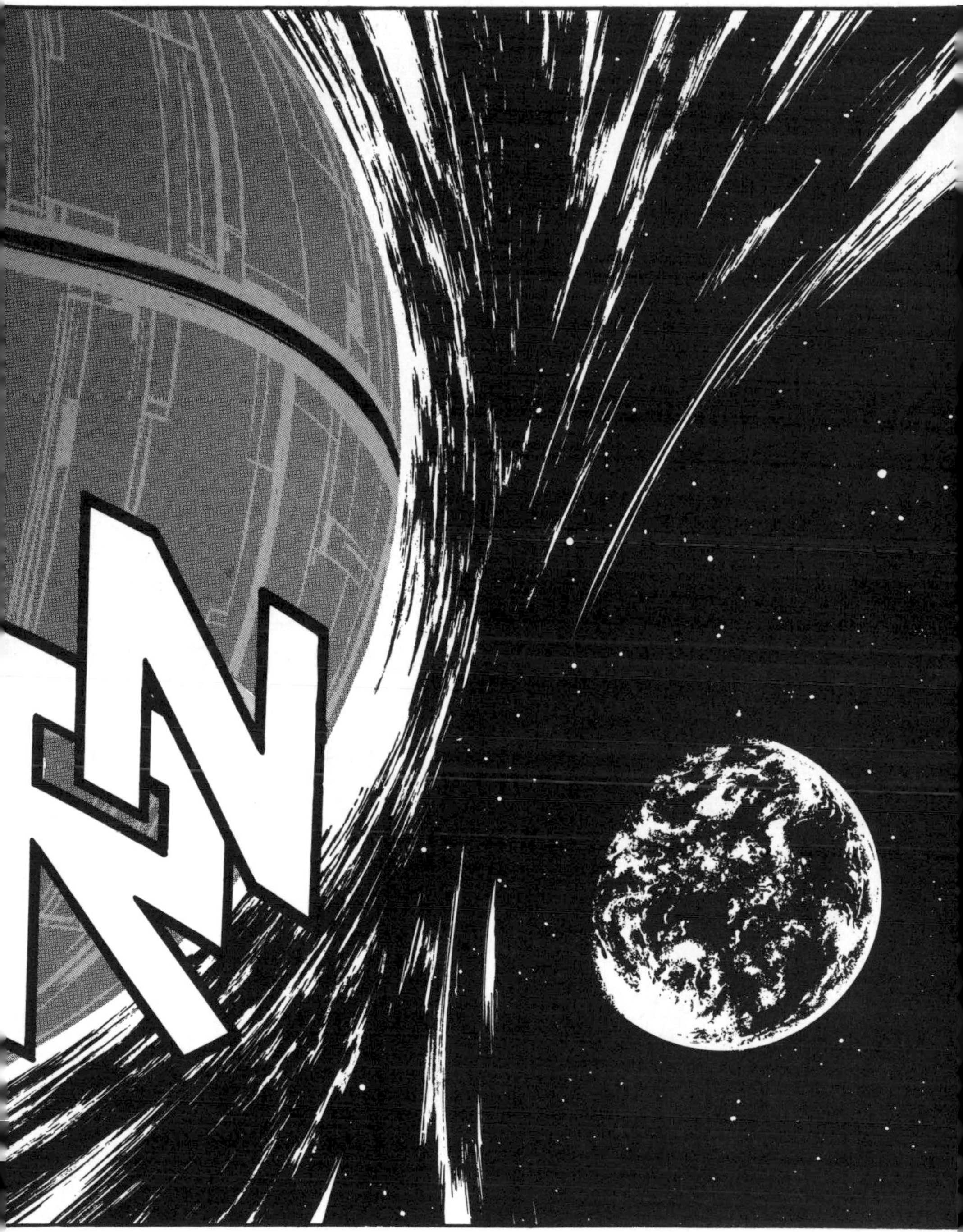

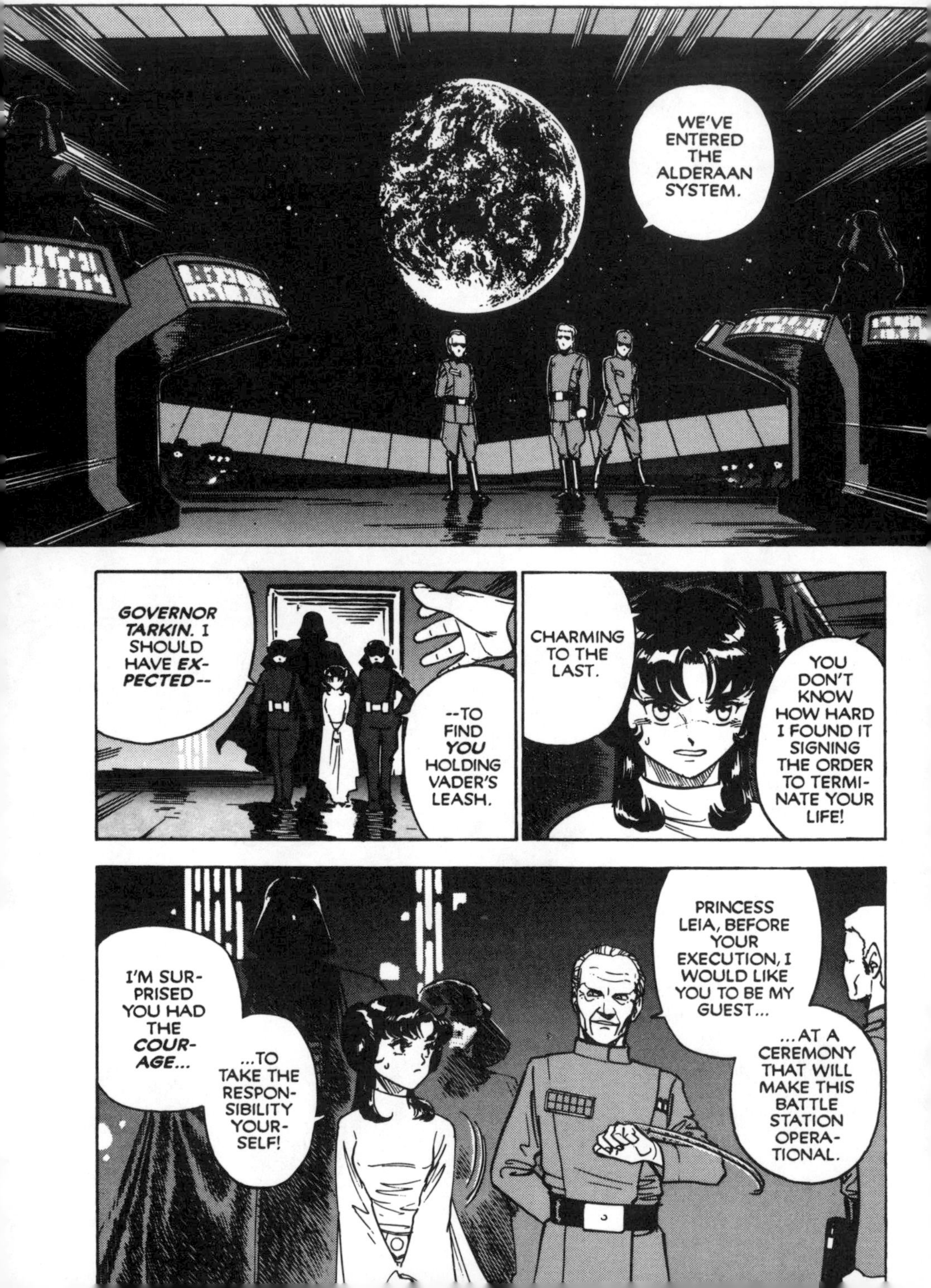
WE'VE ENTERED THE ALDERAAN SYSTEM.
GOVERNOR TARKIN. I SHOULD HAVE EXPECTED--
--TO FIND YOU HOLDING VADER'S LEASH.
CHARMING TO THE LAST.
YOU DON'T KNOW HOW HARD I FOUND IT SIGNING THE ORDER TO TERMINATE YOUR LIFE!
I'M SURPRISED YOU HAD THE COURAGE...
...TO TAKE THE RESPONSIBILITY YOURSELF!
PRINCESS LEIA, BEFORE YOUR EXECUTION, I WOULD LIKE YOU TO BE MY GUEST...
...AT A CEREMONY THAT WILL MAKE THIS BATTLE STATION OPERATIONAL.

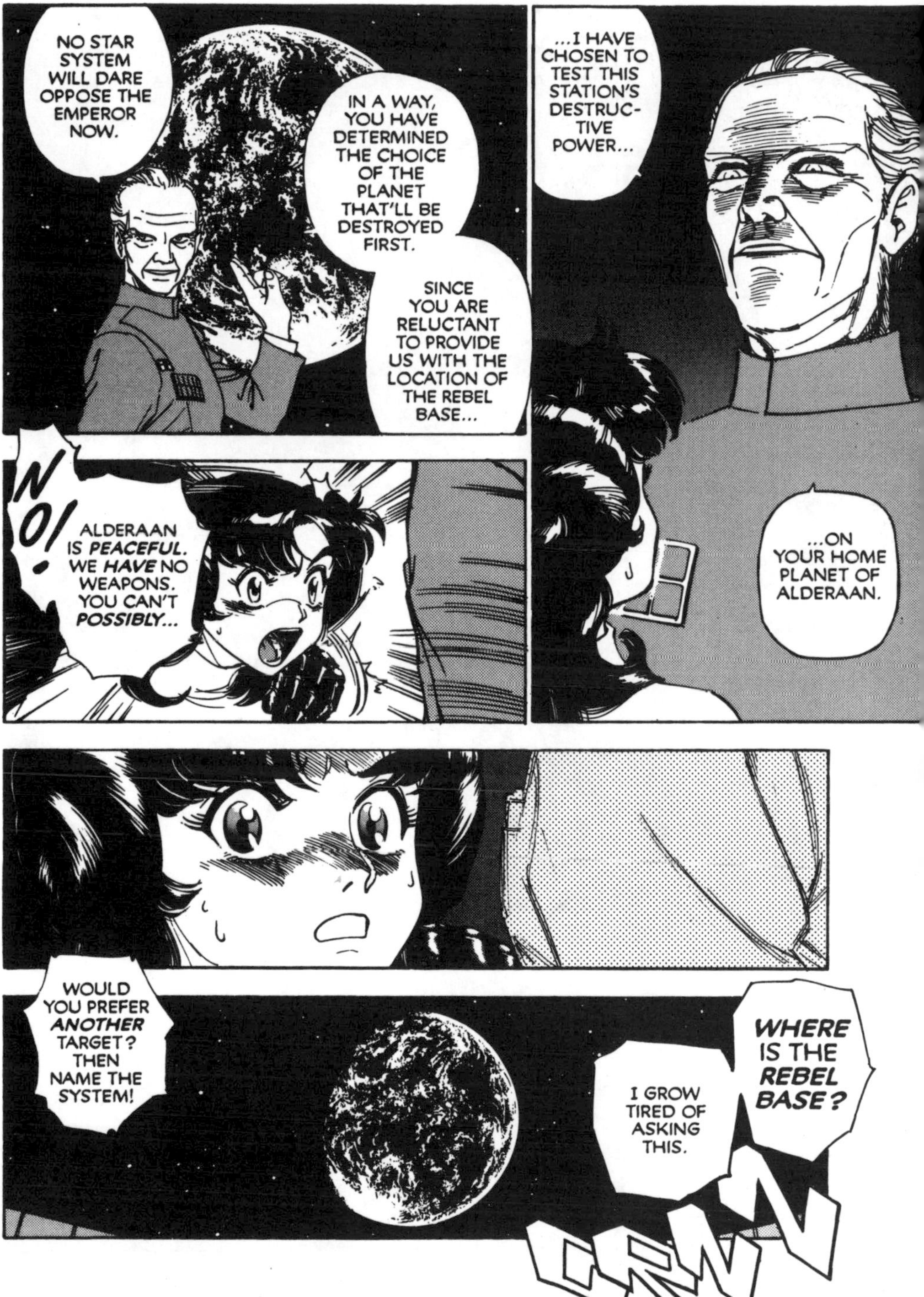
NO STAR SYSTEM WILL DARE OPPOSE THE EMPEROR NOW.
IN A WAY, YOU HAVE DETERMINED THE CHOICE OF THE PLANET THAT'LL BE DESTROYED FIRST.
SINCE YOU ARE RELUCTANT TO PROVIDE US WITH THE LOCATION OF THE REBEL BASE...
...I HAVE CHOSEN TO TEST THIS STATION'S DESTRUC-TIVE POWER...
NO!
ALDERAAN IS *PEACEFUL*. WE *HAVE* NO WEAPONS. YOU CAN'T *POSSIBLY*...
...ON YOUR HOME PLANET OF ALDERAAN.
WOULD YOU PREFER *ANOTHER* TARGET? THEN NAME THE SYSTEM!
I GROW TIRED OF ASKING THIS.
WHERE IS THE *REBEL BASE?*
GRNN

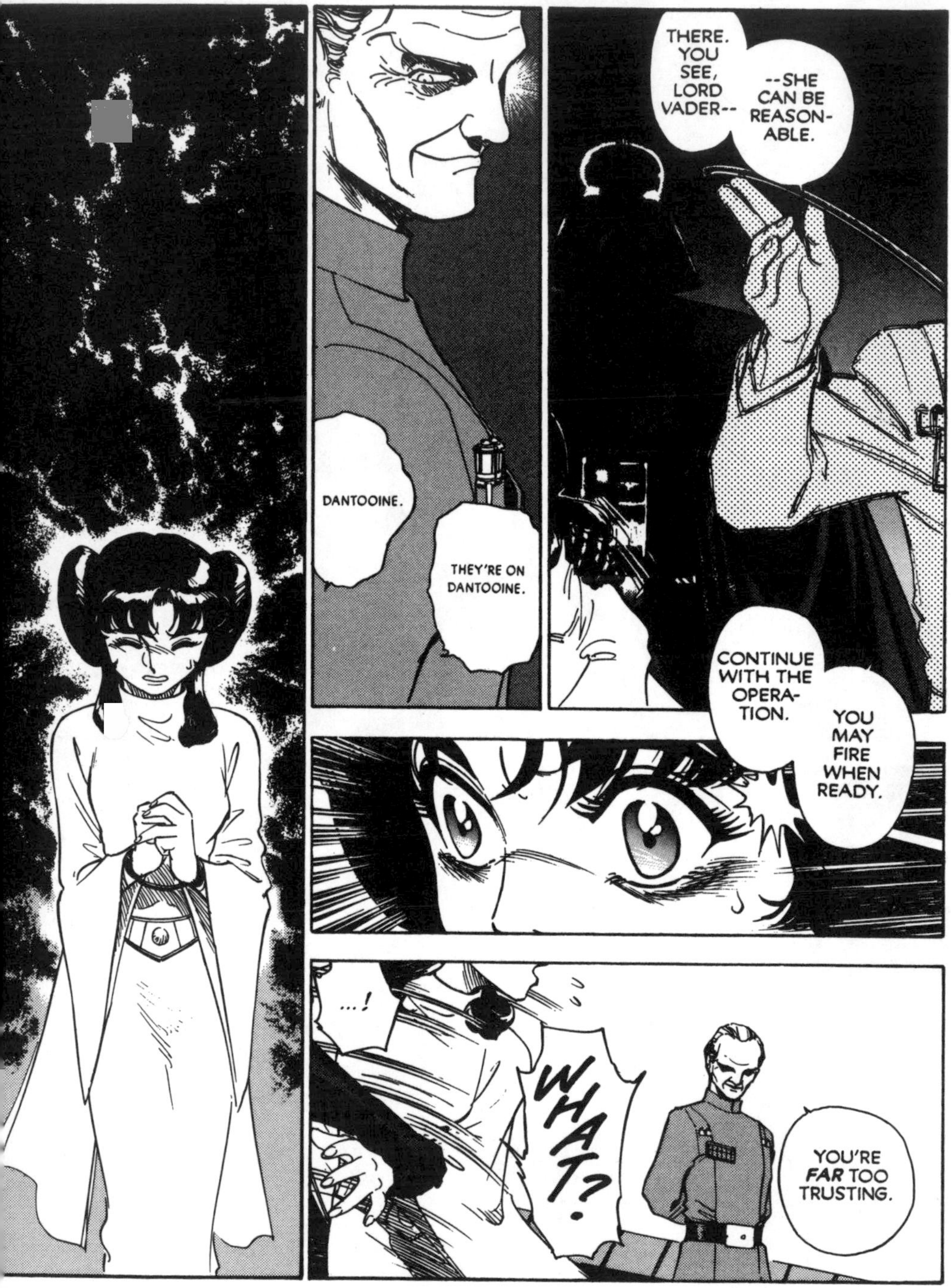
DANTOOINE.
THEY'RE ON DANTOOINE.
THERE. YOU SEE, LORD VADER--
--SHE CAN BE REASONABLE.
CONTINUE WITH THE OPERATION.
YOU MAY FIRE WHEN READY.
...!
WHAT?
YOU'RE **FAR** TOO TRUSTING.

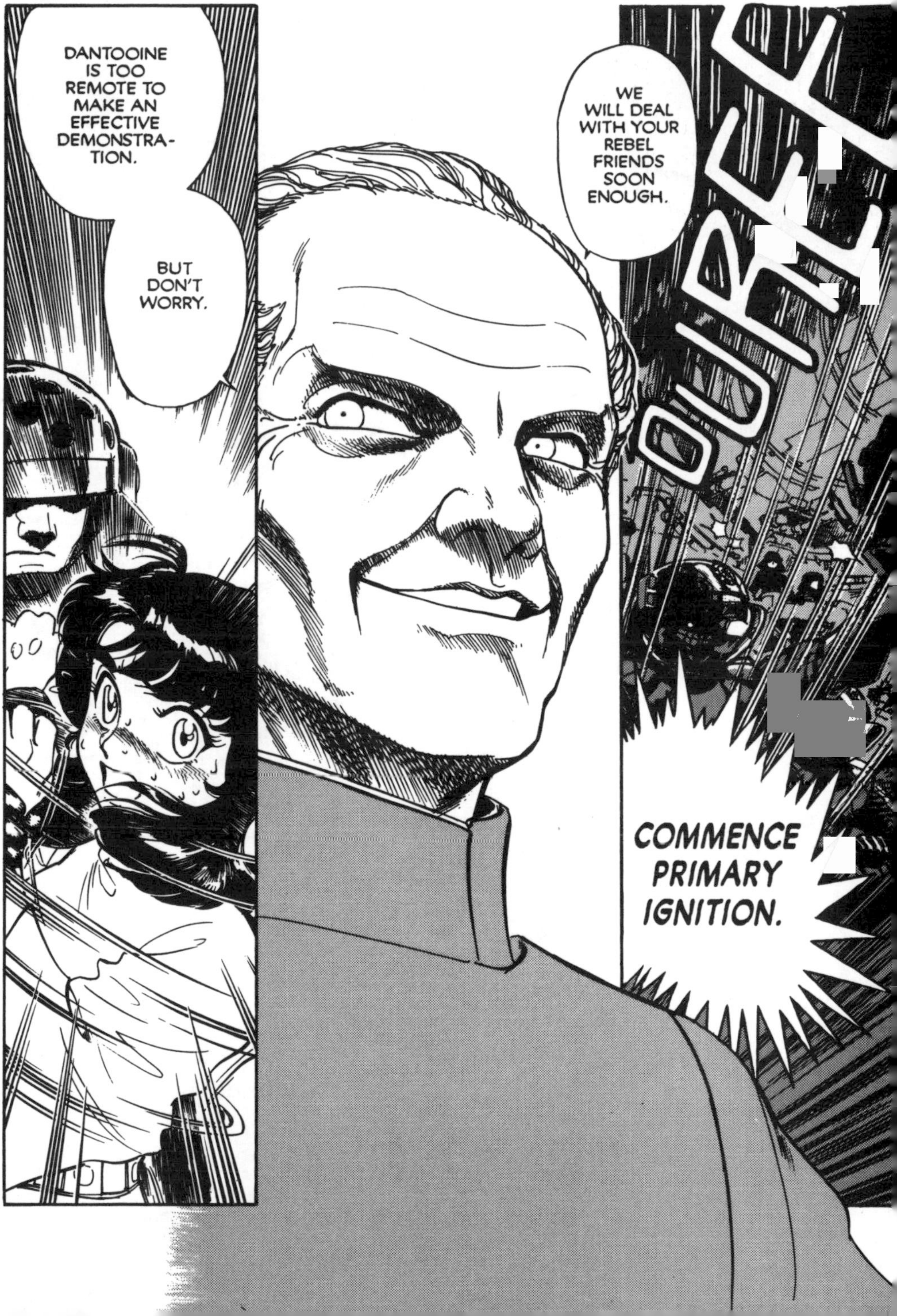
DANTOOINE IS TOO REMOTE TO MAKE AN EFFECTIVE DEMONSTRATION.
BUT DON'T WORRY.
WE WILL DEAL WITH YOUR REBEL FRIENDS SOON ENOUGH.
COMMENCE PRIMARY IGNITION.

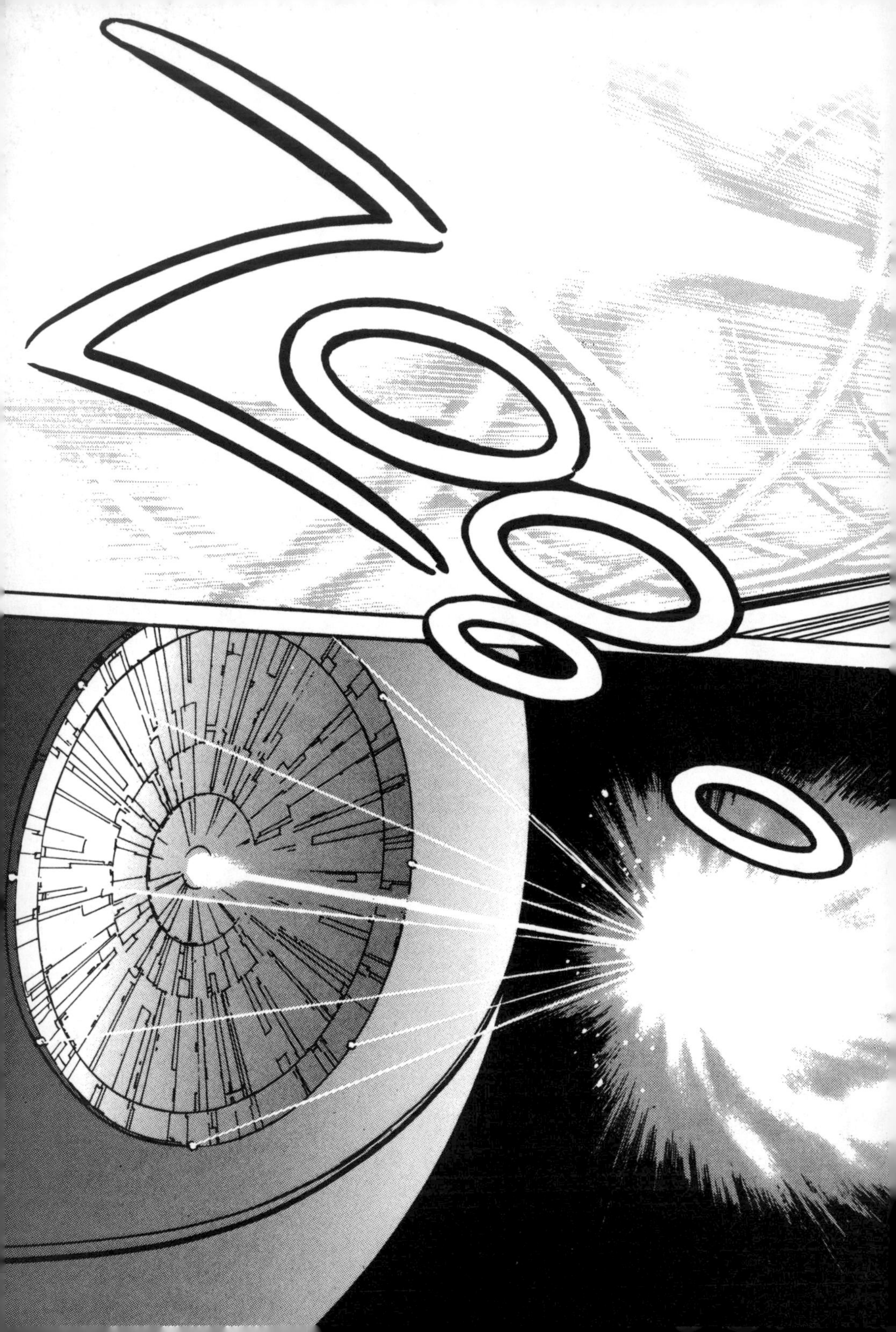
ZOOOO

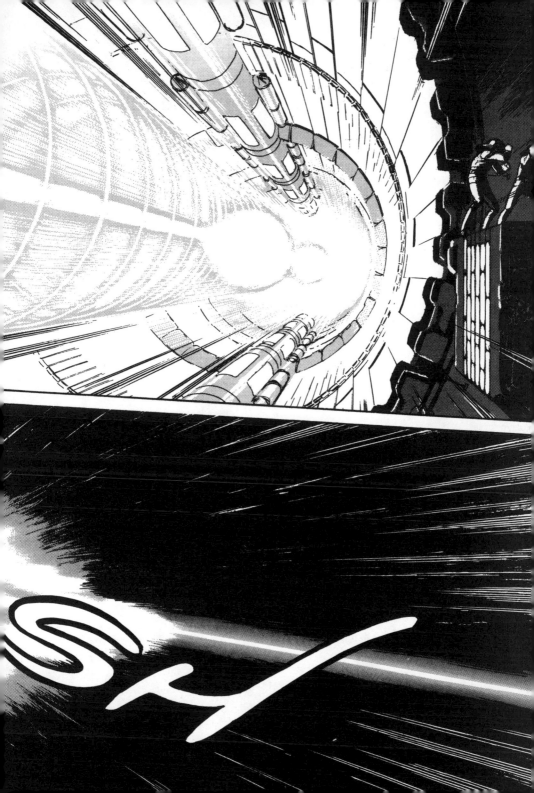

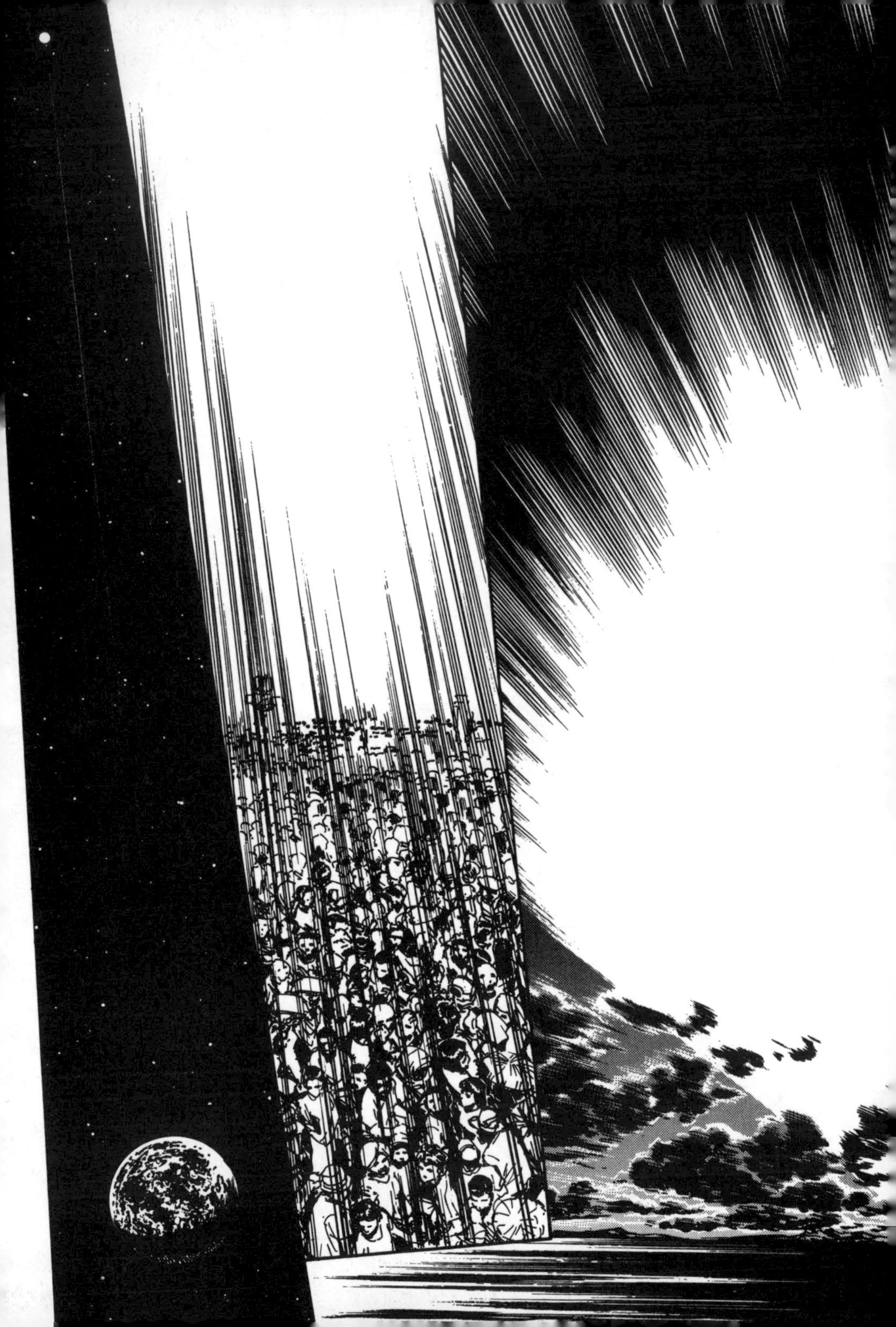

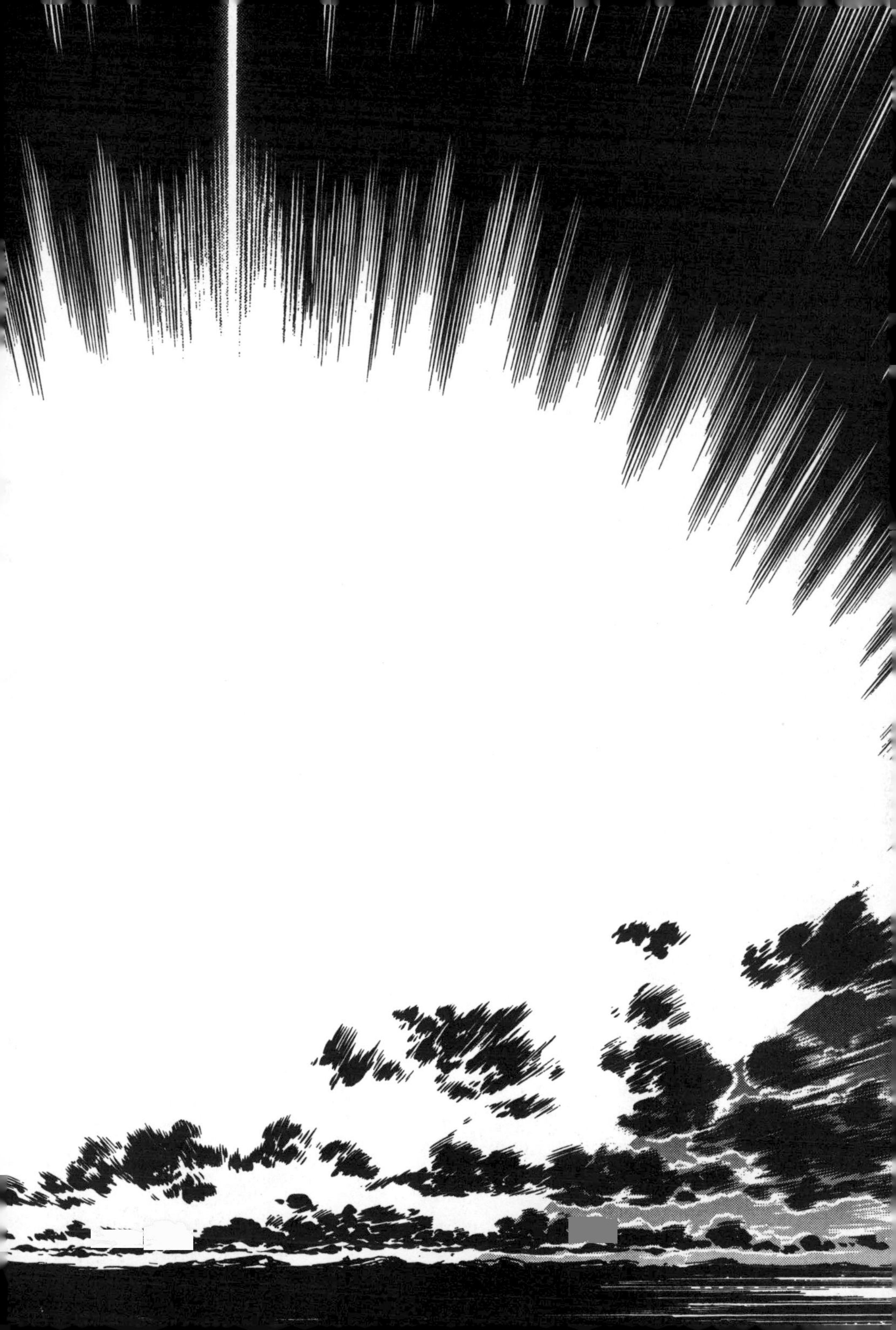

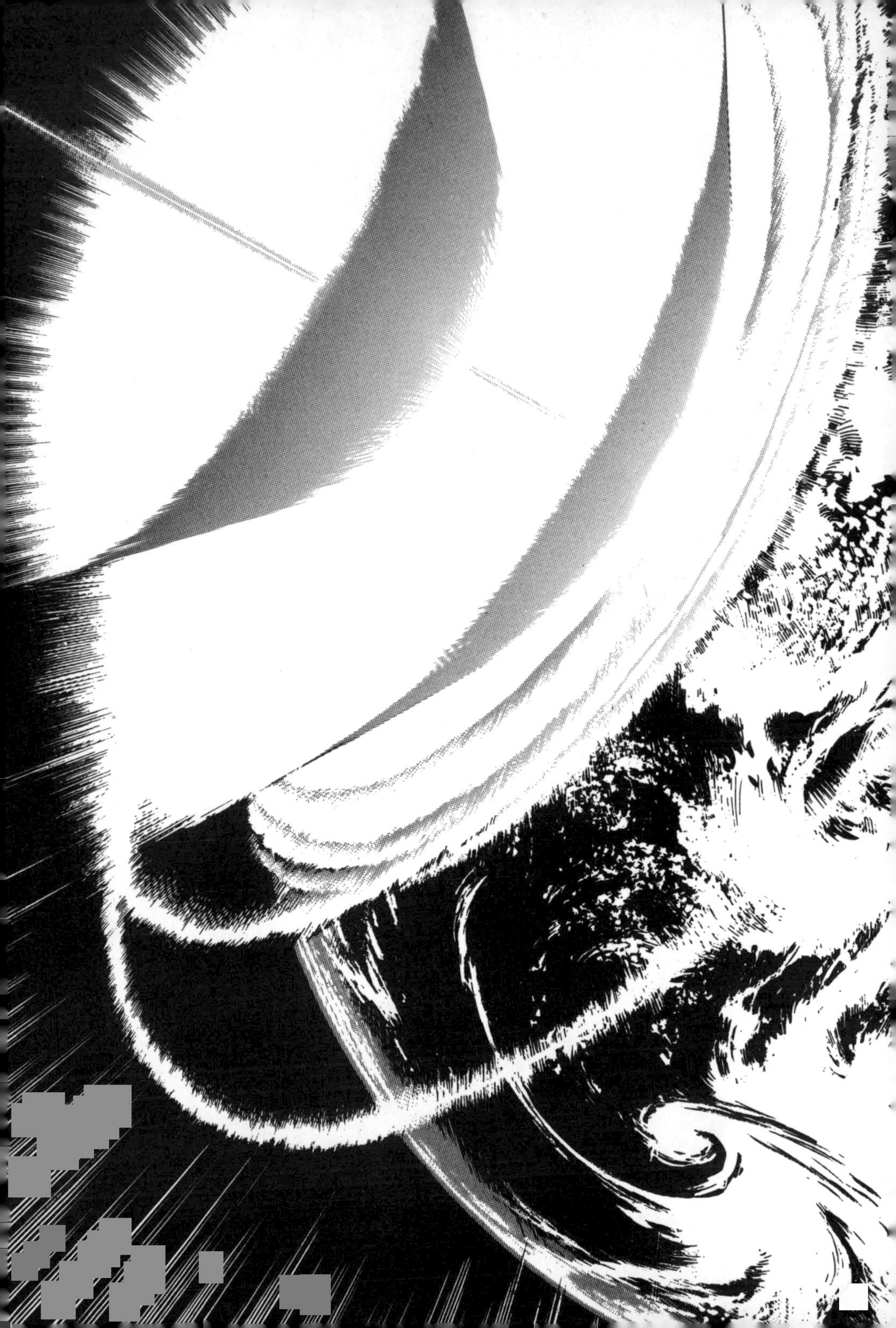

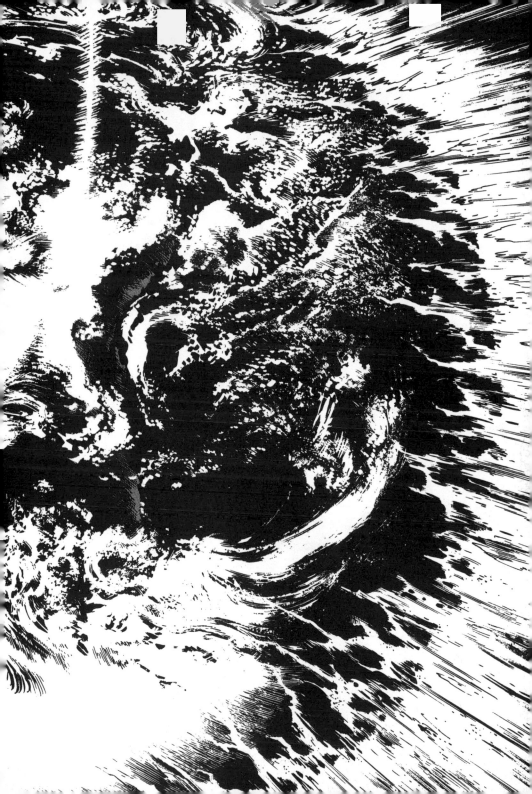

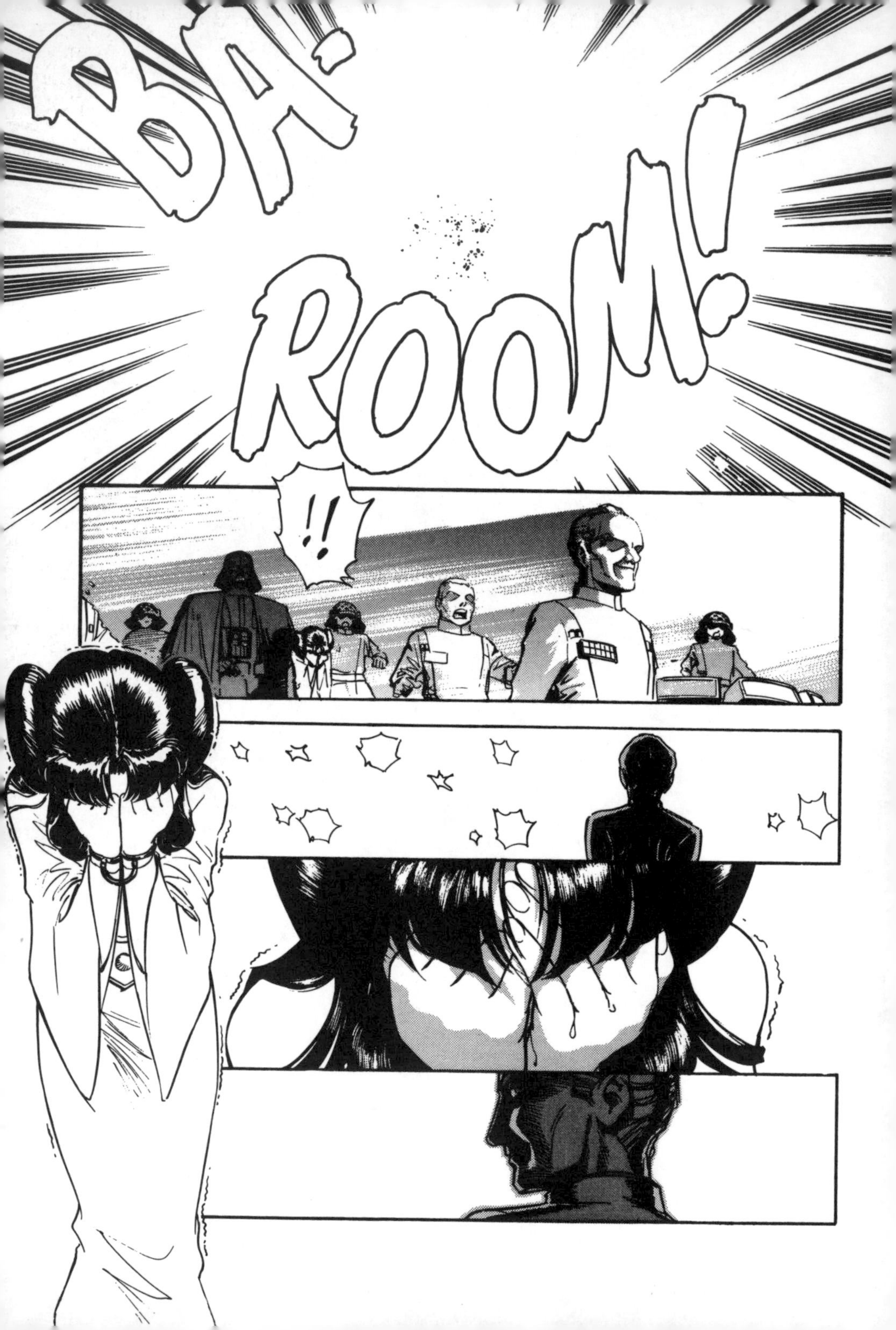
BA-ROOM!
!!

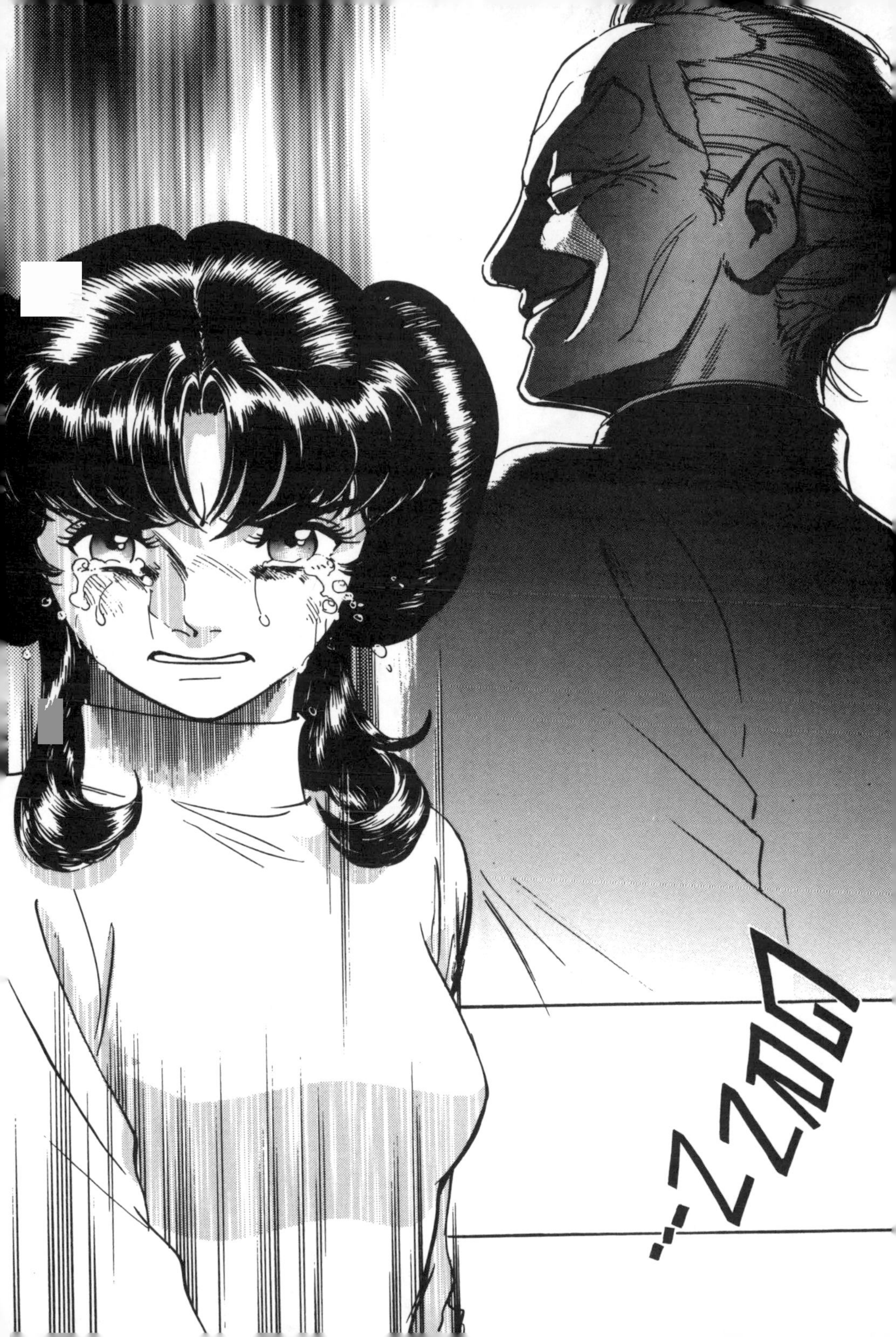
...ZZNG

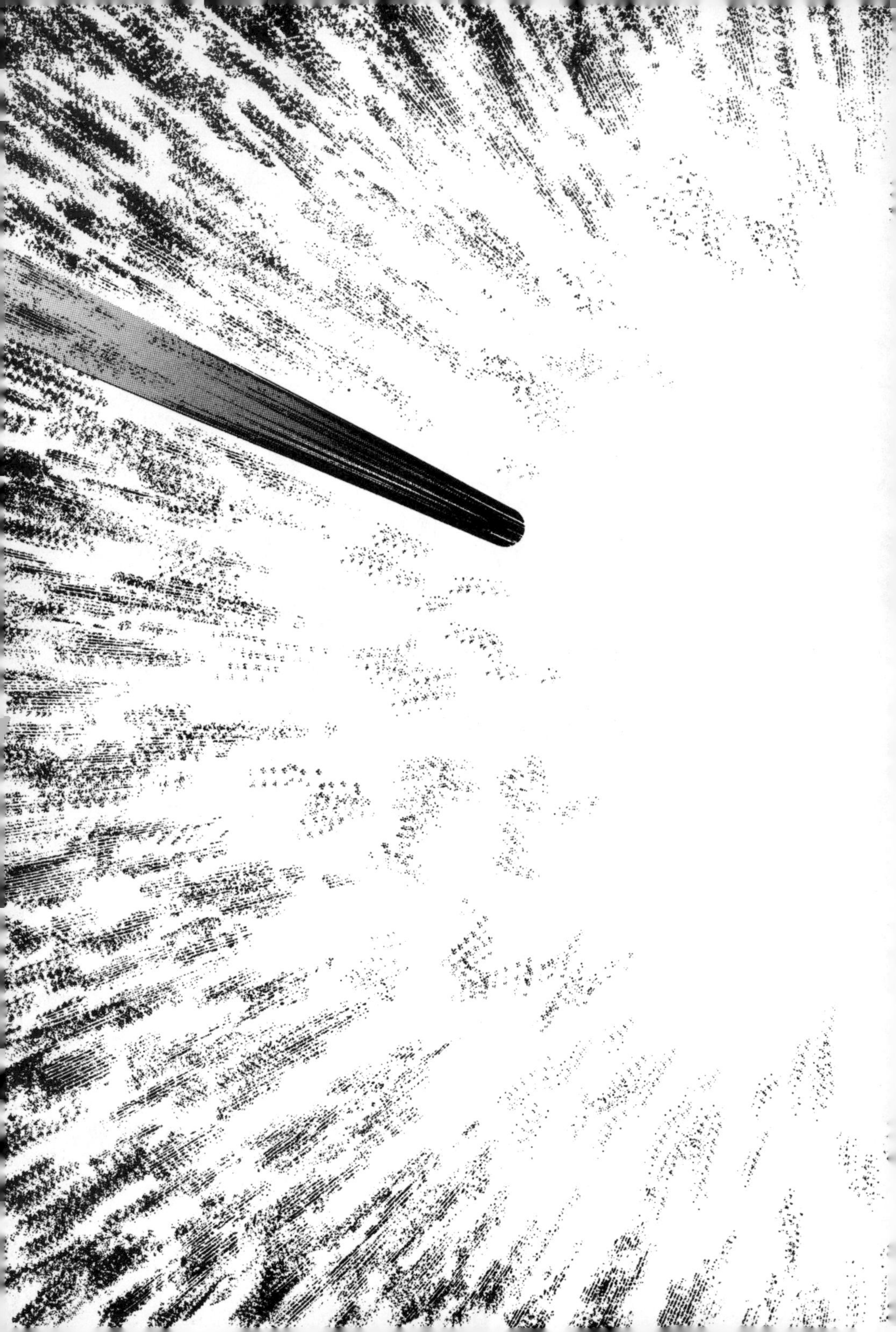

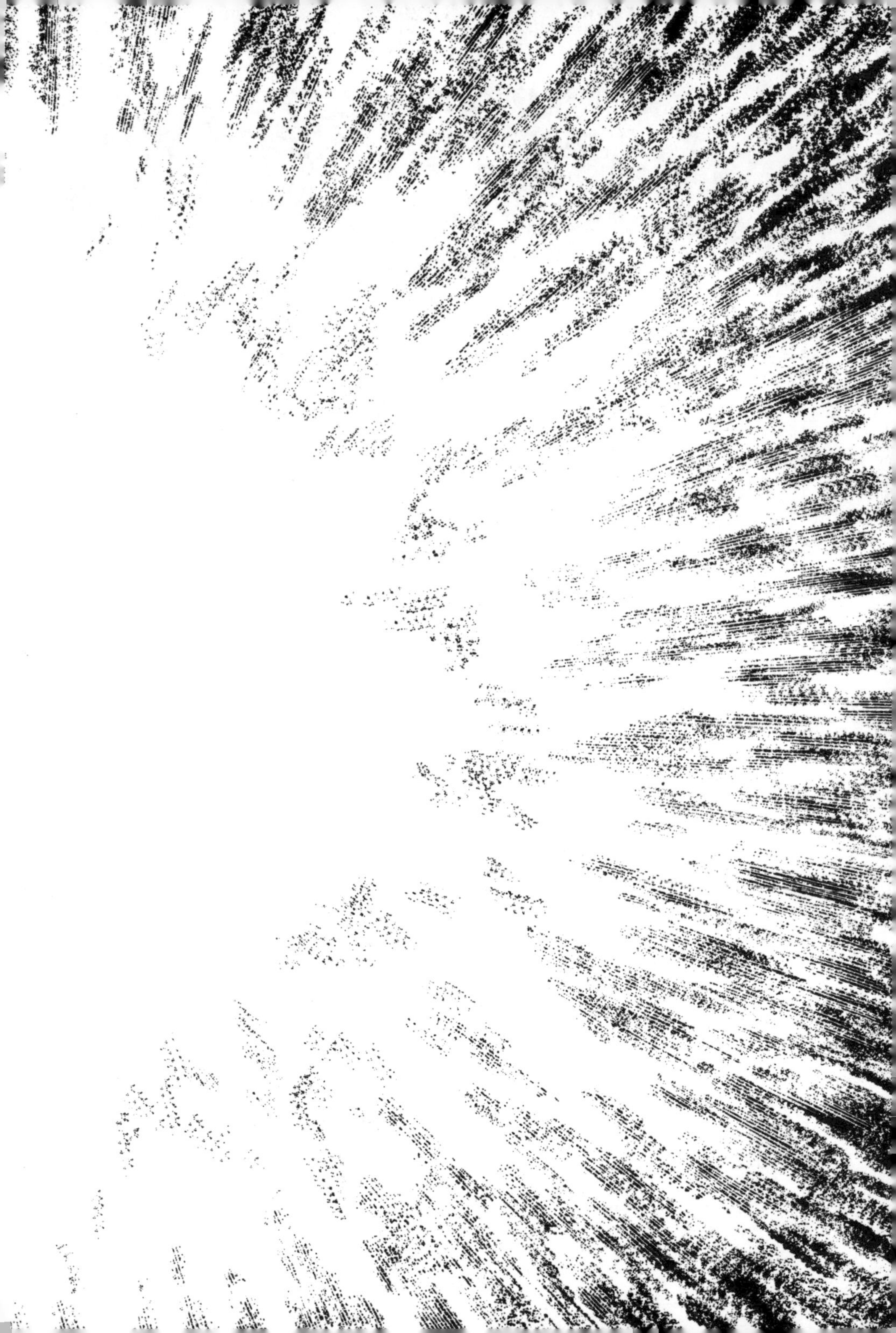

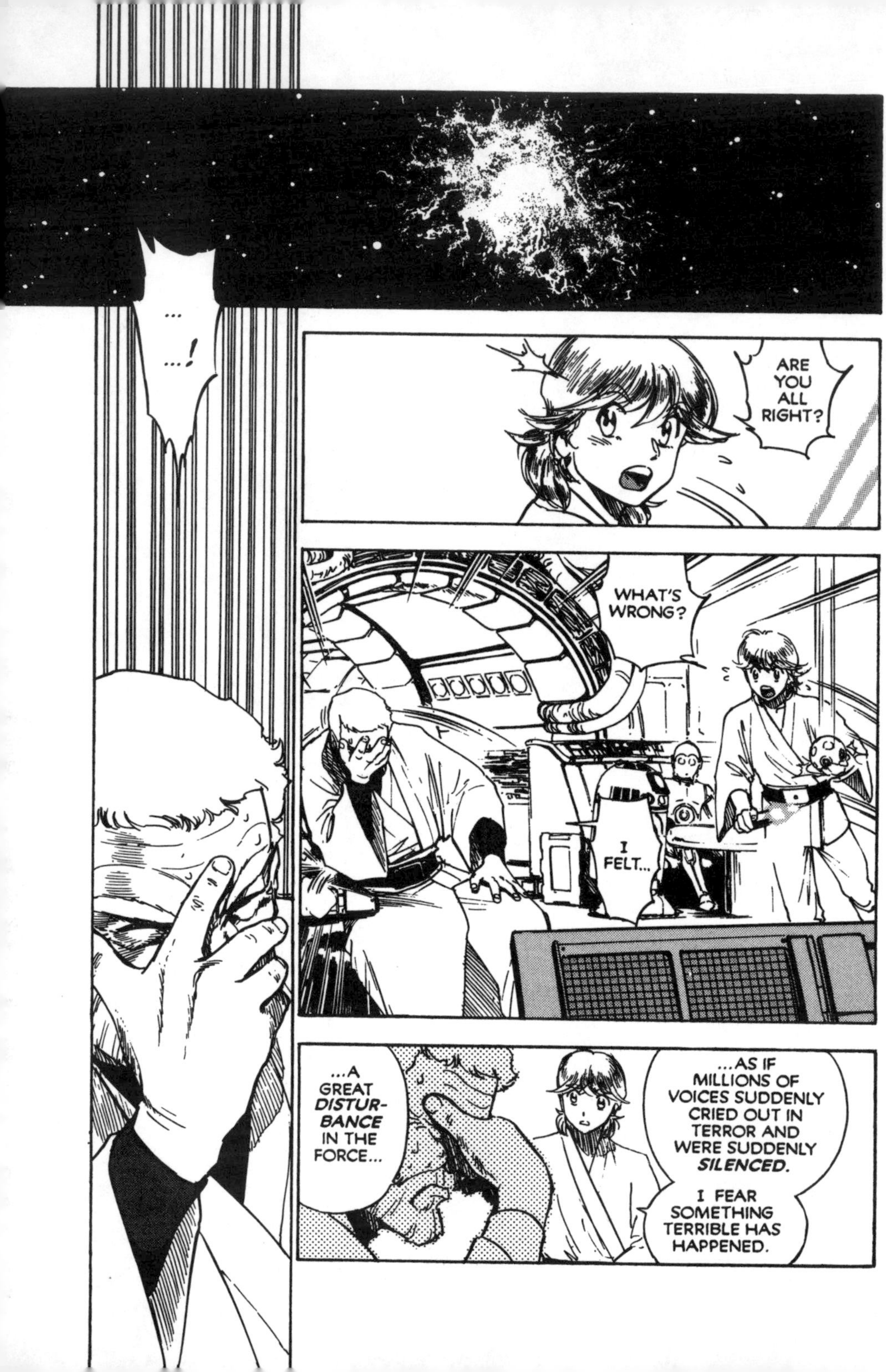
...
...!
ARE YOU ALL RIGHT?
WHAT'S WRONG?
I FELT...
...A GREAT *DISTURBANCE* IN THE FORCE...
...AS IF MILLIONS OF VOICES SUDDENLY CRIED OUT IN TERROR AND WERE SUDDENLY ***SILENCED.***
I FEAR SOMETHING TERRIBLE HAS HAPPENED.

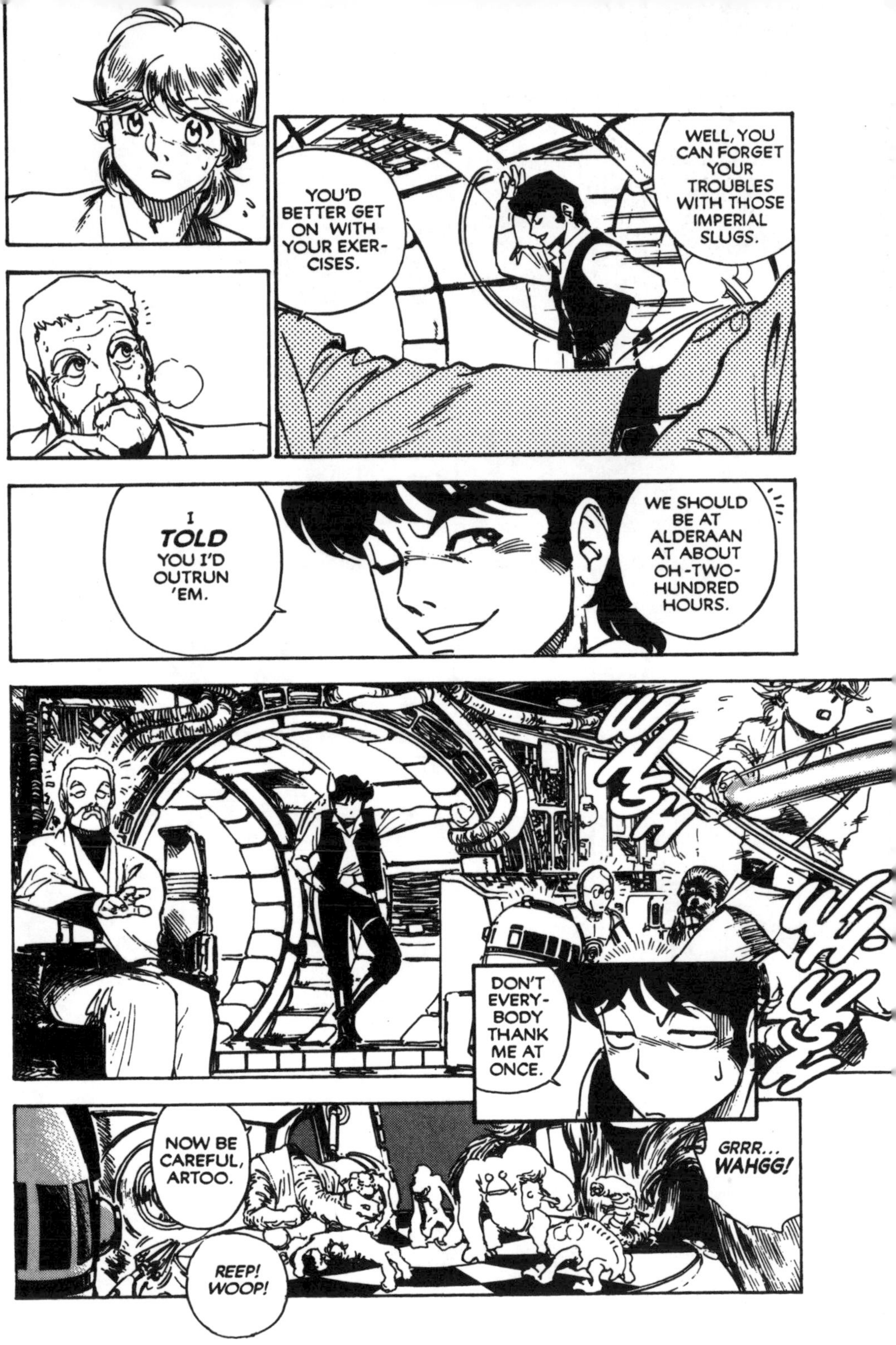
WELL, YOU CAN FORGET YOUR TROUBLES WITH THOSE IMPERIAL SLUGS.
YOU'D BETTER GET ON WITH YOUR EXER-CISES.
I *TOLD* YOU I'D OUTRUN 'EM.
WE SHOULD BE AT ALDERAAN AT ABOUT OH-TWO-HUNDRED HOURS.
DON'T EVERY-BODY THANK ME AT ONCE.
NOW BE CAREFUL, ARTOO.
REEP! WOOP!
GRRR... WAHGG!

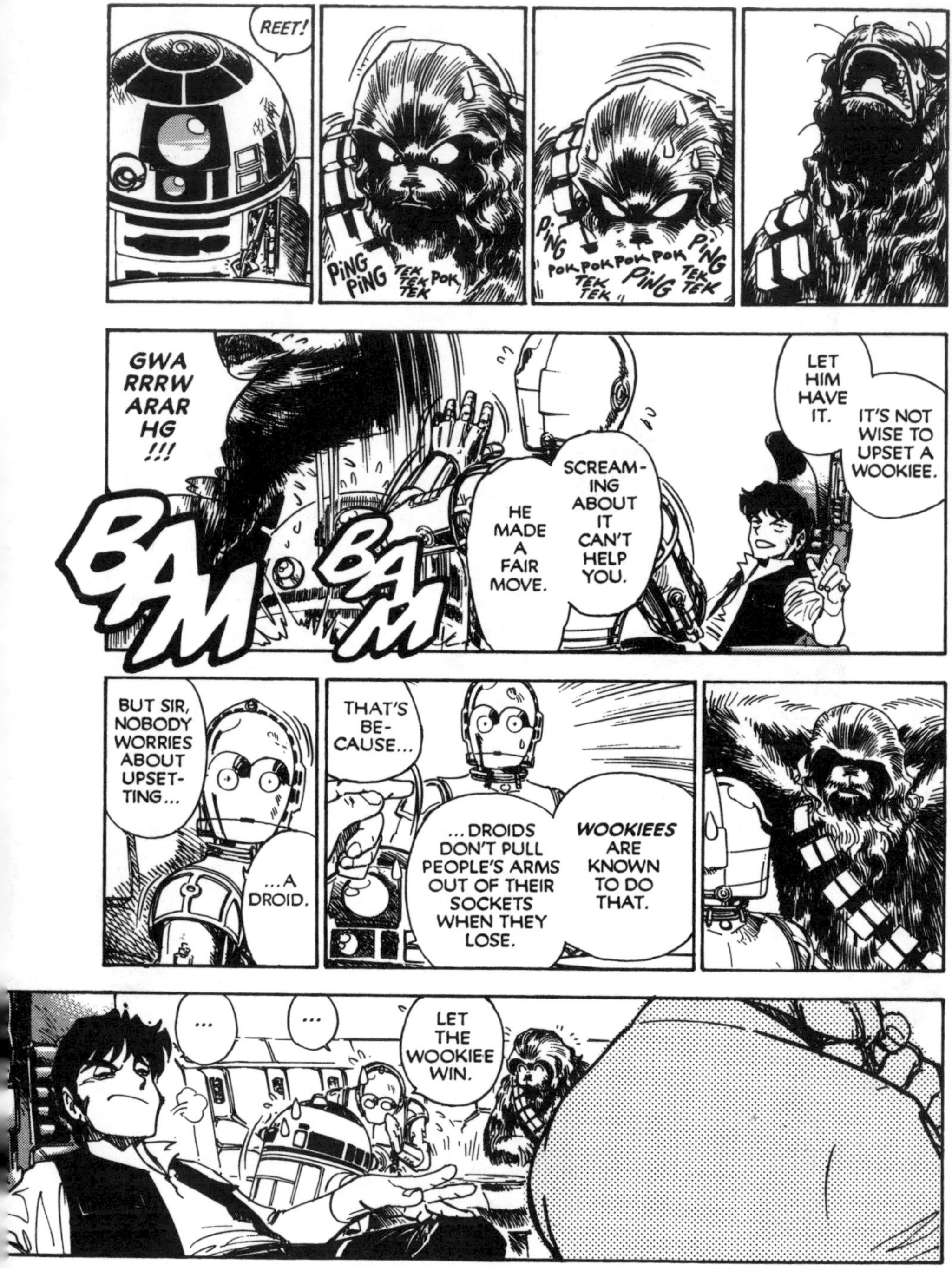
REET!
PING PING TEK TEK TEK POK
PING POK POK POK POK PING TEK TEK PING TEK TEK
GWA RRRW ARAR HG !!!
BAM
BAM
HE MADE A FAIR MOVE.
SCREAM-ING ABOUT IT CAN'T HELP YOU.
LET HIM HAVE IT.
IT'S NOT WISE TO UPSET A WOOKIEE.
BUT SIR, NOBODY WORRIES ABOUT UPSET-TING...
...A DROID.
THAT'S BE-CAUSE...
...DROIDS DON'T PULL PEOPLE'S ARMS OUT OF THEIR SOCKETS WHEN THEY LOSE.
WOOKIEES ARE KNOWN TO DO THAT.
...
...
LET THE WOOKIEE WIN.

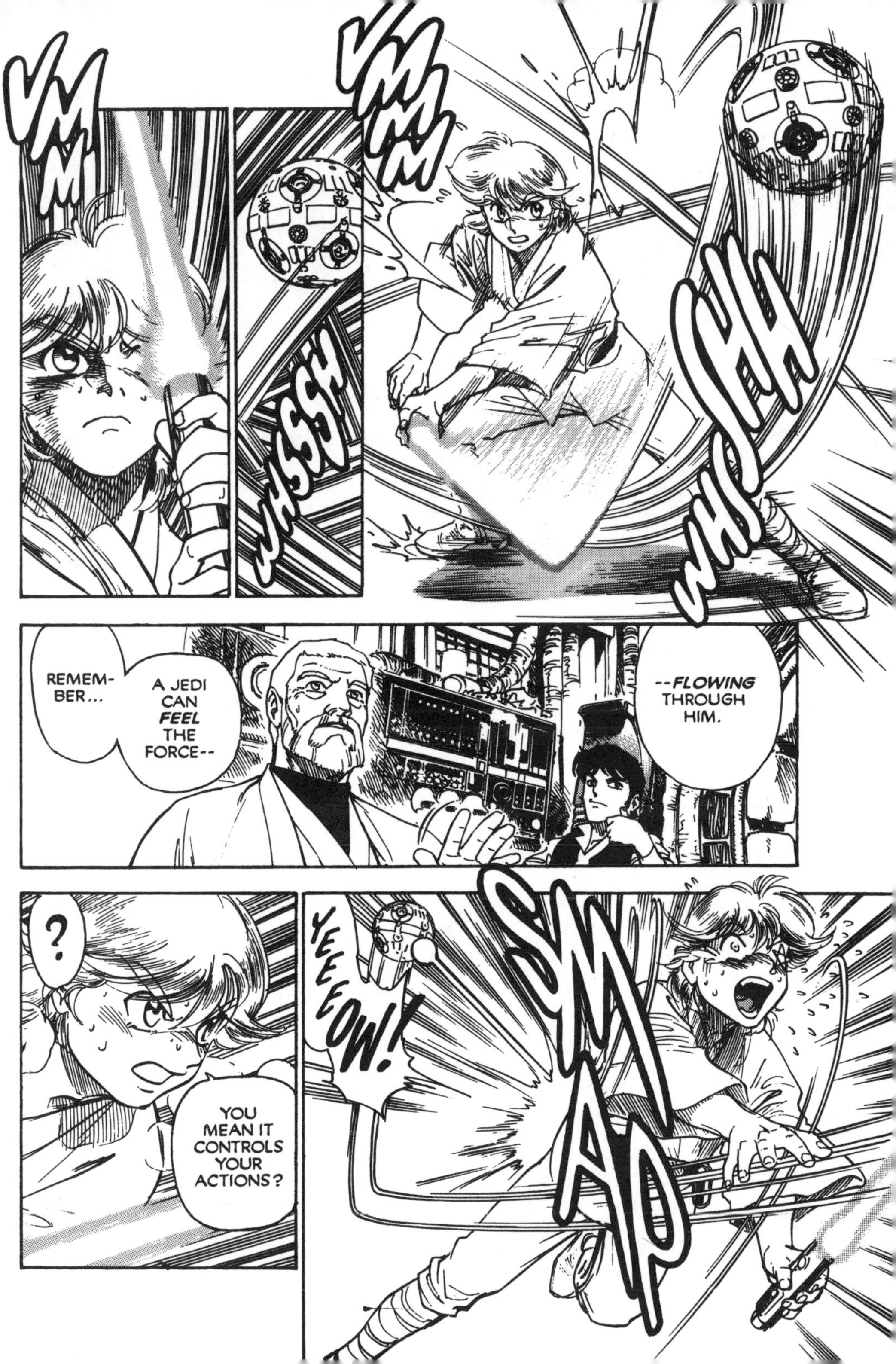

VMMM
WHSSSH
VMMM
WHSHHH
REMEMBER...
A JEDI CAN *FEEL* THE FORCE--
--*FLOWING* THROUGH HIM.
?
YOU MEAN IT CONTROLS YOUR ACTIONS?
YEEEOW!
SMAP

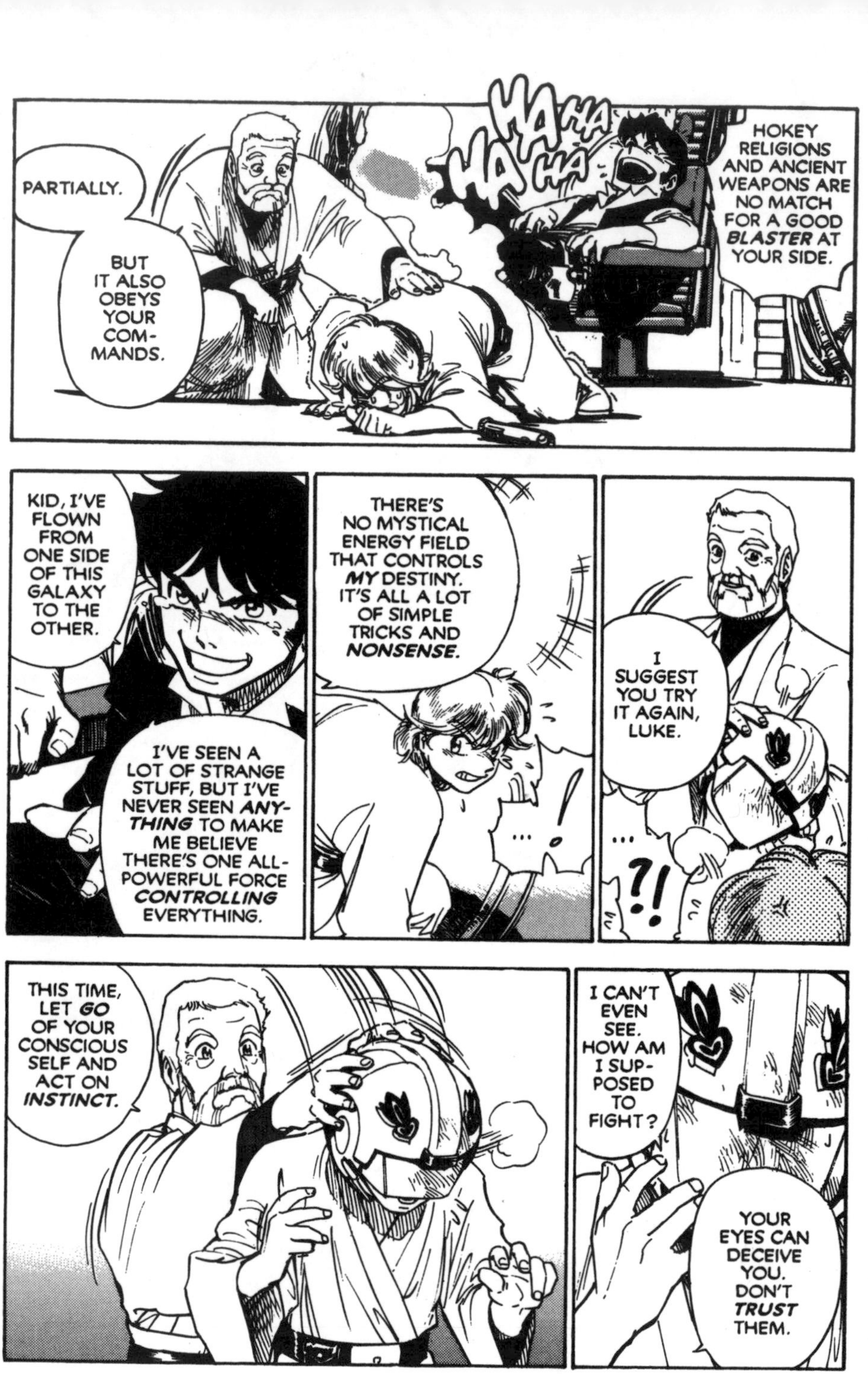
PARTIALLY.
BUT IT ALSO OBEYS YOUR COM-MANDS.
HA HA HA HA HA
HOKEY RELIGIONS AND ANCIENT WEAPONS ARE NO MATCH FOR A GOOD BLASTER AT YOUR SIDE.
KID, I'VE FLOWN FROM ONE SIDE OF THIS GALAXY TO THE OTHER.
I'VE SEEN A LOT OF STRANGE STUFF, BUT I'VE NEVER SEEN ANY-THING TO MAKE ME BELIEVE THERE'S ONE ALL-POWERFUL FORCE CONTROLLING EVERYTHING.
THERE'S NO MYSTICAL ENERGY FIELD THAT CONTROLS MY DESTINY. IT'S ALL A LOT OF SIMPLE TRICKS AND NONSENSE.
... !
I SUGGEST YOU TRY IT AGAIN, LUKE.
...
?!
THIS TIME, LET GO OF YOUR CONSCIOUS SELF AND ACT ON INSTINCT.
I CAN'T EVEN SEE. HOW AM I SUP-POSED TO FIGHT?
YOUR EYES CAN DECEIVE YOU. DON'T TRUST THEM.

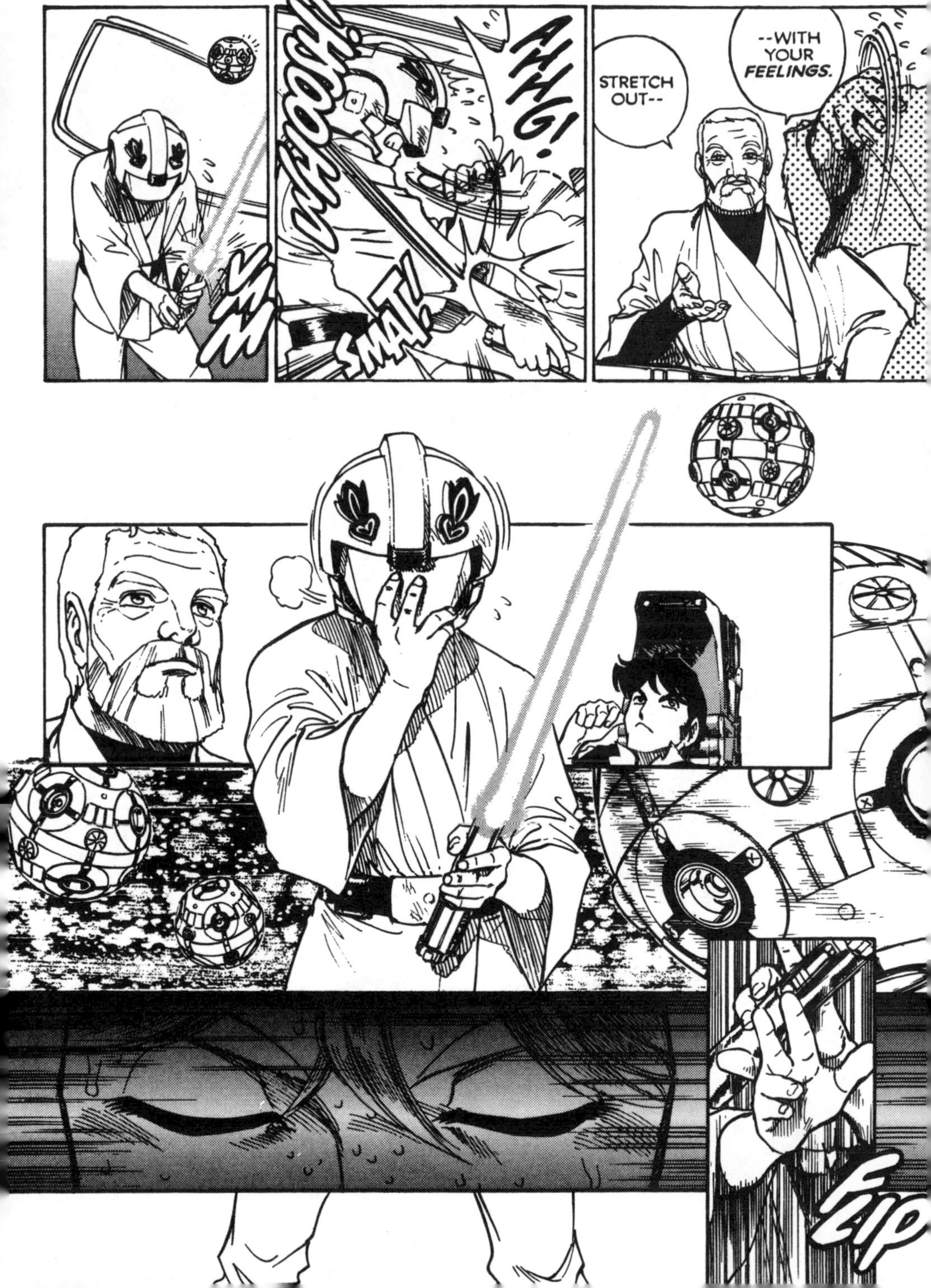
VMM
WHOOM
AHHG!
SMAT!
STRETCH OUT--
--WITH YOUR FEELINGS.
flip

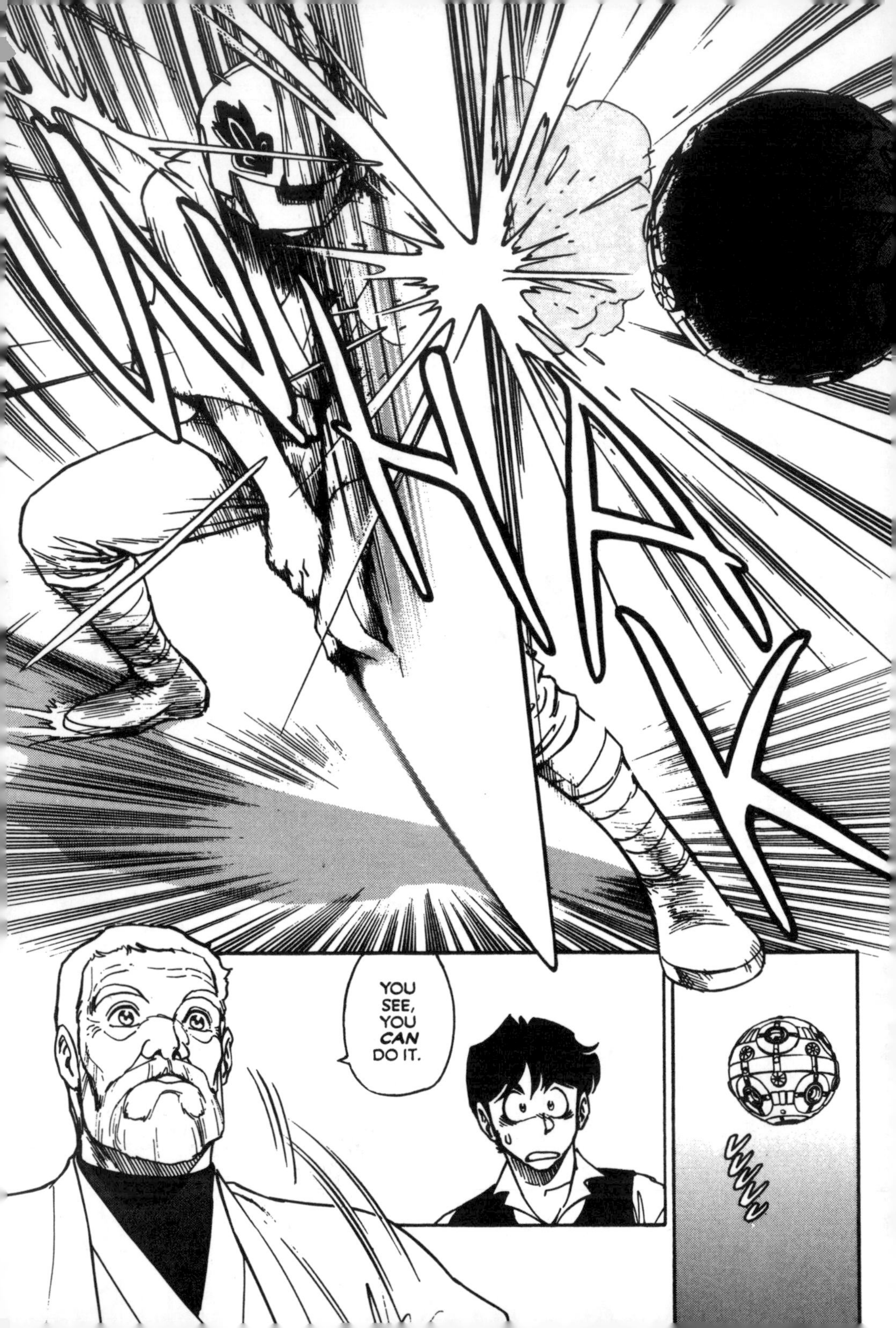
WHAAK
YOU SEE, YOU ***CAN*** DO IT.

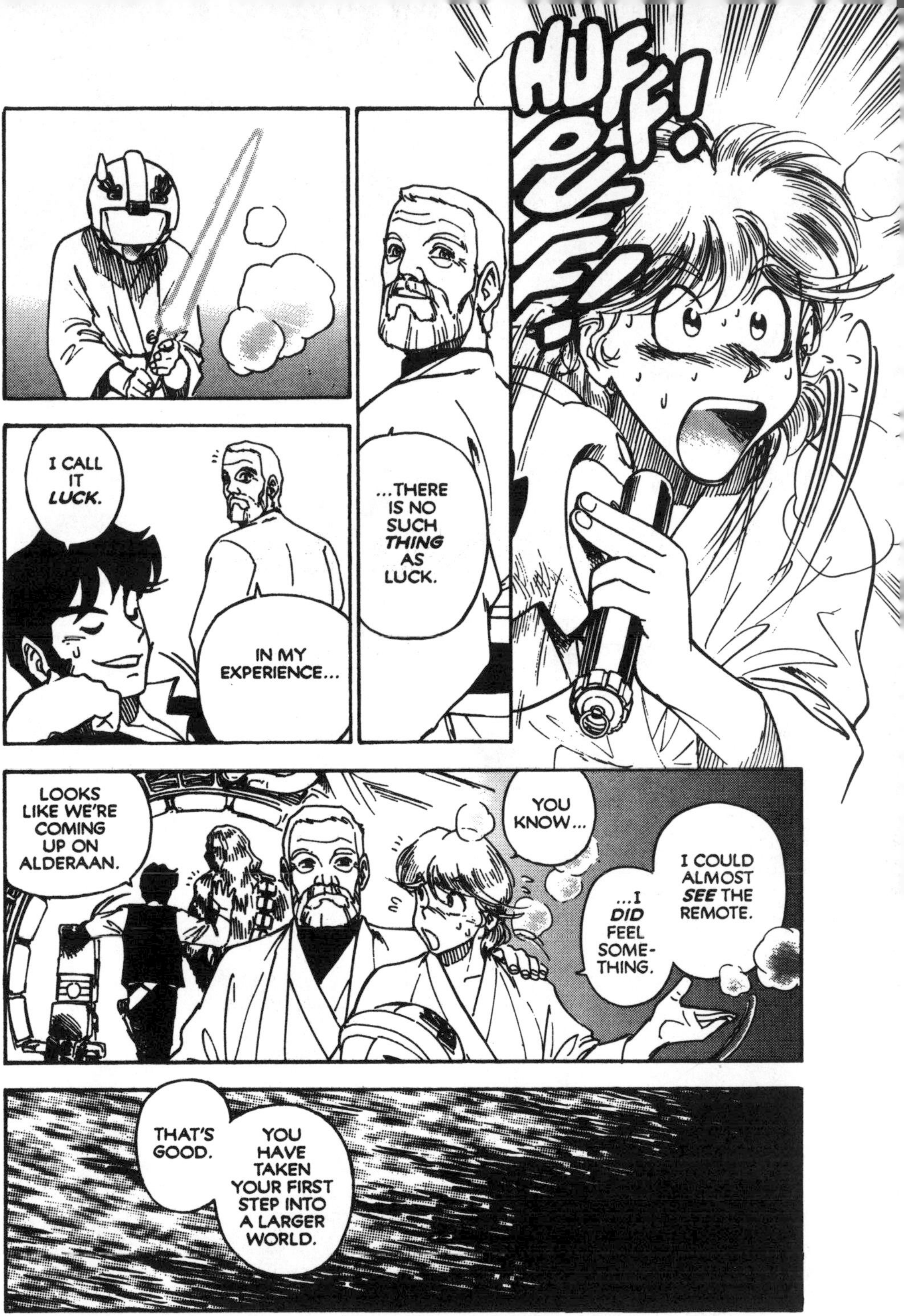

I CALL IT *LUCK*.
IN MY EXPERIENCE...
...THERE IS NO SUCH *THING* AS LUCK.
HUFF! PUFF!
LOOKS LIKE WE'RE COMING UP ON ALDERAAN.
YOU KNOW...
...I *DID* FEEL SOMETHING.
I COULD ALMOST *SEE* THE REMOTE.
THAT'S GOOD.
YOU HAVE TAKEN YOUR FIRST STEP INTO A LARGER WORLD.

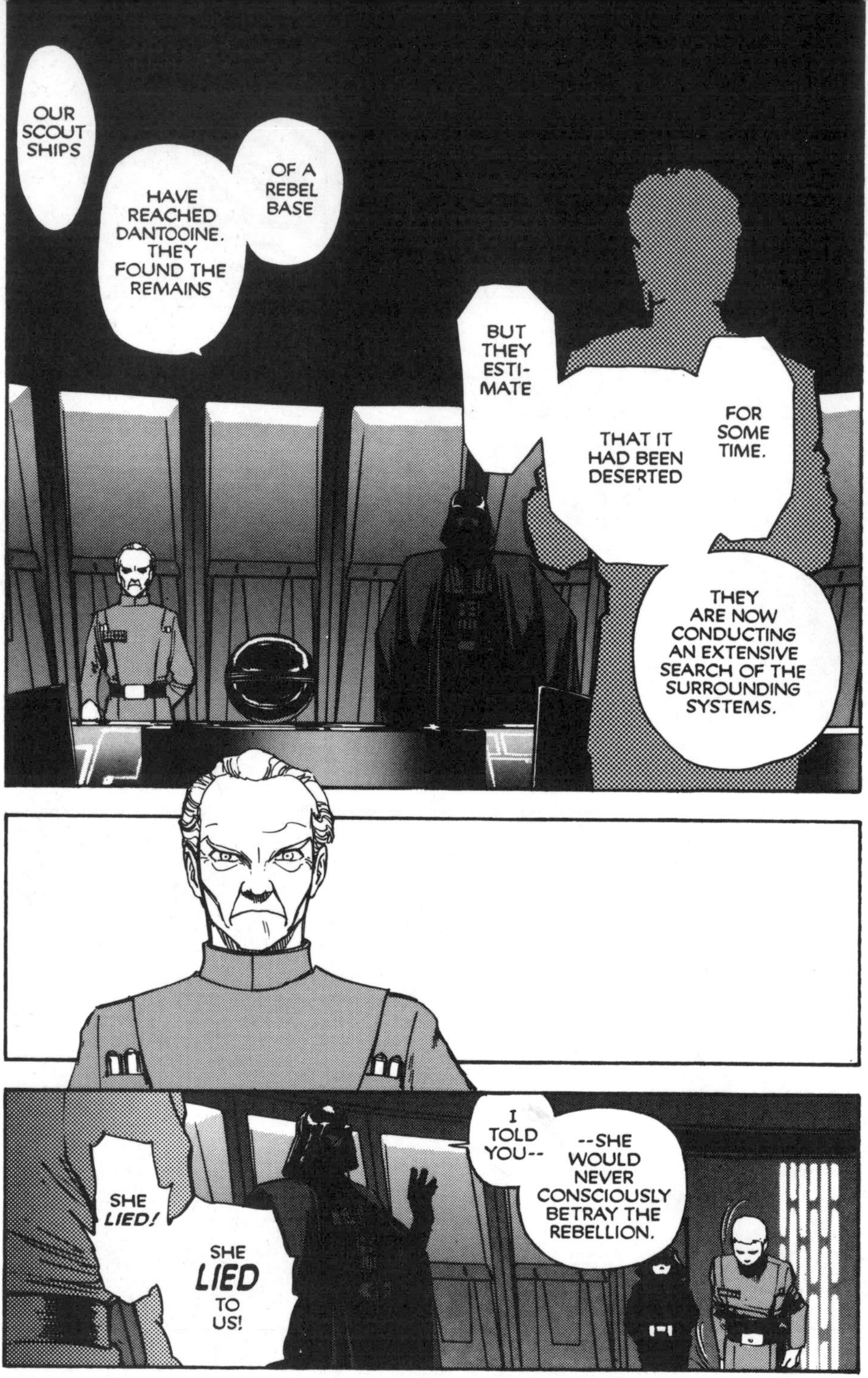
OUR SCOUT SHIPS
HAVE REACHED DANTOOINE. THEY FOUND THE REMAINS
OF A REBEL BASE
BUT THEY ESTI-MATE
THAT IT HAD BEEN DESERTED
FOR SOME TIME.
THEY ARE NOW CONDUCTING AN EXTENSIVE SEARCH OF THE SURROUNDING SYSTEMS.
SHE *LIED!*
SHE **LIED** TO US!
I TOLD YOU--
--SHE WOULD NEVER CONSCIOUSLY BETRAY THE REBELLION.

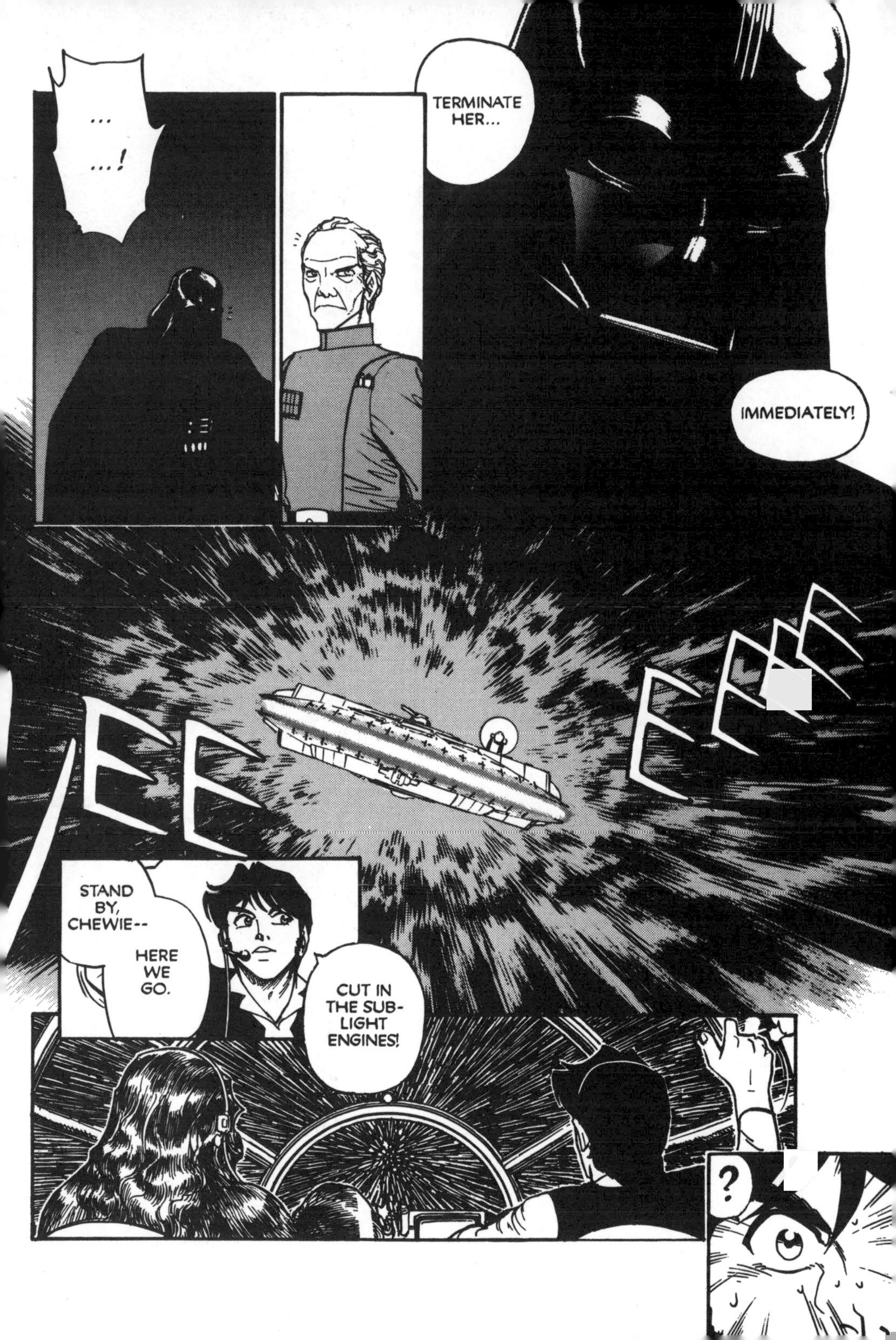
...
...!
TERMINATE HER...
IMMEDIATELY!
EE
EEEEE
STAND BY, CHEWIE--
HERE WE GO.
CUT IN THE SUB-LIGHT ENGINES!
?

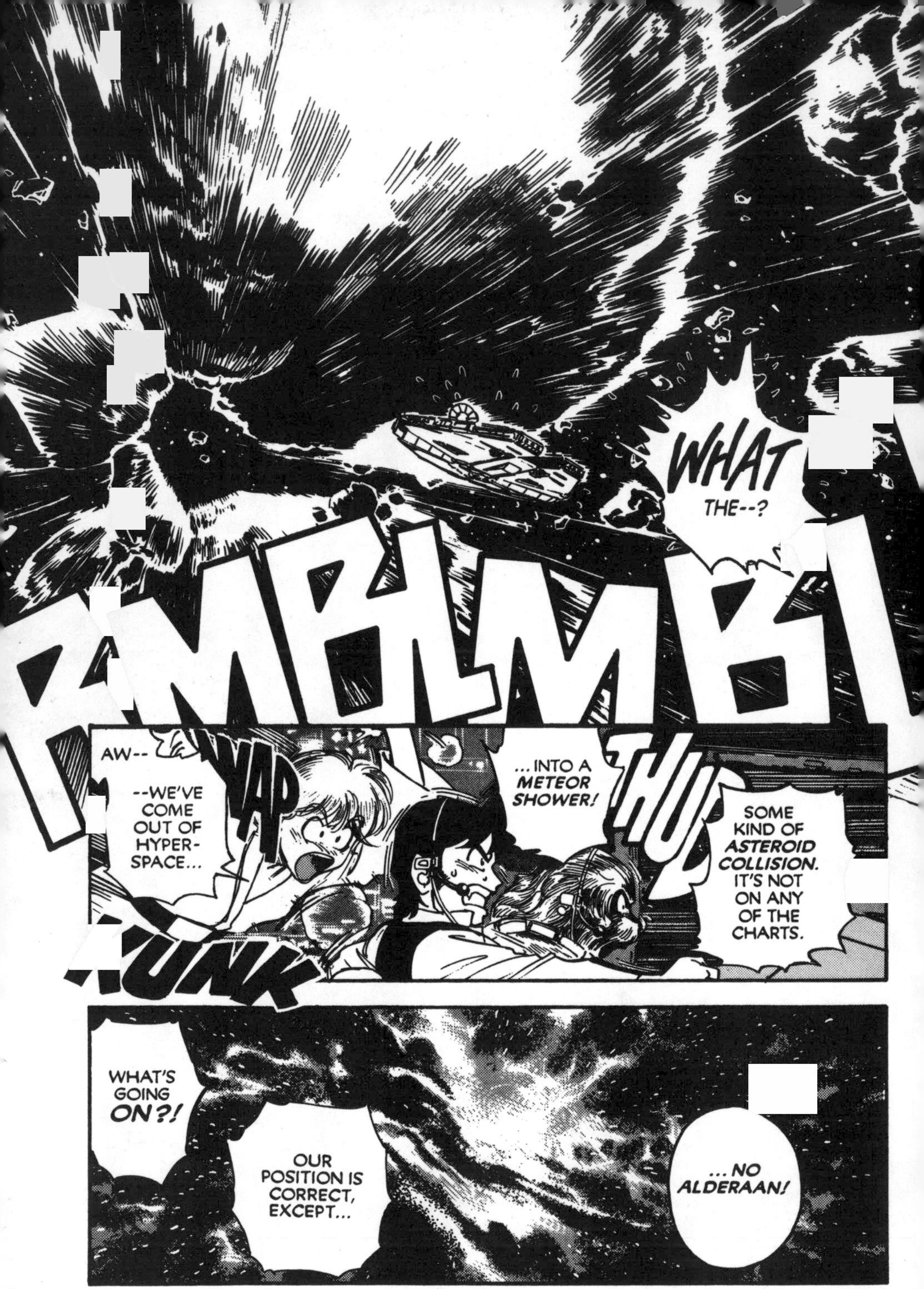
WHAT THE--?
AW--
--WE'VE COME OUT OF HYPER-SPACE...
...INTO A *METEOR SHOWER!*
SOME KIND OF *ASTEROID COLLISION.* IT'S NOT ON ANY OF THE CHARTS.
WHAT'S GOING *ON?!*
OUR POSITION IS CORRECT, EXCEPT...
...NO *ALDERAAN!*

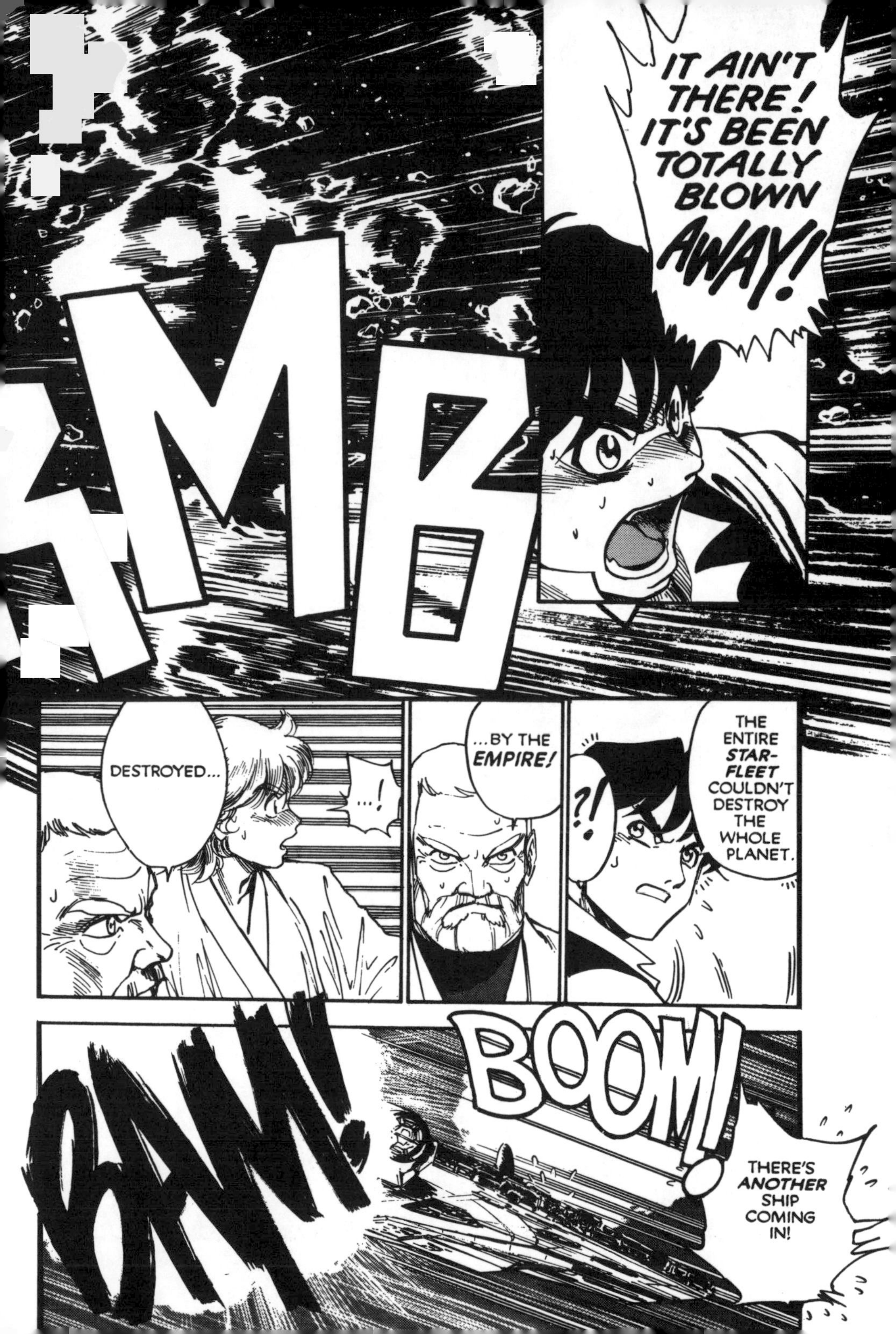
IT AIN'T THERE! IT'S BEEN TOTALLY BLOWN AWAY!
DESTROYED...
...!
...BY THE EMPIRE!
?!
THE ENTIRE STAR-FLEET COULDN'T DESTROY THE WHOLE PLANET.
BAM!
BOOM!
THERE'S ANOTHER SHIP COMING IN!

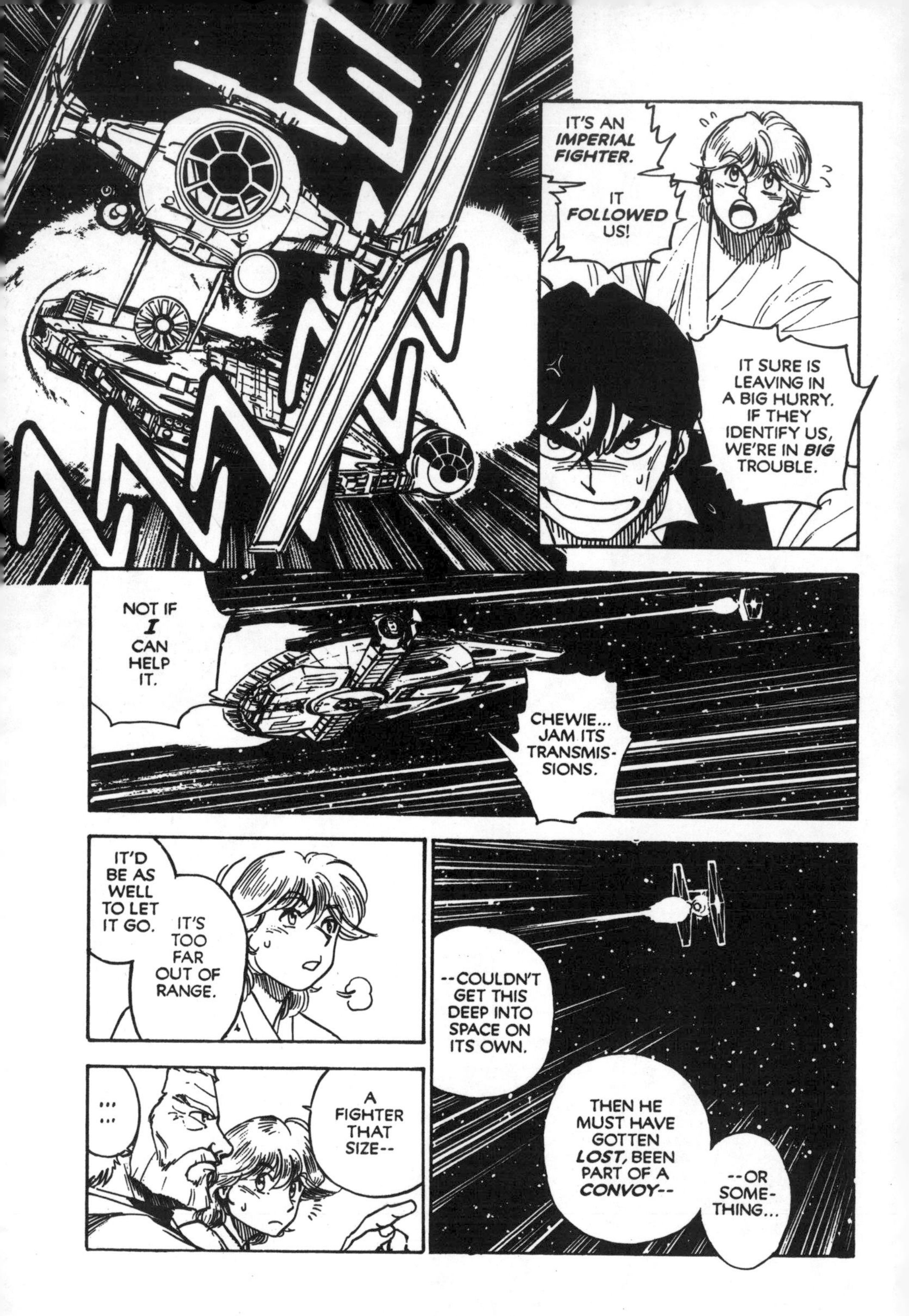
IT'S AN IMPERIAL FIGHTER.
IT FOLLOWED US!
IT SURE IS LEAVING IN A BIG HURRY. IF THEY IDENTIFY US, WE'RE IN BIG TROUBLE.
NOT IF I CAN HELP IT.
CHEWIE... JAM ITS TRANSMIS-SIONS.
IT'D BE AS WELL TO LET IT GO.
IT'S TOO FAR OUT OF RANGE.
...
...
A FIGHTER THAT SIZE--
--COULDN'T GET THIS DEEP INTO SPACE ON ITS OWN.
THEN HE MUST HAVE GOTTEN LOST, BEEN PART OF A CONVOY--
--OR SOME-THING...

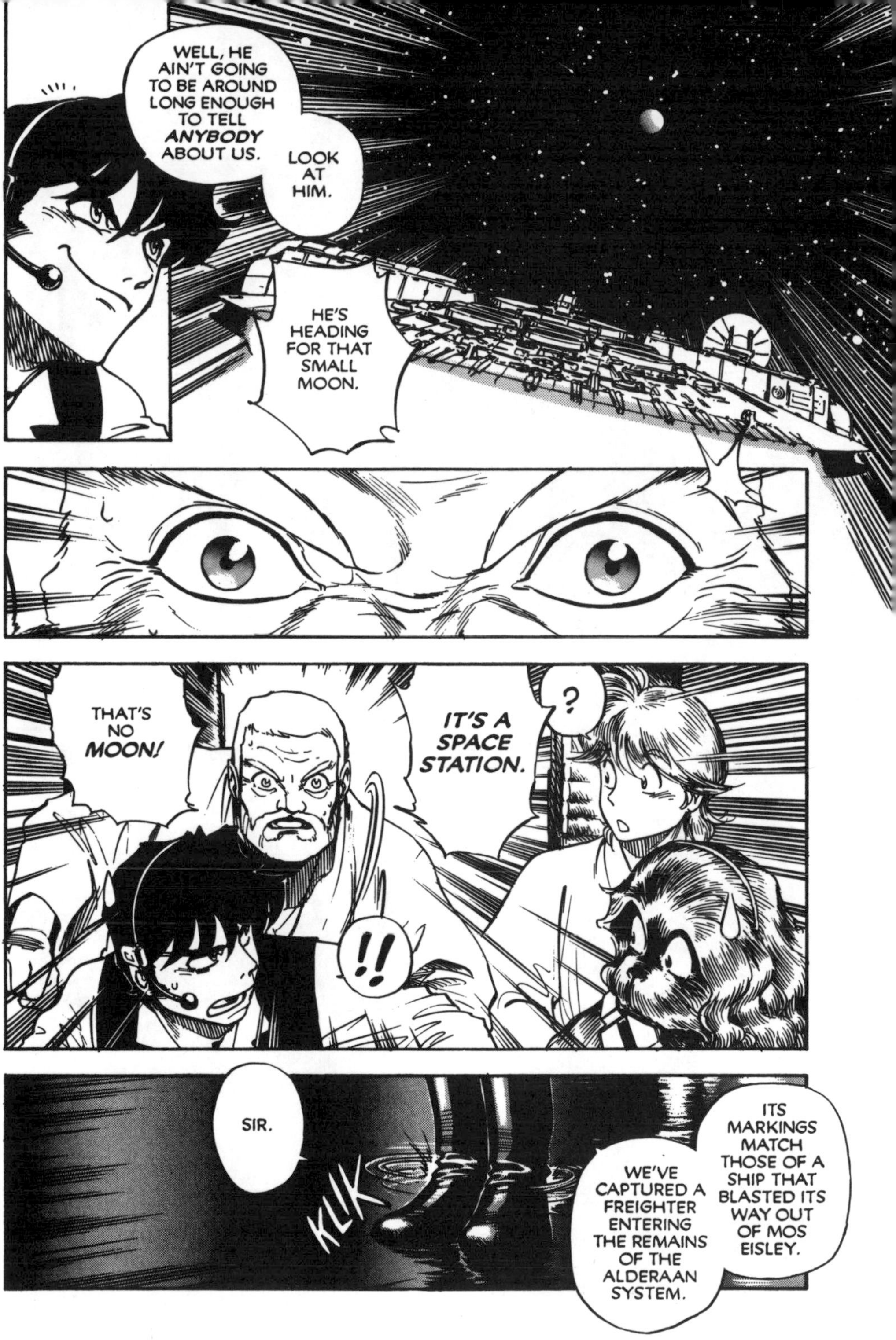
WELL, HE AIN'T GOING TO BE AROUND LONG ENOUGH TO TELL ANYBODY ABOUT US.
LOOK AT HIM.
HE'S HEADING FOR THAT SMALL MOON.
THAT'S NO MOON!
IT'S A SPACE STATION.
?
!!
SIR.
KLIK
WE'VE CAPTURED A FREIGHTER ENTERING THE REMAINS OF THE ALDERAAN SYSTEM.
ITS MARKINGS MATCH THOSE OF A SHIP THAT BLASTED ITS WAY OUT OF MOS EISLEY.

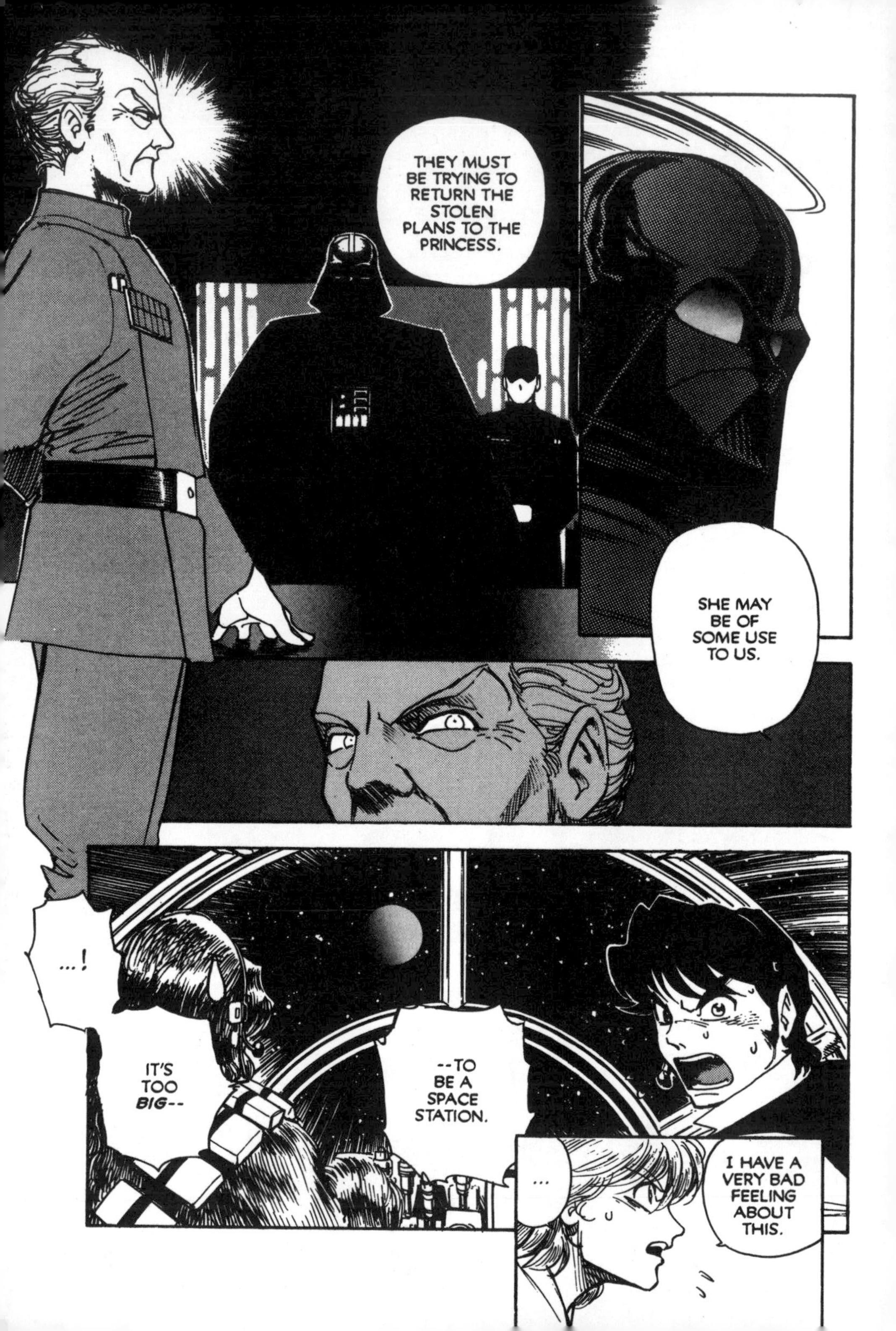
THEY MUST BE TRYING TO RETURN THE STOLEN PLANS TO THE PRINCESS.
SHE MAY BE OF SOME USE TO US.
...!
IT'S TOO *BIG*--
--TO BE A SPACE STATION.
...
I HAVE A VERY BAD FEELING ABOUT THIS.

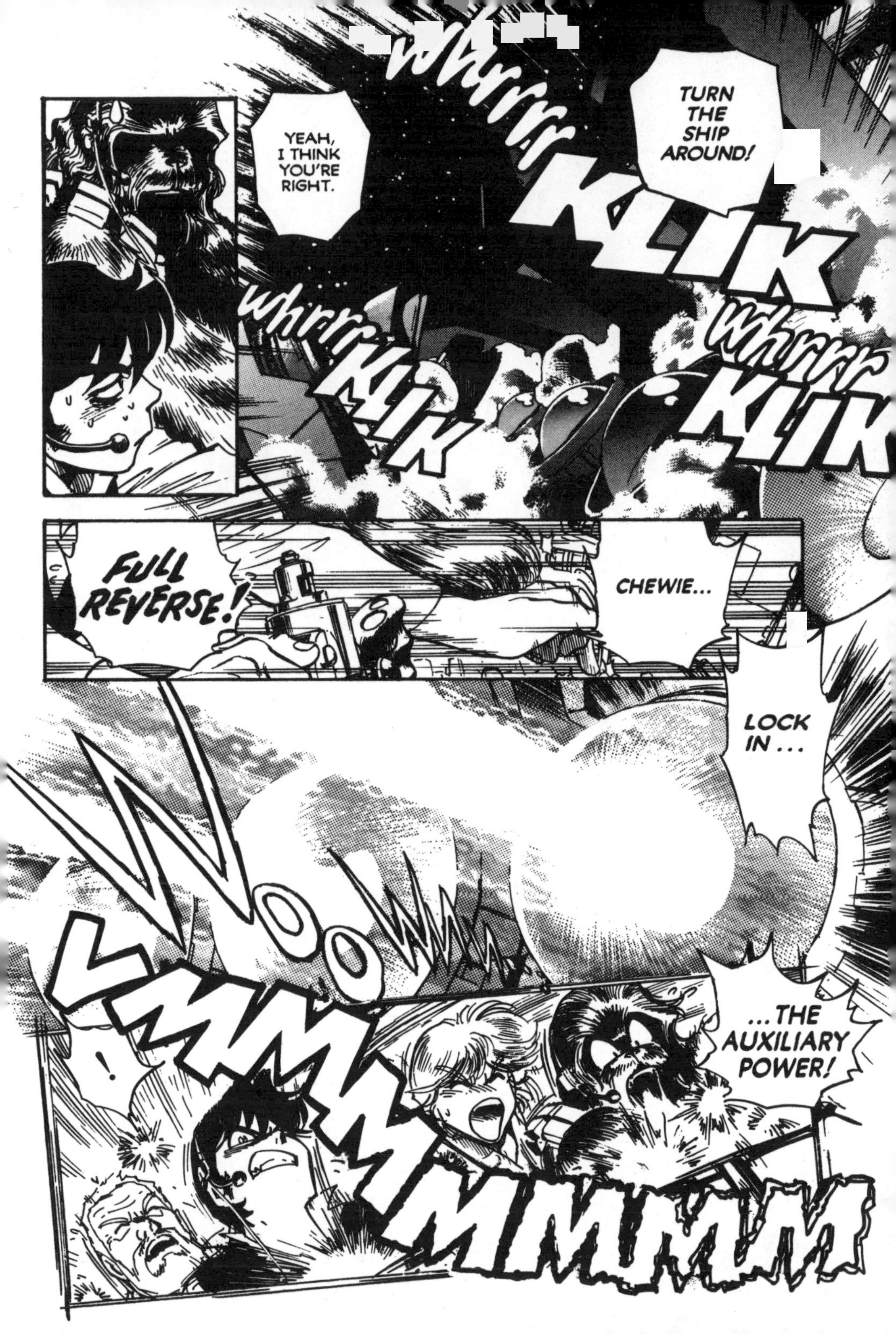

YEAH, I THINK YOU'RE RIGHT.
WHRRRR KLIK
TURN THE SHIP AROUND!
WHRRRR KLIK
WHRRRR KLIK
FULL REVERSE!
CHEWIE...
LOCK IN . . .
!
VOOOWMMMMMMMM
...THE AUXILIARY POWER!

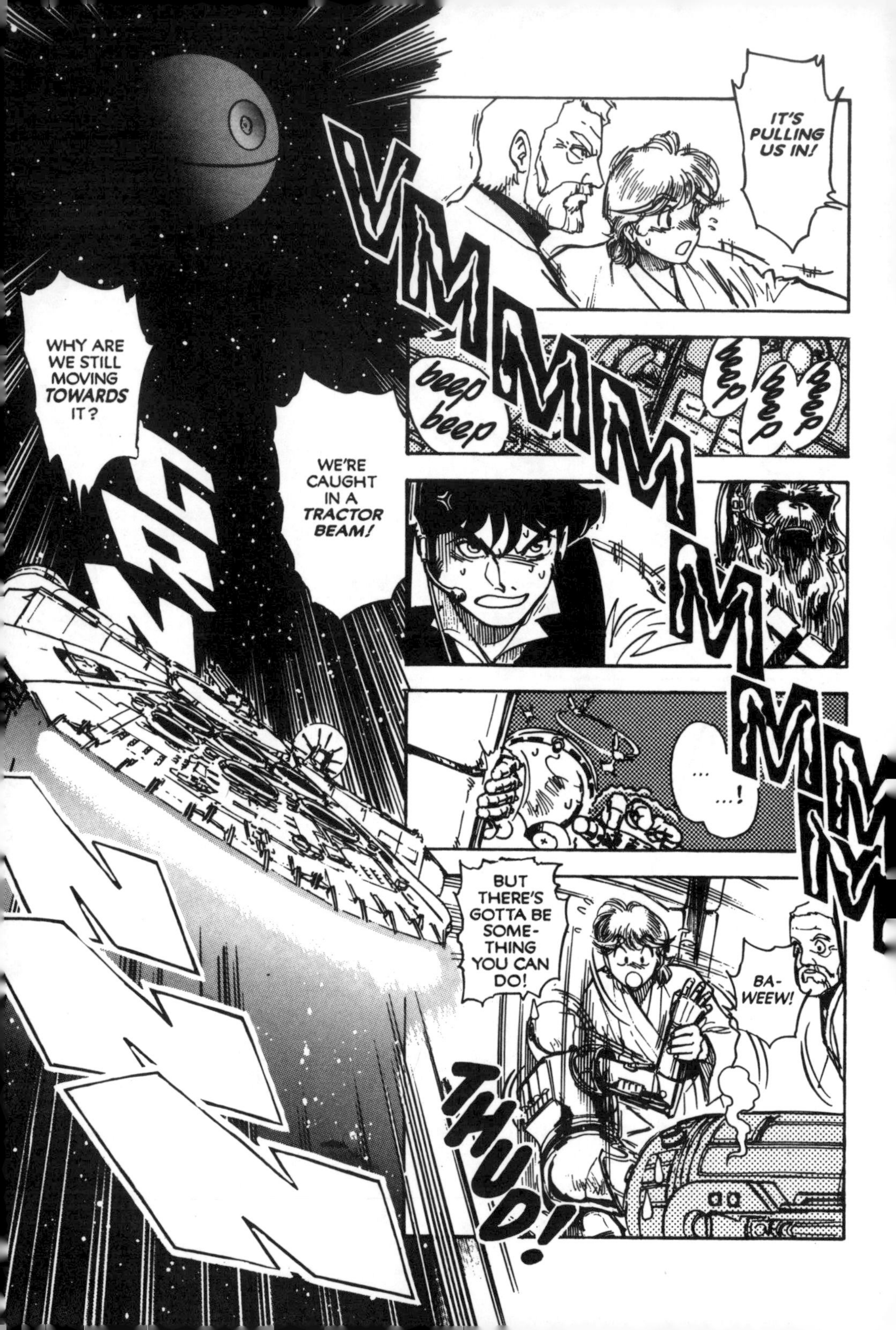
WHY ARE WE STILL MOVING *TOWARDS* IT?
WE'RE CAUGHT IN A *TRACTOR BEAM!*
VMMMMMMMMMM
IT'S PULLING US IN!
beep beep
beep beep
beep beep
beep beep
...
...!
BUT THERE'S GOTTA BE SOME-THING YOU CAN DO!
BA-WEEW!
THUD!

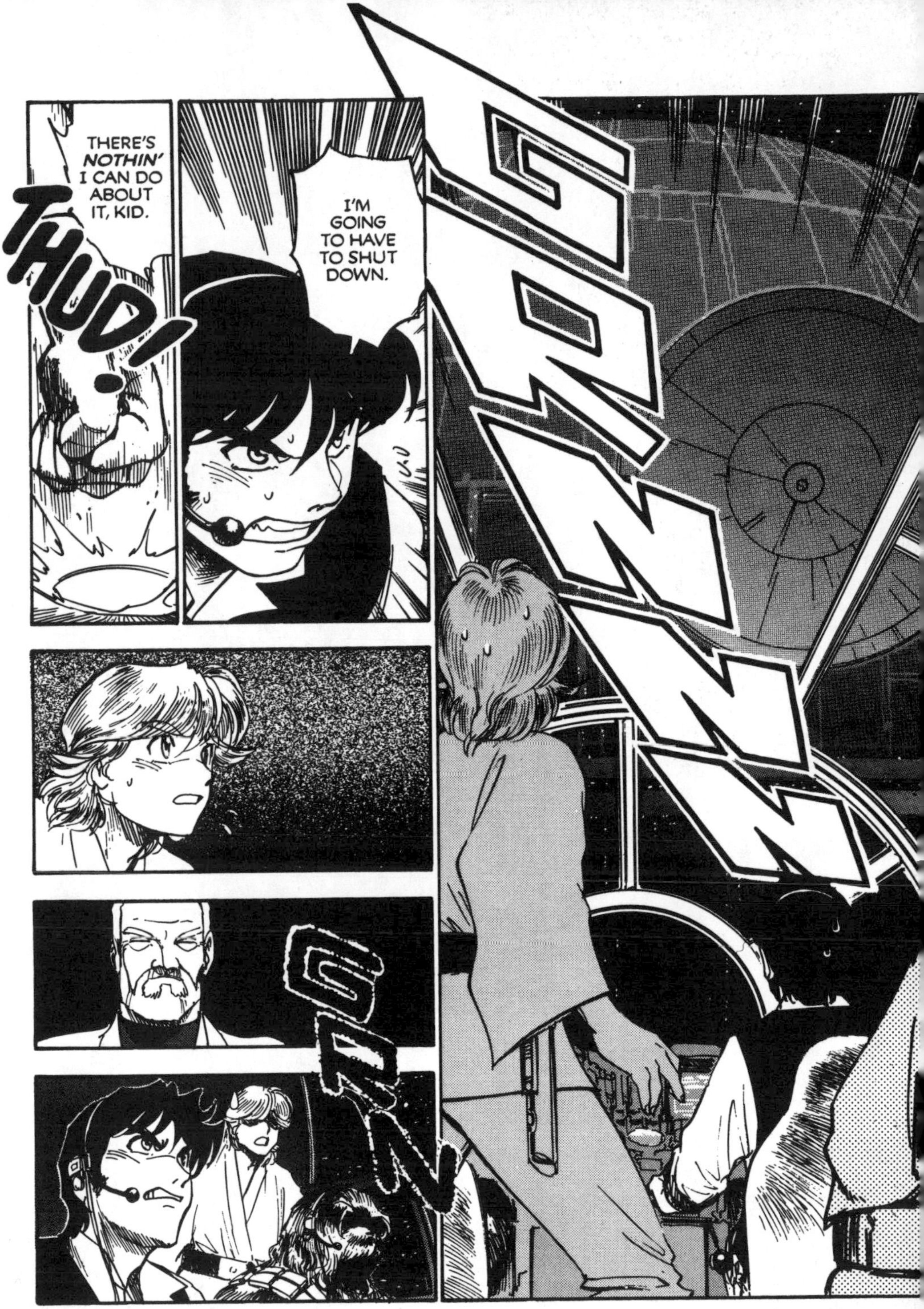
THUD!
THERE'S *NOTHIN'* I CAN DO ABOUT IT, KID.
I'M GOING TO HAVE TO SHUT DOWN.
GRNNNN

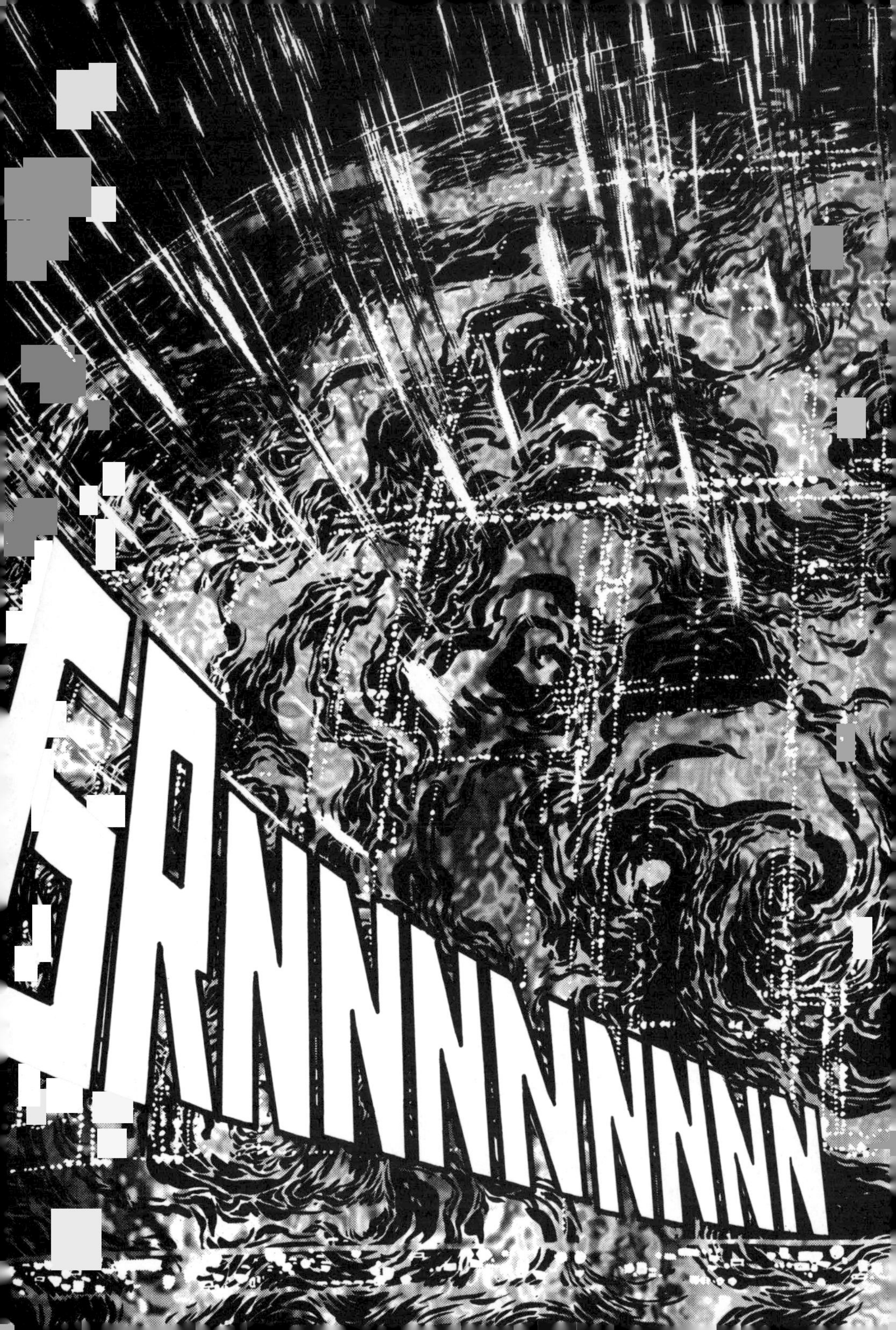
SRNNNNNNNNNN

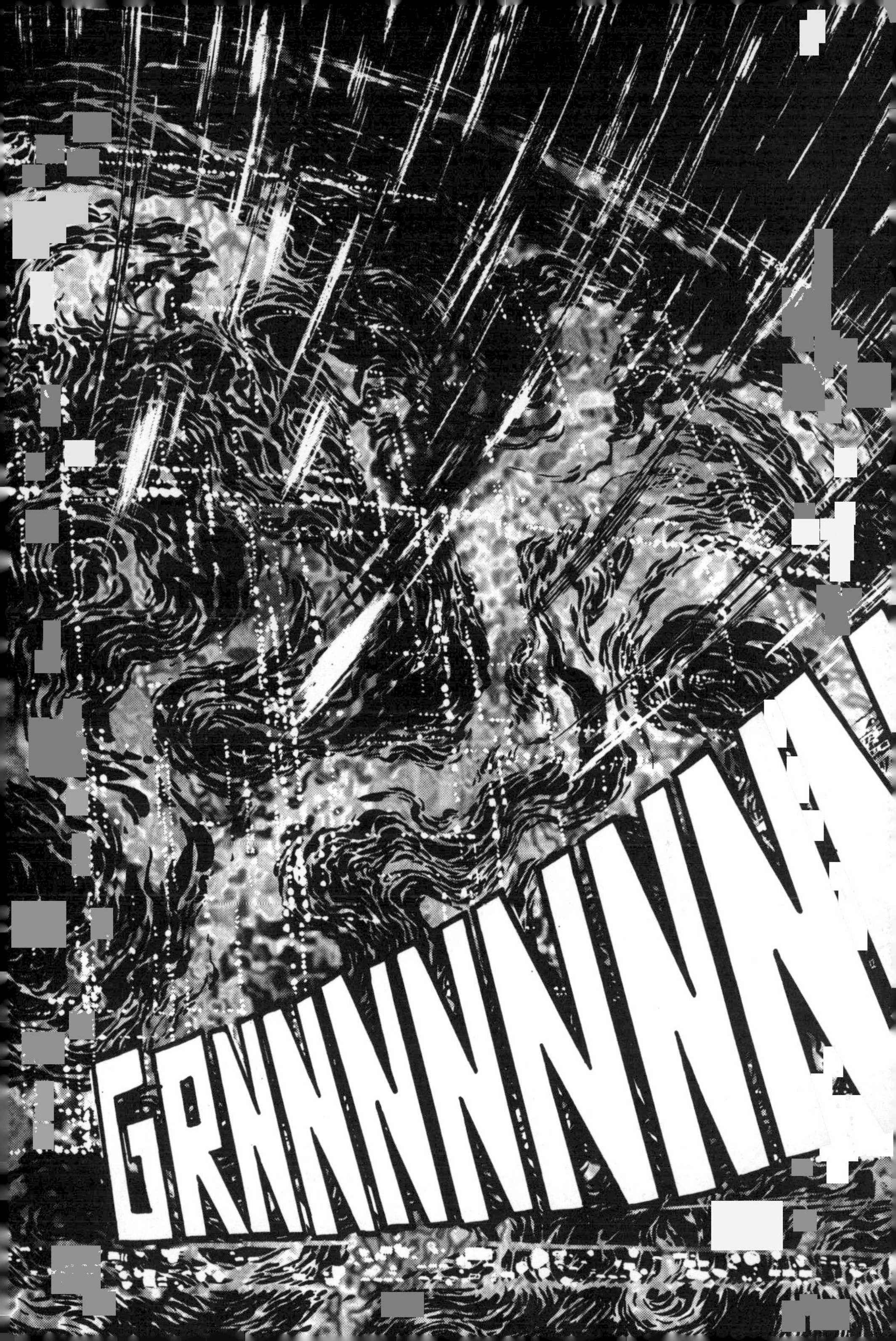
GRNNNNNNNNN

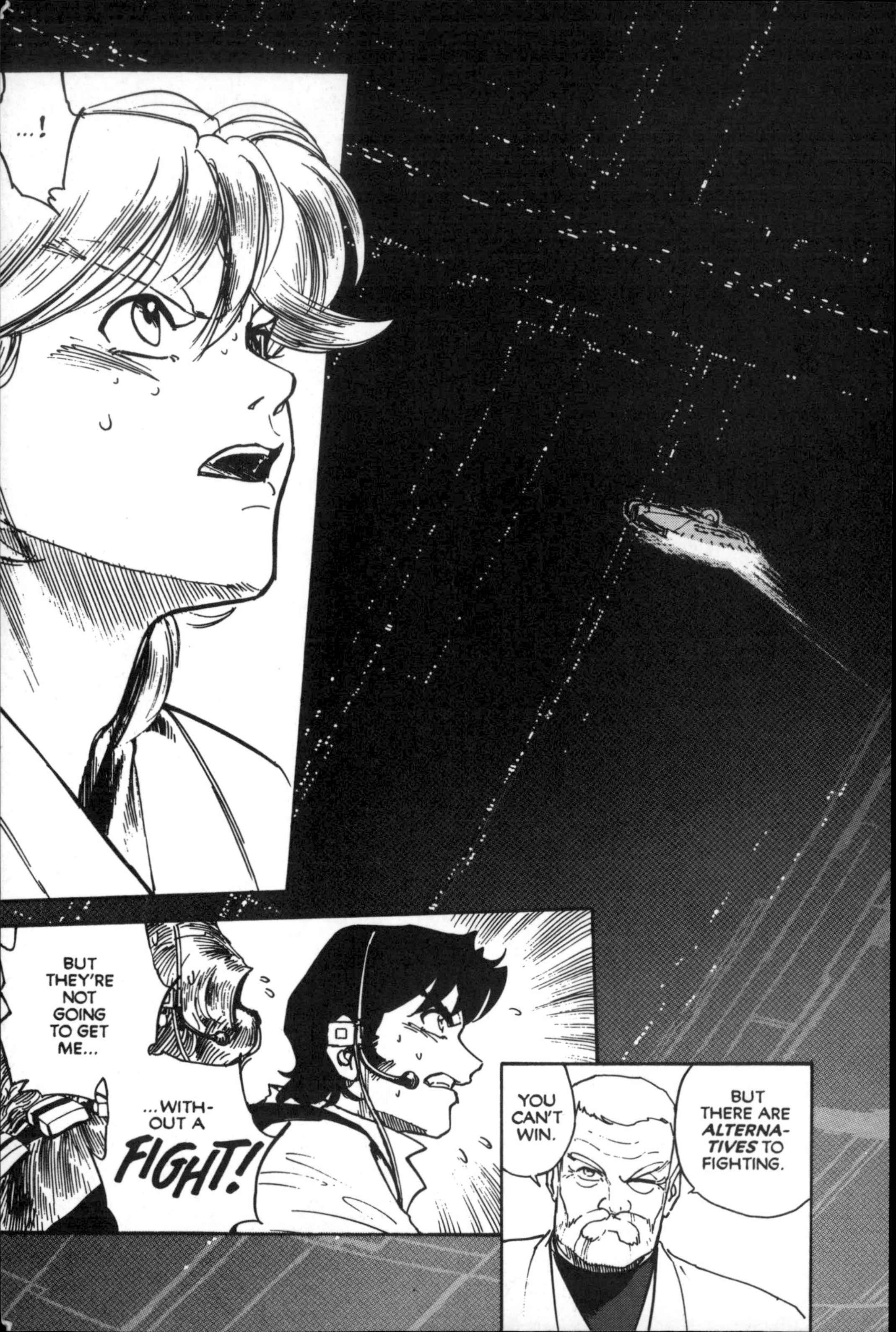
...!
BUT THEY'RE NOT GOING TO GET ME...
...WITH-OUT A FIGHT!
YOU CAN'T WIN.
BUT THERE ARE ALTERNA-TIVES TO FIGHTING.

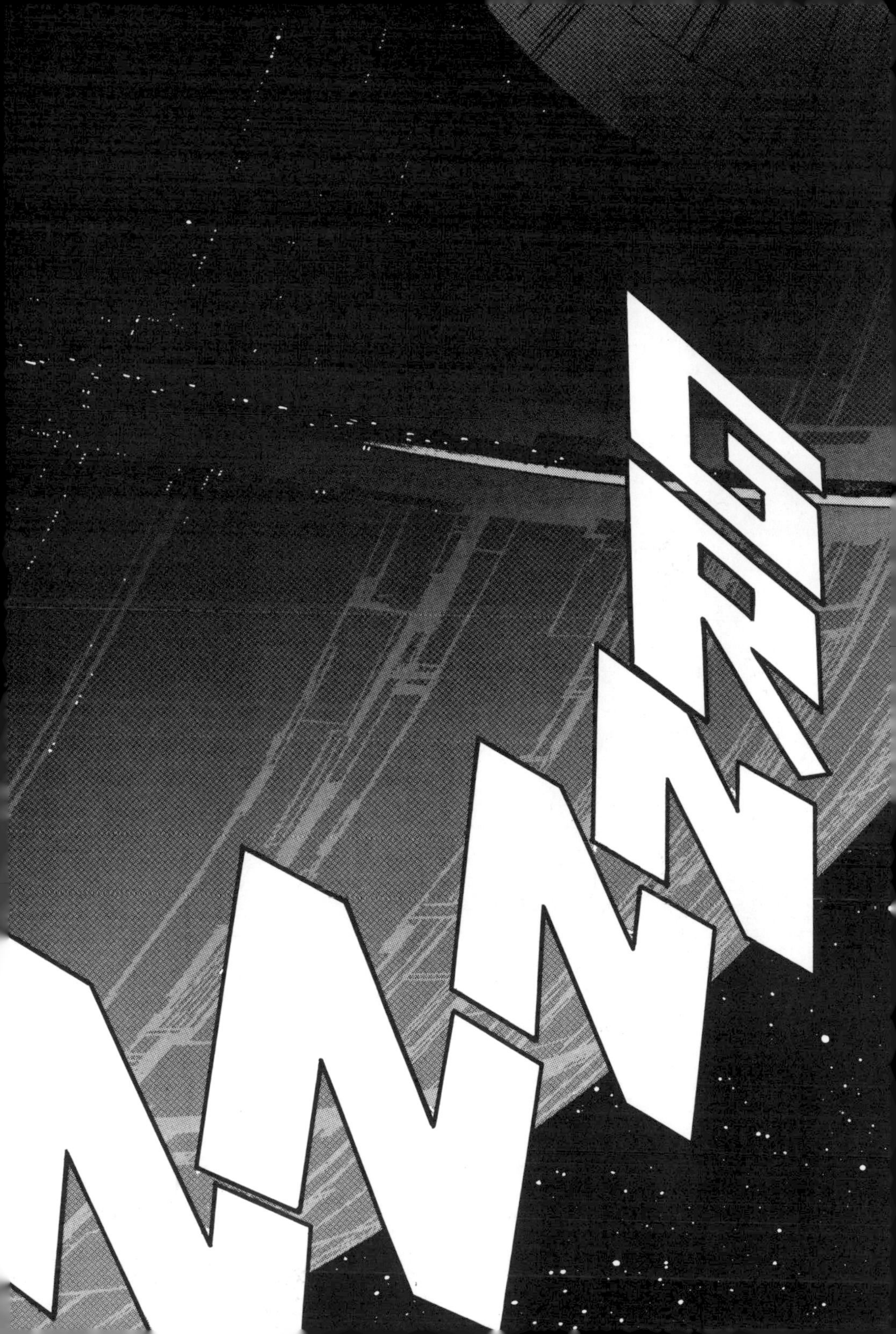
GRNNNN

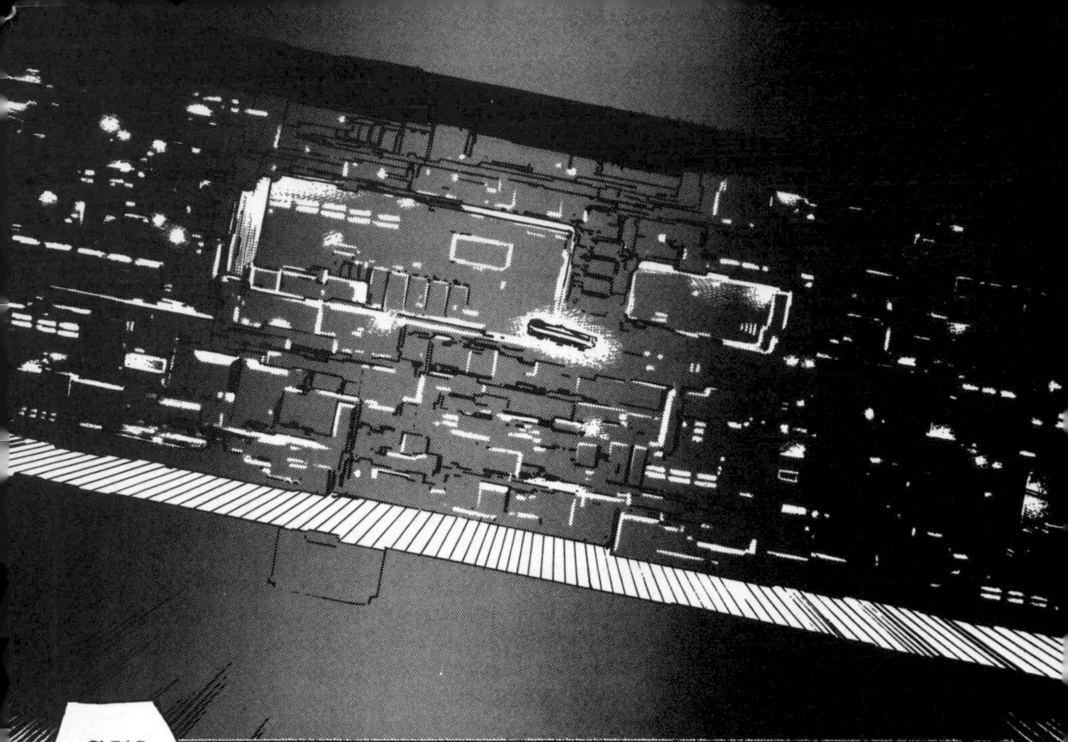

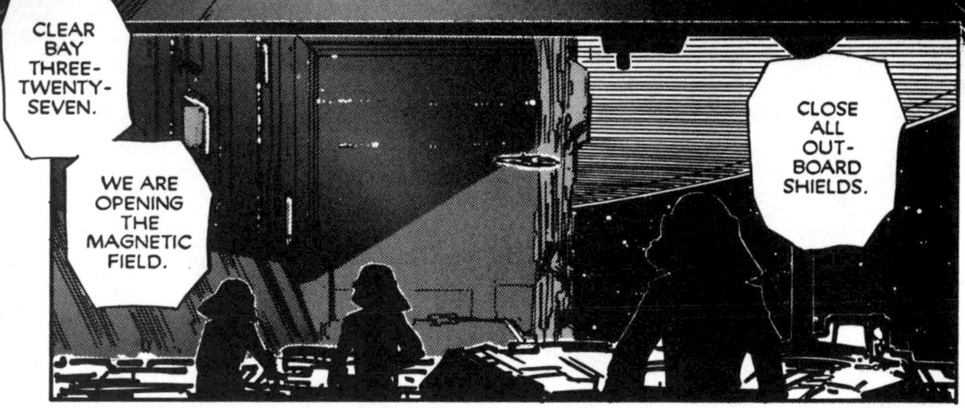

CLEAR BAY THREE-TWENTY-SEVEN.
WE ARE OPENING THE MAGNETIC FIELD.
CLOSE ALL OUT-BOARD SHIELDS.

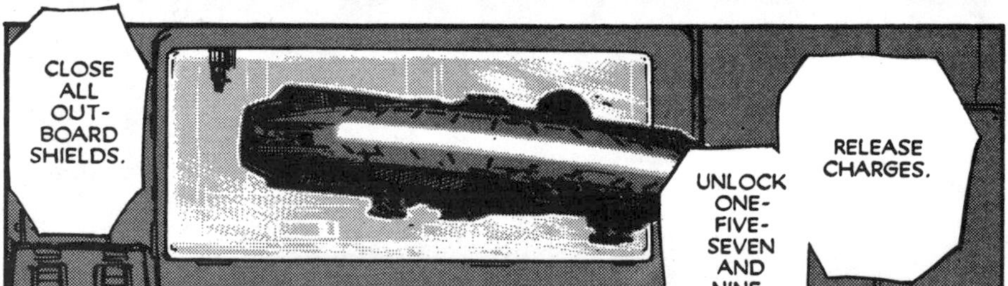

CLOSE ALL OUT-BOARD SHIELDS.
UNLOCK ONE-FIVE-SEVEN AND NINE.
RELEASE CHARGES.

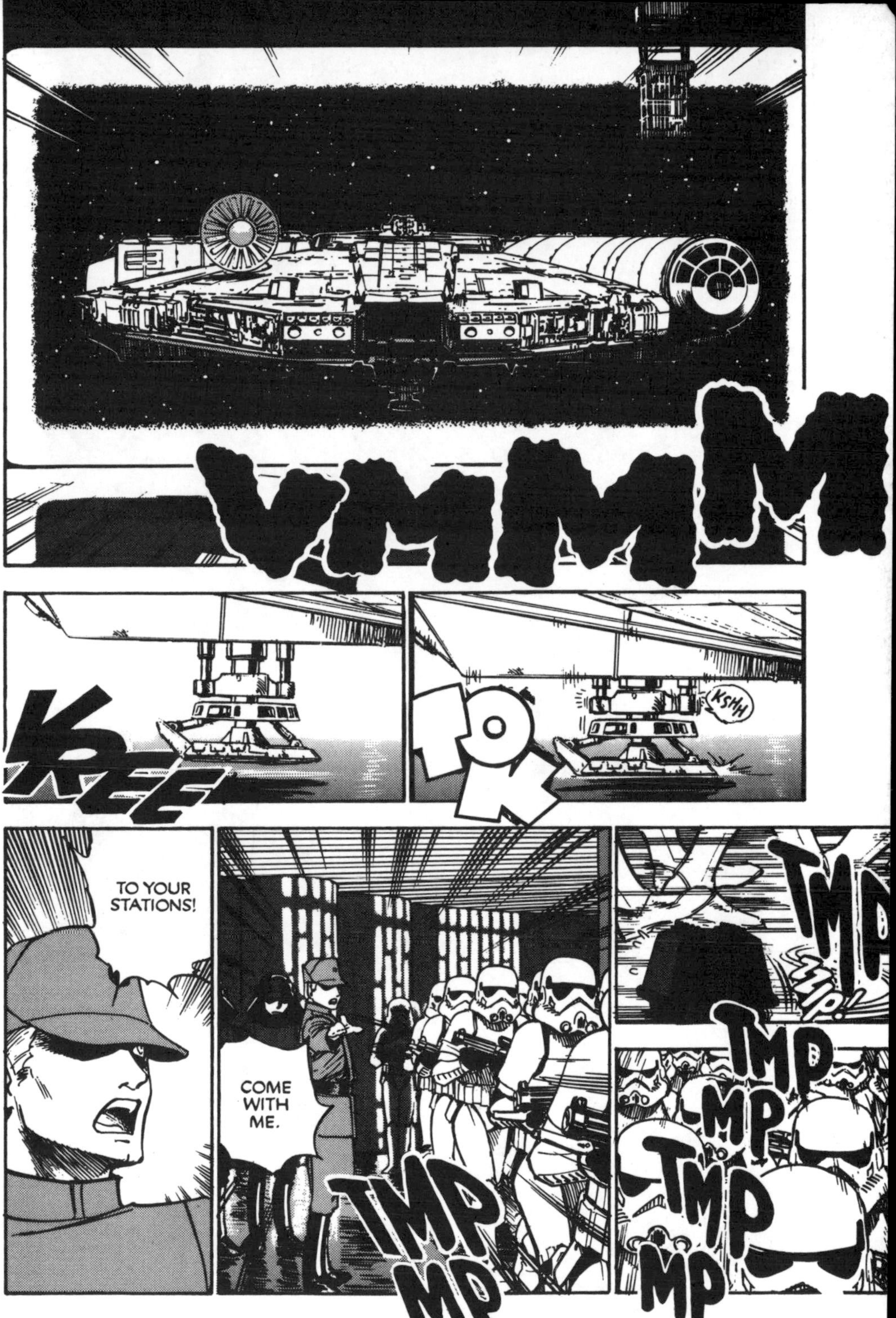
VMMMM
KREE
TONK
KSHH
TO YOUR STATIONS!
COME WITH ME.
TMP MP
TMP
TMP!
TMP MP
TMP MP

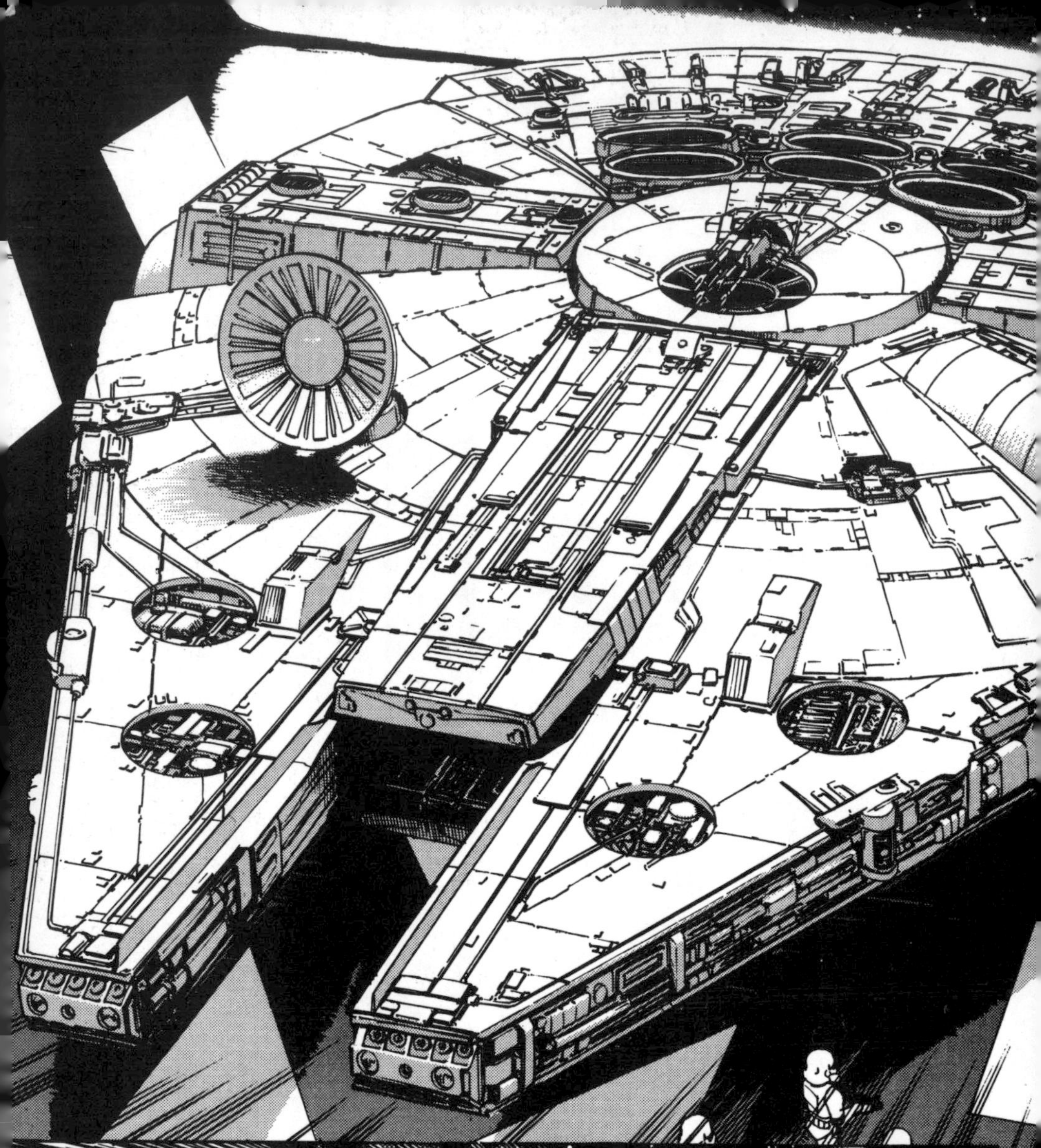
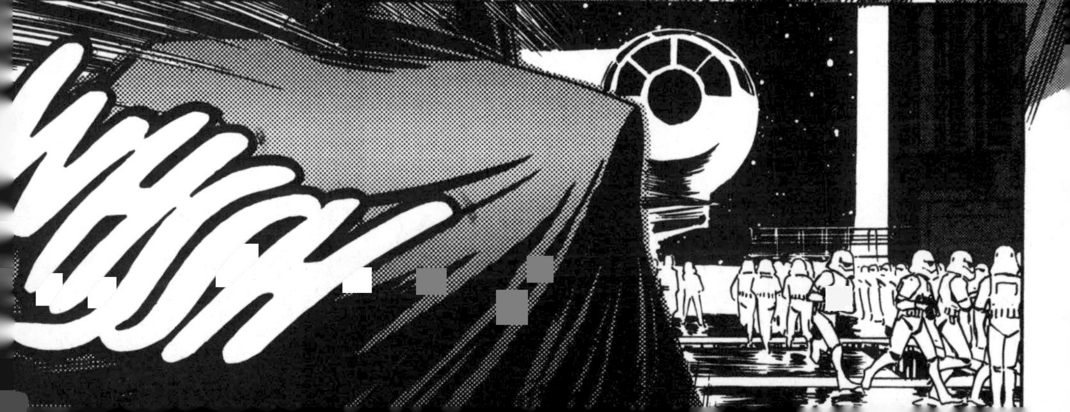

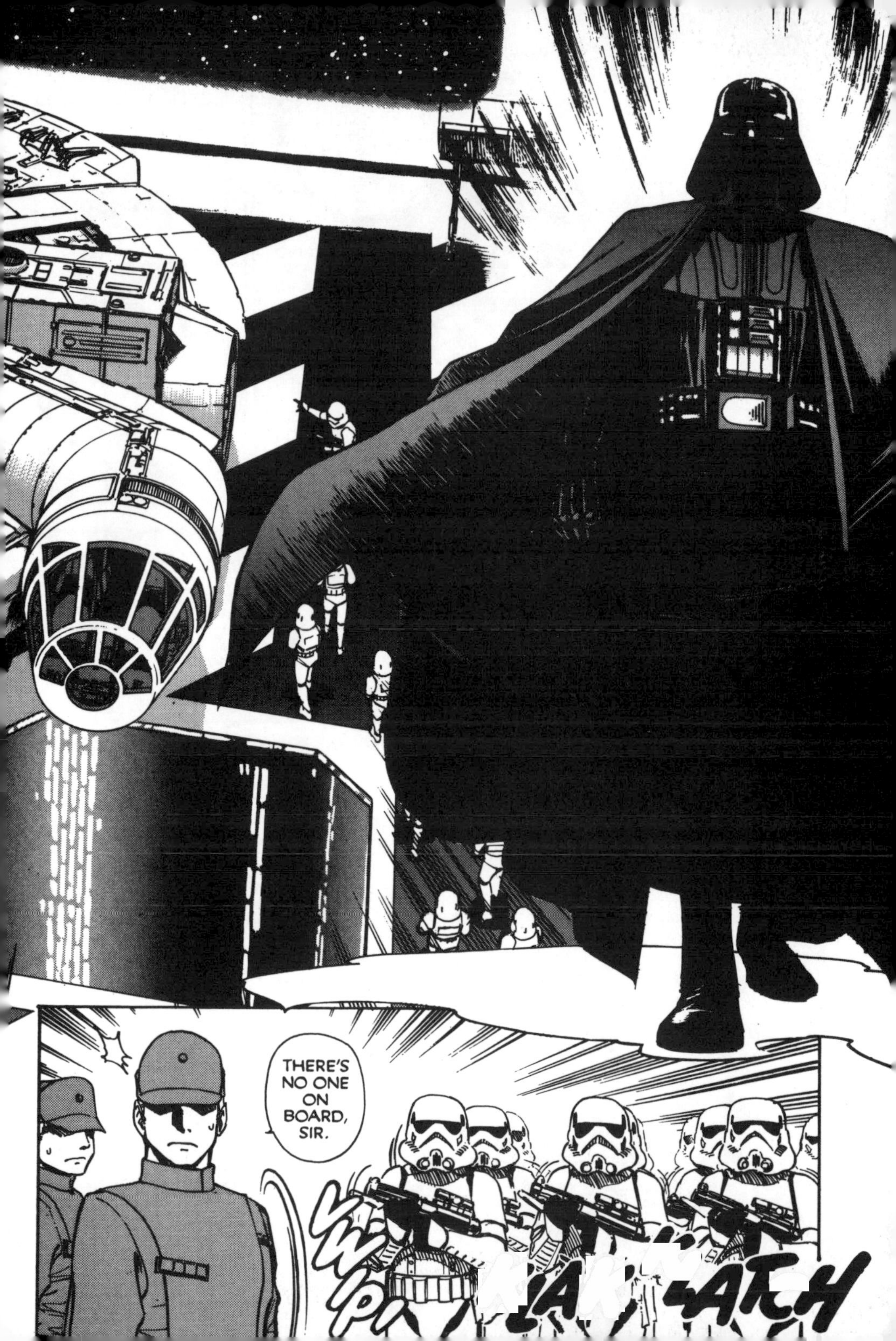
THERE'S NO ONE ON BOARD, SIR.

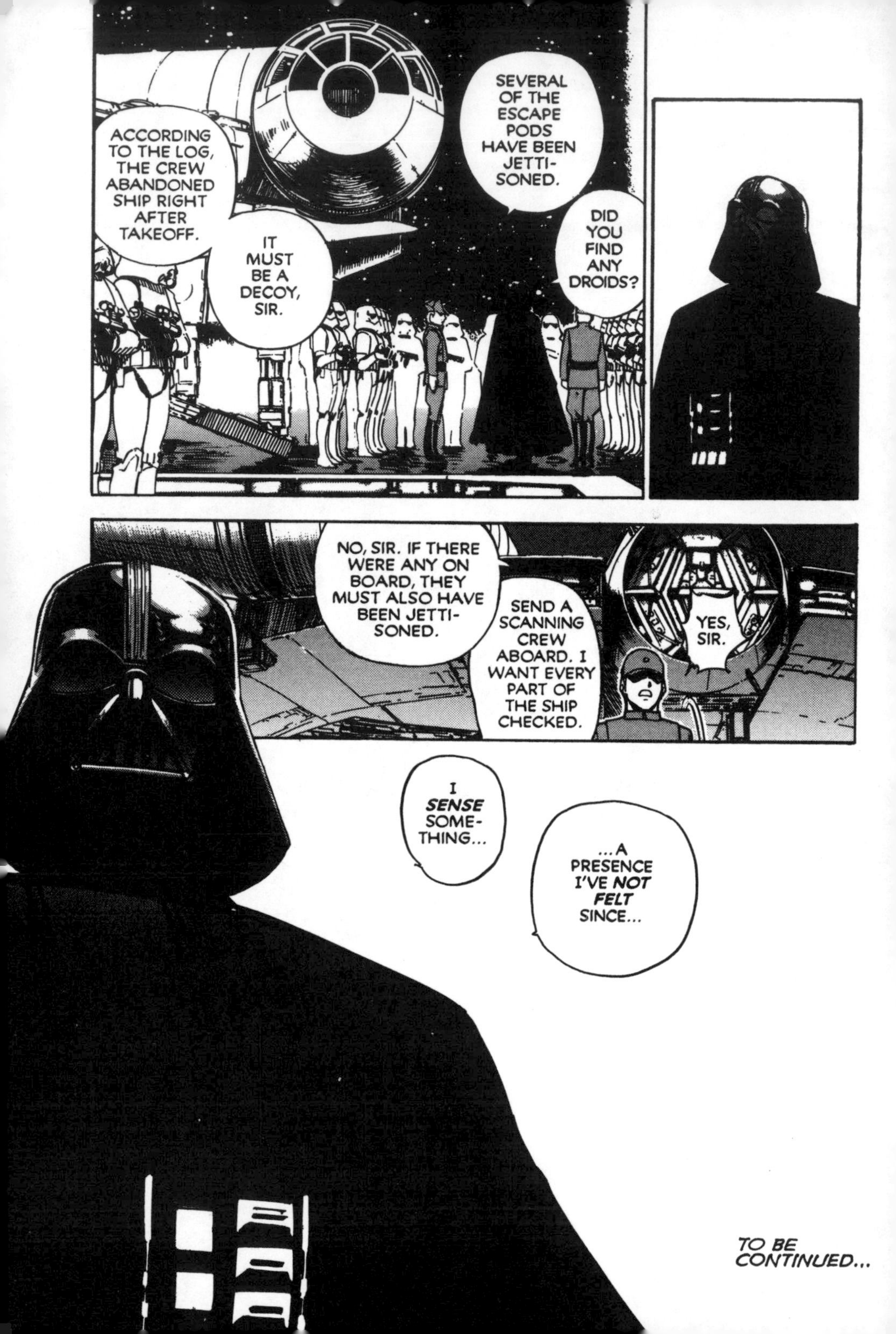
ACCORDING TO THE LOG, THE CREW ABANDONED SHIP RIGHT AFTER TAKEOFF.
IT MUST BE A DECOY, SIR.
SEVERAL OF THE ESCAPE PODS HAVE BEEN JETTI-SONED.
DID YOU FIND ANY DROIDS?
NO, SIR. IF THERE WERE ANY ON BOARD, THEY MUST ALSO HAVE BEEN JETTI-SONED.
SEND A SCANNING CREW ABOARD. I WANT EVERY PART OF THE SHIP CHECKED.
YES, SIR.
I *SENSE* SOME-THING...
...A PRESENCE I'VE *NOT FELT* SINCE...
TO BE CONTINUED...

ADAPTED FROM AN ORIGINAL SCRIPT BY GEORGE LUCAS

ILLUSTRATION BY HISAO TAMAKI

スター・ウォーズ 2
新たなる希望

LETTERING AND ART RETOUCH BY TOM ORZECHOWSKI

COVER ART BY ADAM WARREN

COVER COLORS BY JOSEPH WIGHT

SPECIAL THANKS TO ALLAN KAUSCH AND LUCY AUTREY WILSON AT LUCAS LICENSING

SPECIAL THANKS TO AMADOR CISNEROS

BOOK DESIGN BY CARY GRAZZINI

EDITED BY DAVID LAND

PUBLISHED BY MIKE RICHARDSON

STAR WARS: A NEW HOPE — MANGA VOLUME TWO, August 1998. Published by Dark Horse Comics, Inc., 10956 SE Main Street, Milwaukie, Oregon 97222. Star Wars®: A New Hope — MANGA © 1997, 1998 Lucasfilm Ltd. Title and character and place names protected by all applicable trademark laws. All rights reserved. Used under authorization. This material was originally published in Japan in book form in 1997 by Media Works Inc., Tokyo. Dark Horse Comics® and the Dark Horse logo are registered trademarks of Dark Horse Comics, Inc. All rights reserved. No portion of this publication may be reproduced or transmitted, in any form or by any means, without the express written permission of Dark Horse Comics, Inc. Names, characters, places, and incidents featured in this publication either are the product of the author's imagination or are used fictitiously. Any resemblance to actual persons (living or dead), events, institutions, or locales, without satiric intent, is coincidental.

Published by Dark Horse Comics, Inc., 10956 SE Main Street, Milwaukie, OR 97222

ISBN: 1-56971-363-4   First edition: August 1998

10 9 8 7 6 5 4 3

PRINTED IN THE UNITED STATES OF AMERICA

スター・ウォーズ BACKLIST

DARK HORSE'S COMPLETE LINE OF スター・ウォーズ SPECIALTY BOOKS

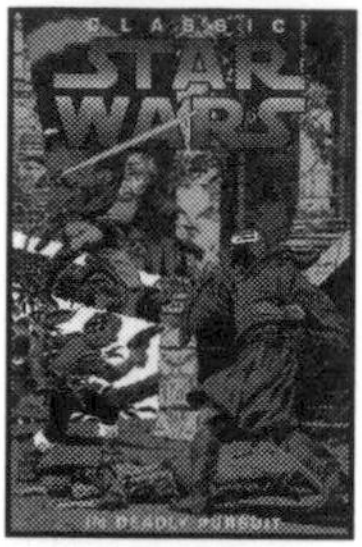
CLASSIC
STAR WARS
IN DEADLY PURSUIT

IN DEADLY PURSUIT
ISBN: 1-56971-109-7 $16.95

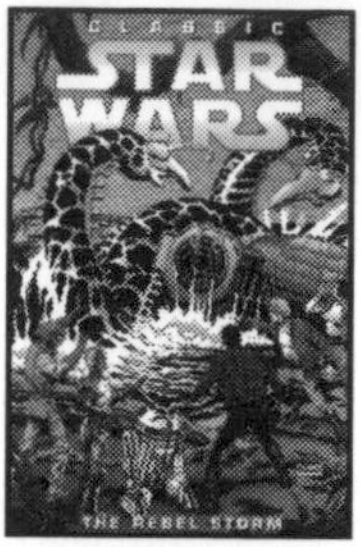
CLASSIC
STAR WARS
THE REBEL STORM

THE REBEL STORM
ISBN: 1-56971-106-2 $16.95

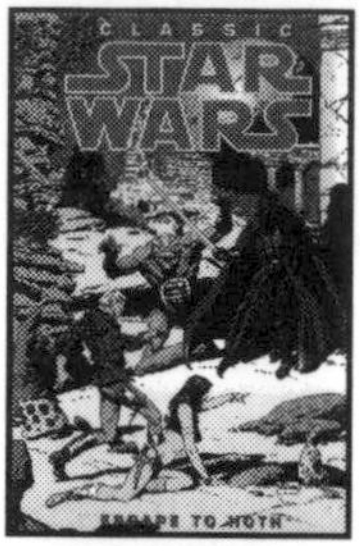
CLASSIC
STAR WARS
ESCAPE TO HOTH

ESCAPE TO HOTH
ISBN: 1-56971-093-7 $16.95

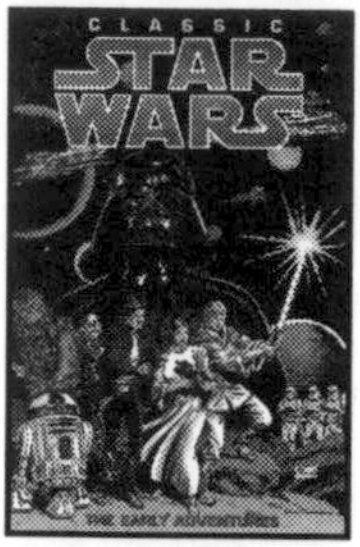
CLASSIC
STAR WARS
THE EARLY ADVENTURES

THE EARLY ADVENTURES
ISBN: 1-56971-178-X $19.95

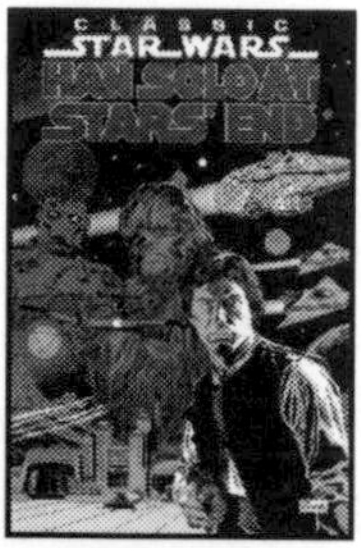
CLASSIC
STAR WARS
HAN SOLO AT STARS' END

HAN SOLO AT STARS' END
ISBN: 1-56971-254-9 $6.95

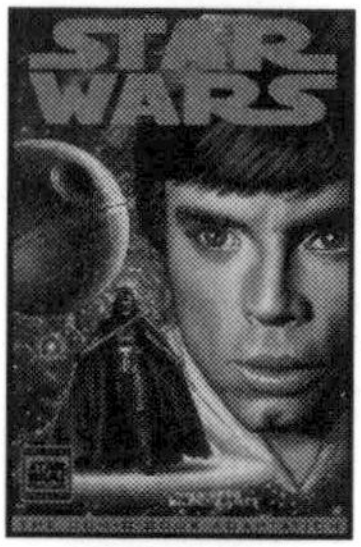
STAR WARS

A NEW HOPE
ISBN: 1-56971-213-1 $9.95

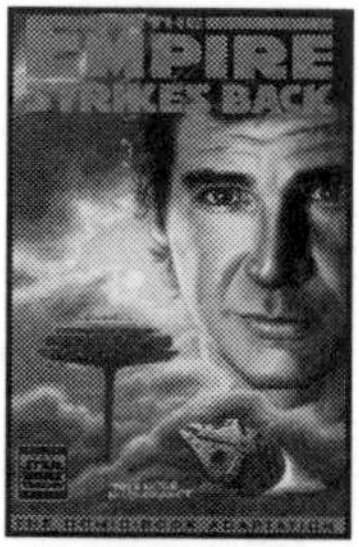
THE EMPIRE STRIKES BACK

THE EMPIRE STRIKES BACK
ISBN: 1-56971-234-4 $9.95

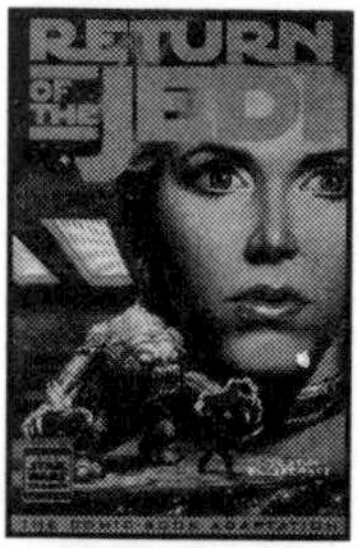
RETURN OF THE JEDI

RETURN OF THE JEDI
ISBN: 1-56971-235-2 $9.95

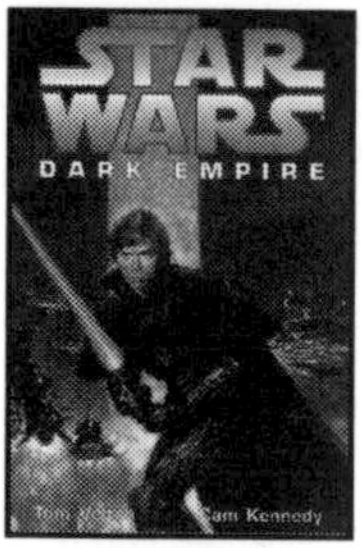
STAR WARS
DARK EMPIRE
Cam Kennedy

DARK EMPIRE
ISBN: 1-56971-073-2 $17.95

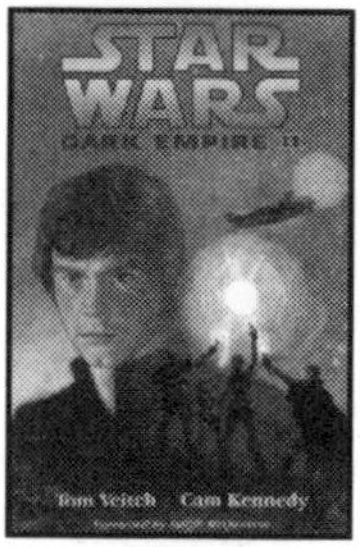
STAR WARS
DARK EMPIRE II
Tom Veitch Cam Kennedy

DARK EMPIRE II
ISBN: 1-56971-119-4 $17.95

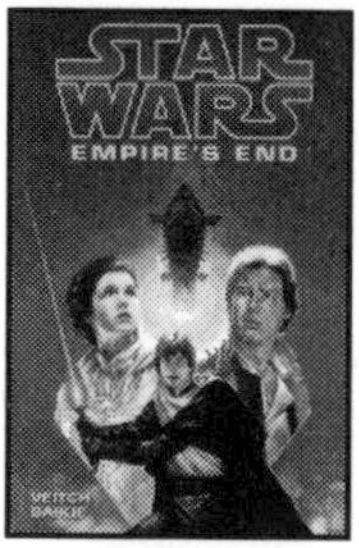
STAR WARS
EMPIRE'S END

EMPIRE'S END
ISBN: 1-56971-306-5 $5.95

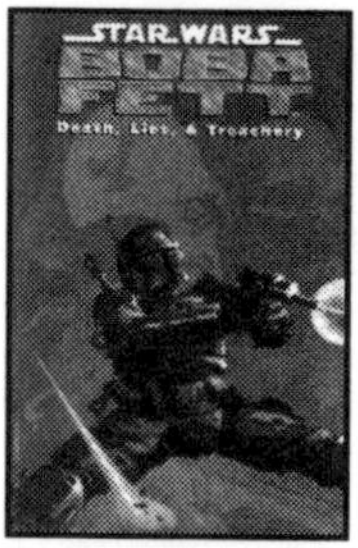
STAR WARS
BOBA FETT
Death, Lies, & Treachery

DEATH, LIES, & TREACHERY
ISBN: 1-56971-311-1 $12.95

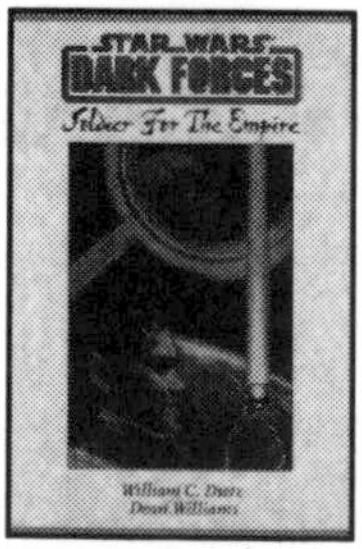
STAR WARS
DARK FORCES
Soldier For The Empire

SOLDIER FOR THE EMPIRE
ISBN: 1-56971-155-0 $24.95

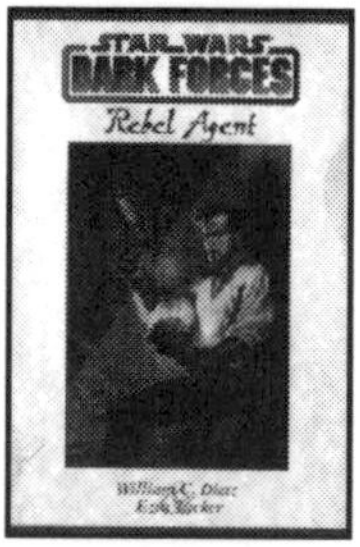
STAR WARS
DARK FORCES
Rebel Agent

REBEL AGENT
ISBN: 1-56971-156-9 $24.95

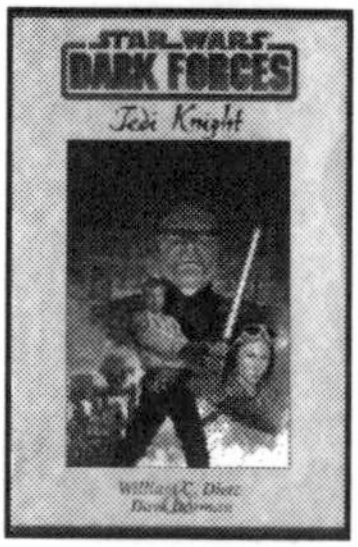
STAR WARS
DARK FORCES
Jedi Knight

JEDI KNIGHT
1-56971-157-7 $24.95

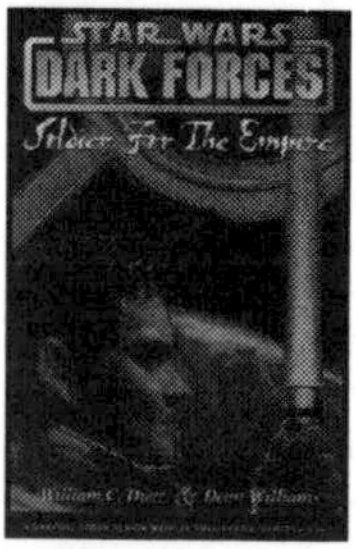
STAR WARS
DARK FORCES
Soldier For The Empire

SOLDIER FOR THE EMPIRE SC
1-56971-348-0 $14.95

漫画 BACKLIST

DARK HORSE'S COMPLETE LINE OF 漫画 SPECIALTY BOOKS

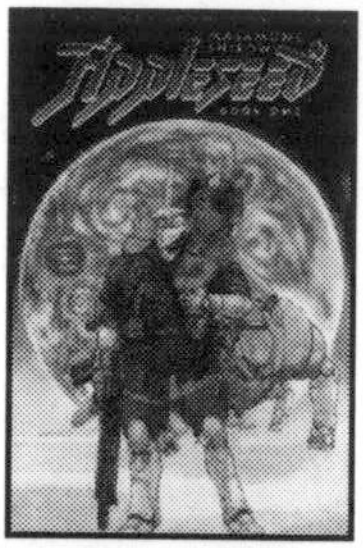
Appleseed
BOOK ONE

BOOK ONE
ISBN: 1-56971-070-8 $14.95

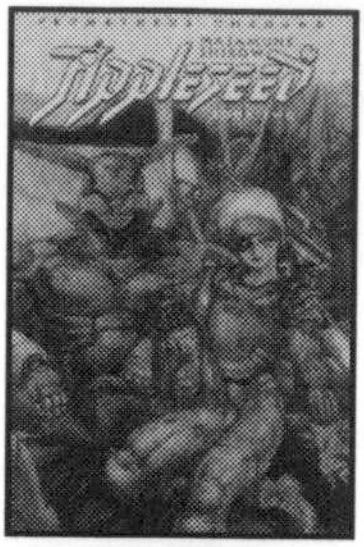
Appleseed

BOOK TWO
ISBN: 1-56971-071-6 $14.95

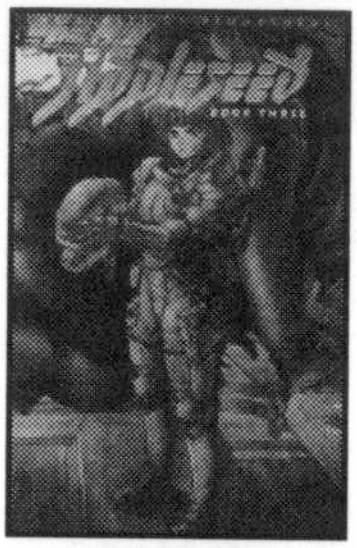
Appleseed
BOOK THREE

BOOK THREE
ISBN: 1-56971-072-4 $14.95

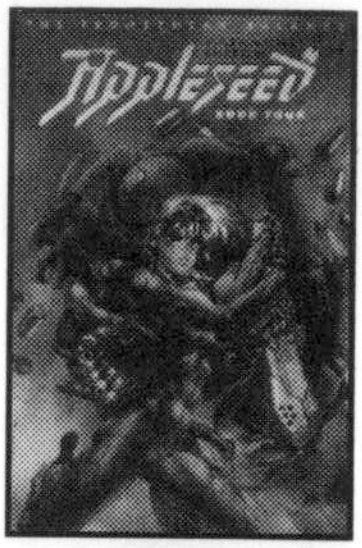
Appleseed

BOOK FOUR
ISBN: 1-56971-074-0 $14.95

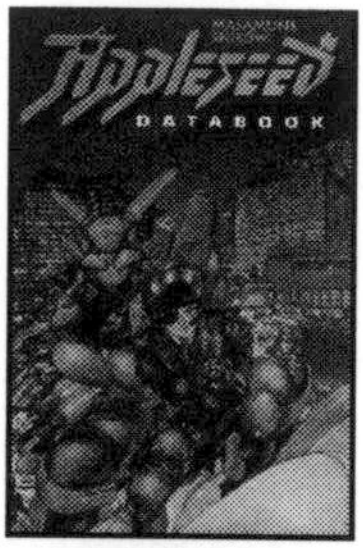
Appleseed
DATABOOK

DATABOOK
ISBN: 1-56971-103-8 $12.95

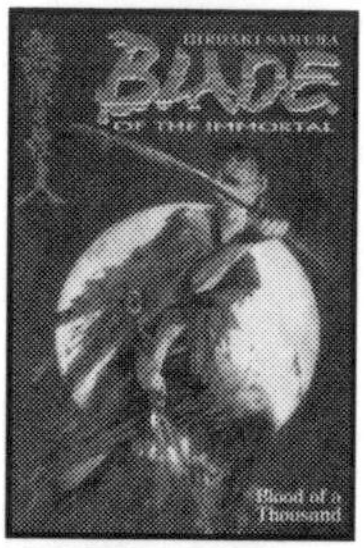
HIROAKI SAMURA
BLADE
OF THE IMMORTAL
Blood of a Thousand

BLOOD OF A THOUSAND
ISBN: 1-56971-239-5 $12.95

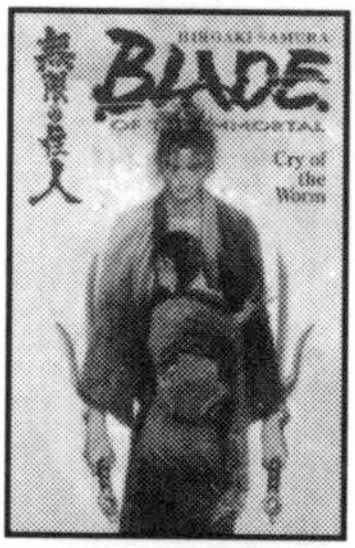
HIROAKI SAMURA
BLADE
Cry of the Worm

CRY OF THE WORM
ISBN: 1-56971-300-6 $12.95

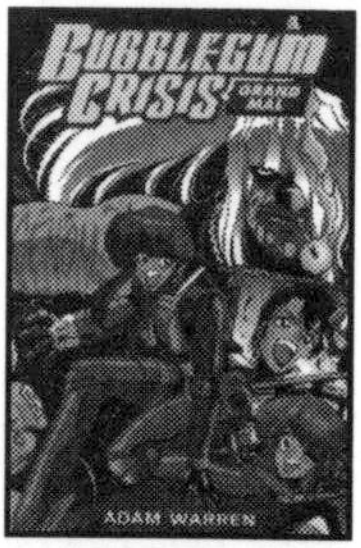
BUBBLEGUM CRISIS
GRAND MAL
ADAM WARREN

GRAND MAL
ISBN: 1-56971-120-8 $14.95

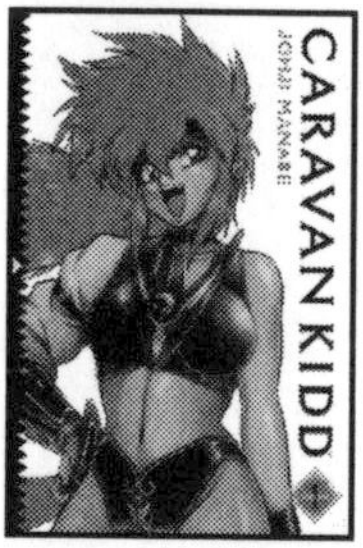
CARAVAN KIDD
JOHJI MANABE

VOLUME ONE
ISBN: 1-56971-260-3 $19.95

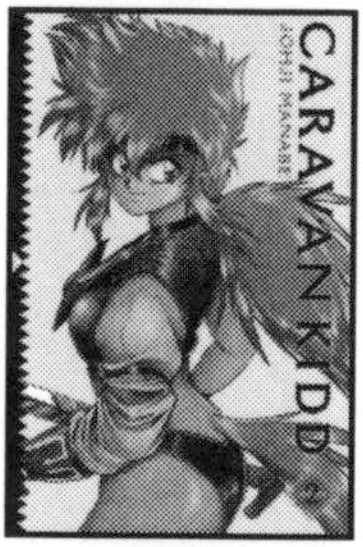
CARAVAN KIDD
JOHJI MANABE

VOLUME TWO
ISBN: 1-56971-324-3 $19.95

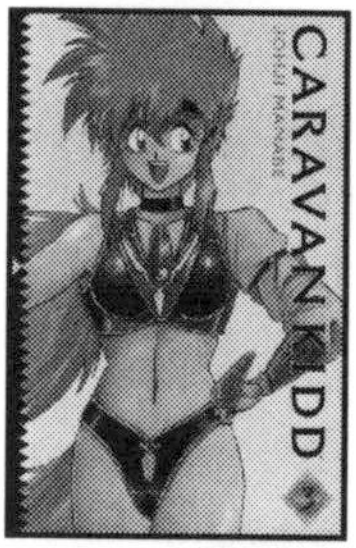
CARAVAN KIDD
JOHJI MANABE

VOLUME THREE
ISBN: 1-5-6971-338-3 $19.95

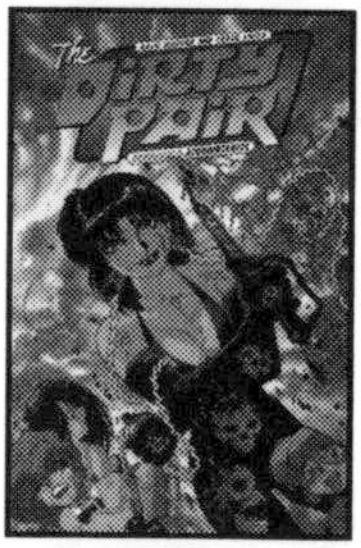
The Dirty Pair

DANGEROUS ACQUAINTANCES
ISBN: 1-56971-227-1 $12.95

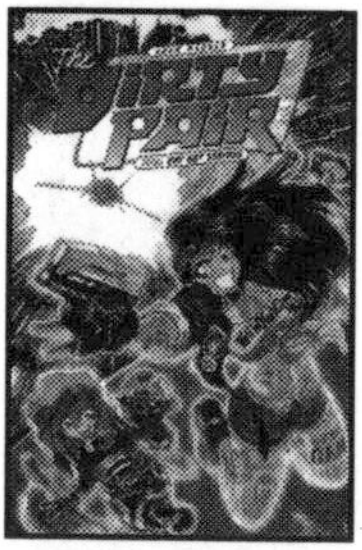
The Dirty Pair

FATAL BUT NOT SERIOUS
ISBN: 1-56971-172-0 $14.95

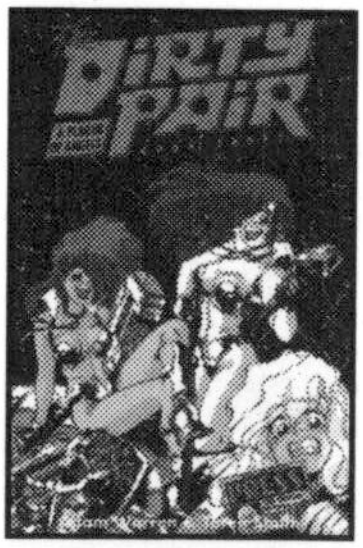
Dirty Pair

A PLAGUE OF ANGELS
ISBN: 1-56971-029-5 $12.95

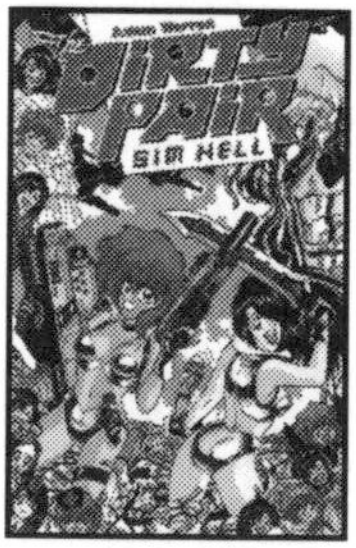
Dirty Pair
SIM HELL

SIM HELL
ISBN: 1-56971-159-3 $13.95

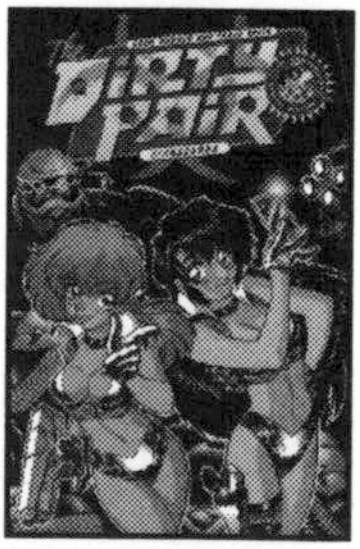
Dirty Pair

BIOHAZARDS
ISBN:1-56917-339-1 $12.95

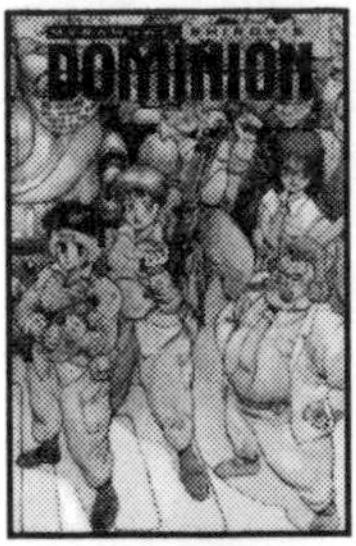
DOMINION

DOMINION
ISBN: 1-56971-160-7 $14.95

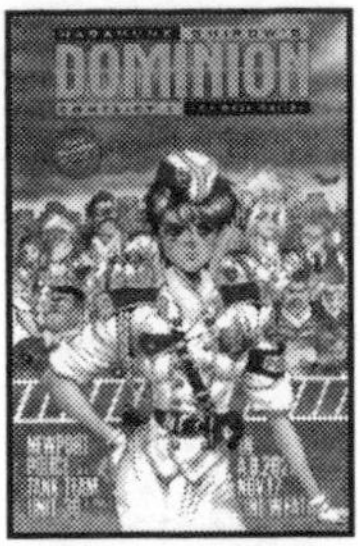
DOMINION

CONFLICT 1: NO MORE NOISE
ISBN: 1-56971-233-6 $14.95

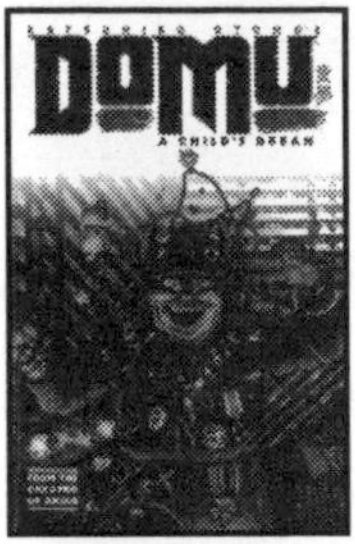
DOMU
A CHILD'S DREAM

A CHILD'S DREAM
ISBN: 1-56971-140-2 $17.95

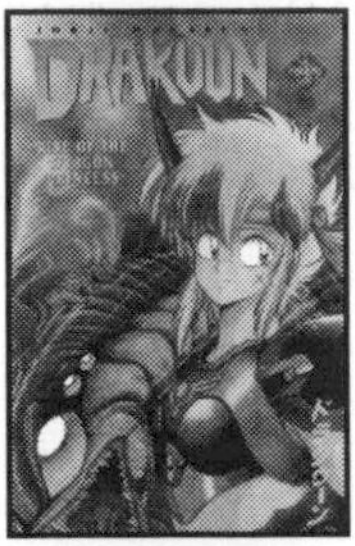
DRAKUUN

RISE OF THE DRAGON PRINCESS
ISBN: 1-56971-302-2 $12.95

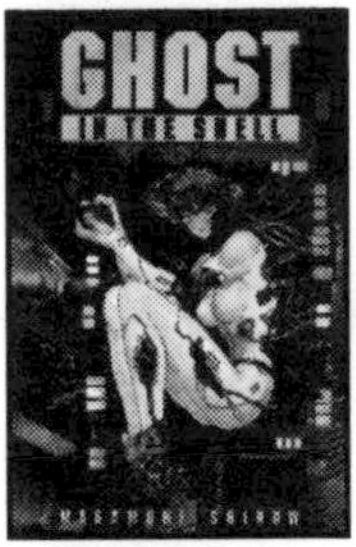
GHOST
IN THE SHELL

GHOST IN THE SHELL
ISBN: 1-56971-081-3 $24.95

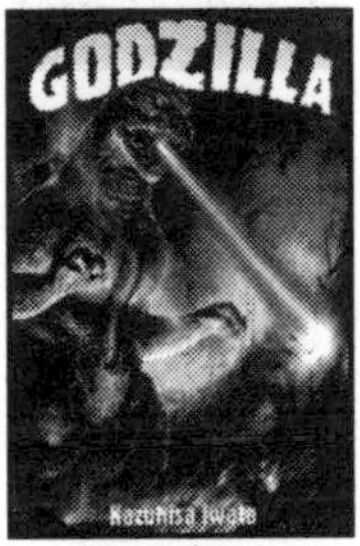
GODZILLA
Kazuhisa Iwata

GODZILLA
ISBN: 1-56971-063-5 $17.95

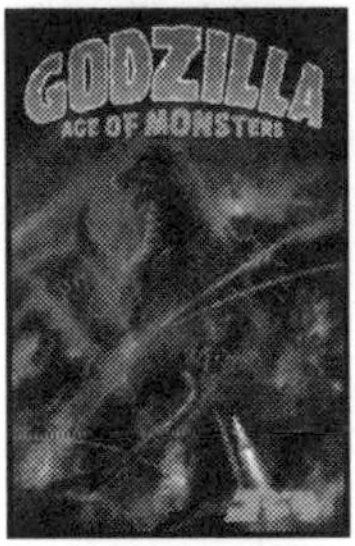
GODZILLA
AGE OF MONSTERS

AGE OF MONSTERS
ISBN: 1-56971-277-8 $17.95

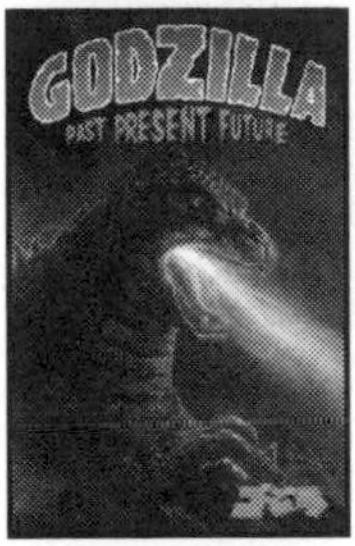
GODZILLA
PAST PRESENT FUTURE

PAST, PRESENT, AND FUTURE
ISBN: 1-56971-278-6 $17.95

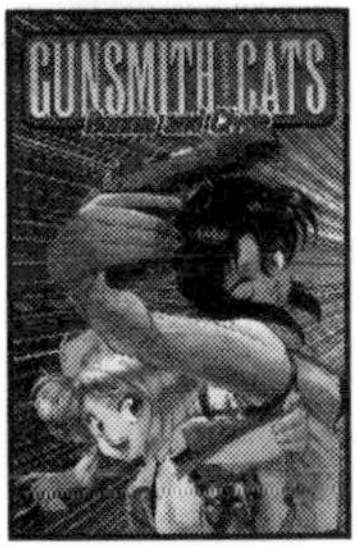
GUNSMITH CATS

BONNIE & CLYDE
ISBN: 1-56971-215-8 $12.95

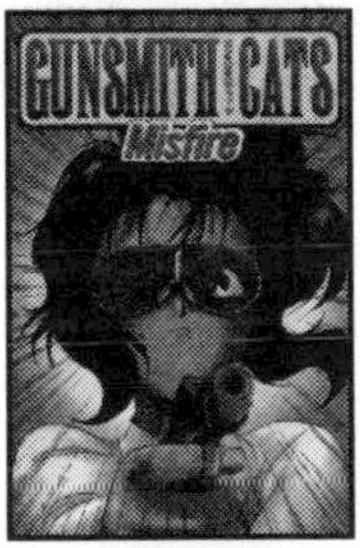
GUNSMITH CATS
Misfire

MISFIRE
ISBN: 1-56971-253-0 $12.95

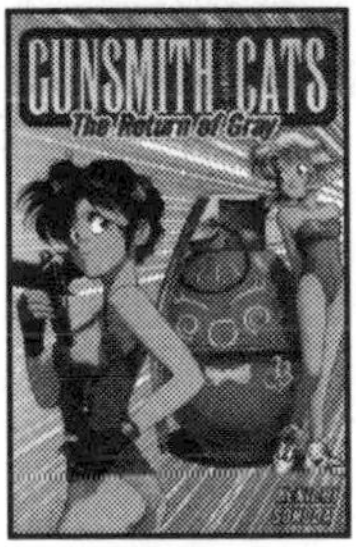
GUNSMITH CATS
The Return of Gray

RETURN OF GRAY
ISBN: 1-56971-299-9 $17.95

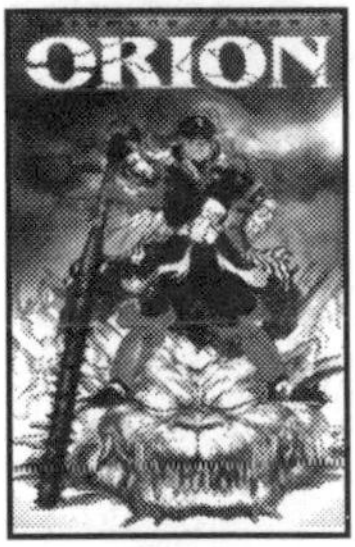
ORION

ORION
ISBN: 1-56971-148-8 $17.95

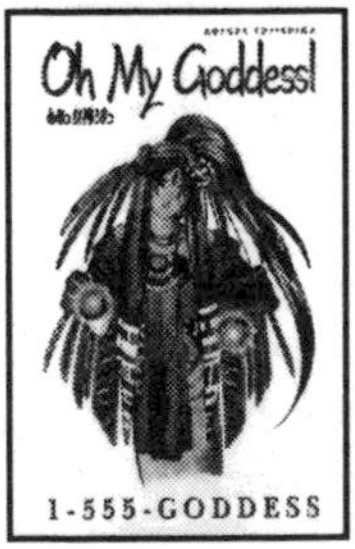
Oh My Goddess!
1-555-GODDESS

1-555-GODDESS
ISBN: 1-56971-207-7 $12.95

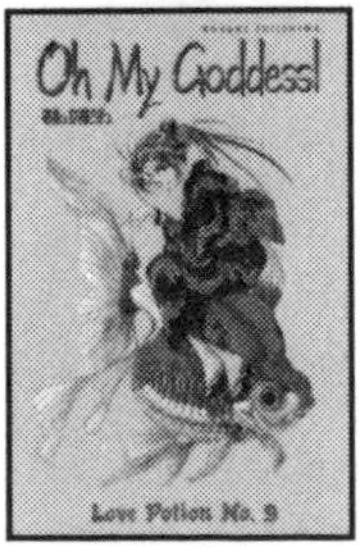
Oh My Goddess!
Love Potion No. 9

LOVE POTION NO. 9
ISBN: 1-56971-252-2 $12.95

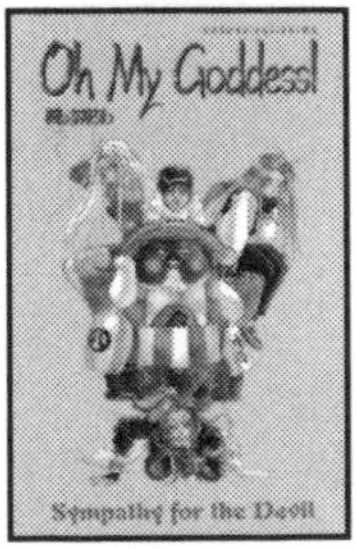
Oh My Goddess!
Sympathy for the Devil

SYMPATHY FOR THE DEVIL
ISBN: 1-56971-329-4 $12.95

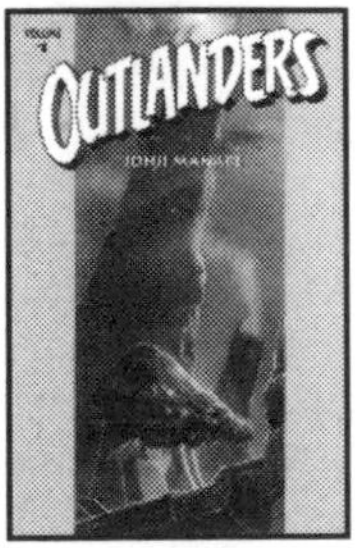
OUTLANDERS

VOLUME 1
ISBN: 1-56971-161-5 $13.95

3 1901 05327 8661